The Cultural Politics of Lifestyle Sports

D0303902

This important new study examines the changing place and meaning of lifestyle sports – parkour, surfing, skateboarding, kite-surfing and others – and asks whether they continue to pose a challenge to the dominant meanings and experience of 'sport' and physical culture.

Drawing on a series of in-depth, empirical case studies, the book offers a re-evaluation of theoretical frameworks with which lifestyle sports have been understood and focuses on aspects of their cultural politics that have received little attention, particularly the racialisation of lifestyle sporting spaces. Centrally, it re-assesses the political potential of lifestyle sports, considering if lifestyle sport cultures present alternative identities and spaces that challenge the dominant ideologies of sport, and the broader politics of identity, in the twenty-first century.

It explores a range of key contemporary themes in lifestyle sport including:

- identity and the politics of difference
- commercialisation and globalisation
- sportscapes, media discourse and lived reality
- risk and responsibility
- governance and regulation
- the racialisation of lifestyle sport spaces
- lifestyle sports outside of the Global North
- the use of lifestyle sport to engage non-privileged youth.

Casting new light on the significance of sport and sporting subcultures within contemporary society, this book is essential reading for students or researchers working in the sociology of sport, leisure studies or cultural studies.

Belinda Wheaton is Principal Research Fellow in Sport and Leisure Cultures at the University of Brighton, UK. Her extensive research on lifestyle sport cultures has been published across a wide range of international journals and edited collections. She is also the editor of *Understanding Lifestyle Sports: Consumption, Identity and Difference* (Routledge, 2004) and *The Consumption and Representation of Lifestyle Sports* (Routledge, 2012).

LIVERPOOL JMU LIBRARY

3 1111 01424 068

Routledge Critical Studies in Sport
Series Editors
Jennifer Hargreaves and Ian McDonald
University of Brighton

The Routledge Critical Studies in Sport series aims to lead the way in developing the multi-disciplinary field of Sport Studies by producing books that are interrogative, interventionist and innovative. By providing theoretically sophisticated and empirically grounded texts, the series will make sense of the changes and challenges facing sport globally. The series aspires to maintain the commitment and promise of the critical paradigm by contributing to a more inclusive and less exploitative culture of sport.

The Cultural Politics of Lifestyle Sports

Belinda Wheaton

Routledge
Taylor & Francis Group

LONDON AND NEW YORK

First published 2013
by Routledge
2 Park Square, Milton Park, Abingdon, Oxon OX14 4RN

Simultaneously published in the USA and Canada
by Routledge
711 Third Avenue, New York, NY 10017

Routledge is an imprint of the Taylor & Francis Group, an informa business

© 2013 Belinda Wheaton

The right of Belinda Wheaton to be identified as author of this work has
been asserted by her in accordance with sections 77 and 78 of the
Copyright, Designs and Patents Act 1988.

All rights reserved. No part of this book may be reprinted or reproduced or
utilised in any form or by any electronic, mechanical, or other means, now
known or hereafter invented, including photocopying and recording, or in
any information storage or retrieval system, without permission in writing
from the publishers.

Trademark notice: Product or corporate names may be trademarks or
registered trademarks, and are used only for identification and explanation
without intent to infringe.

British Library Cataloguing in Publication Data
A catalogue record for this book is available from the British Library

Library of Congress Cataloging in Publication Data
Wheaton, Belinda, 1966-
The cultural politics of lifestyle sports / Belinda Wheaton.
   pages cm
   1. Sports–Sociological aspects. 2. Extreme sports–Sociological aspects.
   3. Sports and society. I. Title.
   GV706.5.W49 2014
   306.4'83–dc23   2013004535

ISBN: 978-0-415-47857-1 (hbk)
ISBN: 978-0-415-47858-8 (pbk)
ISBN: 978-0-203-88817-9 (ebk)

Typeset in Times
by Wearset Ltd, Boldon, Tyne and Wear

Printed and bound in Great Britain by
TJ International Ltd, Padstow, Cornwall

Contents

Acknowledgements

There are many people who have inspired and supported me intellectually, professionally and personally along this slow, and at times painful and frustrating, journey. Carving out time to complete a project such as this book, which is based on a number of different research projects, is becoming harder and harder in the neoliberal university of the twenty-first century. For a working mother, with young children, the challenges and compromises are even more acutely felt.

I would like to acknowledge the support of the University of Brighton, and particularly my colleagues in Sport and Leisure Cultures: Dan Burdsey, Thomas Carter, Jayne Caudwell, Paul Gilchrist, Marc Keech, Gill Lines, Ian McDonald, John Sugden and Alan Tomlinson. They have provided a unique working environment, infused with intellectual passion and rigour, even in the face of increasing challenges. They have been patient and supportive, allowing me the time and space to complete this book. I am sure I have driven many of you round the bend and I sincerely apologise.

To Simon Whitmore and his team at Routledge I apologise, again, for being (somewhere near) the top of your list of 'bad authors' and am relieved that I have now relinquished that position to someone else! My heartfelt thanks to the series editors Jennifer Hargreaves and Ian McDonald who, despite my numerous changes in direction and tardiness, retained their confidence in me! Jenny's commitment to nurturing the development of sport sociology continues to amaze me, and her meticulous editing was well beyond the call of duty, and I am truly grateful.

There are so many people across the international academic community I would like to thank who, over the past decade, have informed my work immeasurably. Whether it was through formal academic exchanges, teaching courses, sharing offices or informal conversations at conferences, in pubs, on trains and aeroplanes, you know who you are! Particular thanks to Toni Bruce, Paul Gilchrist and Holly Thorpe, colleagues with whom I have greatly enjoyed working on projects that underpin parts of the book. Your openness and our conversations have enhanced my understanding and analysis. Of course, all the errors here are my own. There are also several individuals who have given their *time*, that most precious of commodities, to read parts of this manuscript; with particular thanks to: Mike Atkinson, Becky Beal, Toni Bruce, Dan Burdsey,

Jayne Caudwell, Joanne Kay, Kyle Kusz and Louise Mansfield. Lastly, to my family, my partner Stuart, my kids Poppy and Ollie, and parents John and Marietta, I apologise for all the evenings spent in my office, the bedtime books not shared, school assemblies missed, family activities postponed. Thank you for giving me the time and space to complete this. I love you all.

1 Introduction

An academic journey

My own academic interest in what I have termed lifestyle sports began back in the mid-1990s when I embarked on a Ph.D. based on the culture of windsurfing. As one of only a handful of scholars worldwide who shared this interest, I remember vividly my excitement when, during the research, Becky Beal's paper on skateboarding in Colorado was published (Beal, 1995). This was the first in-depth empirical study to emerge in English publications, and it was thrilling to learn that I was not the only person who thought there was something interesting and potentially different about lifestyle sports that needed articulating. Since then, there has been an explosion of academic interest in what has been variously labelled alternative, new, extreme, adventure, panic, action, whiz and lifestyle sport (see Midol, 1993; Midol and Broyer, 1995; Rinehart, 2000; Rinehart and Sydor, 2003; Wheaton, 2004c; Booth and Thorpe, 2007c). These labels encompass a wide range of participatory and made-for-television sporting activities, including residual cultural forms such as climbing and emergent activities such as kite-surfing.[1] While commentators have differed in their use of nomenclature, many are agreed in seeing such activities as having presented an alternative and potential challenge to traditional ways of 'seeing', 'doing' and understanding sport (cf. Wheaton, 2004a). A steady stream of exciting work has emerged over the past two decades, research that has contributed to comprehending the significance of these sporting activities, their cultures and identities. It has also provided valuable insights into understanding the complexities of social relations in late modernity and the role sports can, and have, played in reconfiguring individual and collective identities.

Initially this body of work on alternative/extreme/lifestyle sports was dominated by scholars from North America and, to a lesser extent, Australasia. The founding work of French scholars, including Nancy Midol (Midol, 1993; Midol and Broyer, 1995), was also important, but as not all of it has been translated into English, it has tended to be overlooked by Anglophone scholars (e.g. Loret, 1995). This North American dominance is not surprising as the USA is considered the home of the extreme sport phenomena – and as Bourdieu (1984) observed, the spiritual hub of many lifestyle sports. However, it is also where commercialisation and institutionalisation processes are most developed and, as a consequence, many activities have experienced fundamental shifts in their meanings. For example, as Beal's work has illustrated, the emergence and success of ESPN's X Games has had a profound impact on the growth and trajectory of North American skateboarding culture and industry (Beal and Wilson, 2004). Empirical work is now emerging from a wider and more international range of sites, including Europe, New Zealand, Africa (e.g. Thompson, 2001), China (Booth and Thorpe, 2007a) and Brazil (Knijnik *et al.*, 2010), illustrating both commonalities and diversity in participants' experiences. Over these decades, the academic interest in lifestyle sport has also broadened, encompassing a range of different academic (inter)disciplines, including cultural geography (e.g. Chiu, 2009), architecture and urban planning (e.g. Borden, 2001), anthropology (e.g. Laviolette, 2007, 2010), gender studies (e.g. Pomerantz *et al.*, 2004; Robinson, 2008), philosophy (e.g. McNamee, 2006) and psychology (e.g. Lyng, 1990; Thorpe, 2009b), stimulating the emergence of new theoretical developments and productive avenues of enquiry.

The lifestyle sportscape in the twenty-first century

Since their emergence in the 1960s, lifestyle sports have experienced unprecedented growth both in participation and in their increased visibility across public and private space. Evolving in a unique historical conjuncture of global communication, corporate sponsorship, entertainment industries and a growing global, young and affluent demographic, lifestyle sports have spread around the world far faster than most established sports (Thorpe and Wheaton, 2011a). In Britain, for example, the BBC draws on imagery of street-running, surfing and extreme kite-flying in idents,[2] and in advertising imagery 'extreme' has become a metaphor to sell products and services, from food to financial services. Lifestyle sports have also been the focus of numerous 'mainstream' television shows and films, such as *Point Break*, *Blue Crush*, *Touching The Void* and *Dogtown and Z-Boys*, which present the danger but also the vertigo inspired by the sports, demonstrating what Beck (1992, cited in Ormrod, 2009: ix) describes as the importance of reflexively experiencing danger and 'living life to the full' in a 'risk society'. Specialist magazines still fill newsagents' shelves, as well as online spaces, and are sustained by a multi-million-dollar industry selling commodities and lifestyles to 'hard-core' aficionados and grazers alike. Thus extreme sports have an importance that 'far transcends' the relatively low numbers of dedicated active participants (Booth and Thorpe, 2007a: ix).

The media's appetite for such sports is exemplified by the continued and still-growing success of ESPN's X Games, which by 2003, less than ten years after its inauguration (1995), had commanded a global audience of 50 million. Conversely, during this time period, the youth audience for the Olympics was steadily declining (Thorpe and Wheaton, 2011a, 2011b) and television contracts for the Big 3 – (North American) football, baseball and basketball – lost the North American networks billions of dollars (Booth and Thorpe, 2007c: 190). The emergence and increasing media support for action sports, but particularly snowboarding in the Olympics – the bastion of 'traditional achievement sport' – is testament to their ability to adapt across contexts and appeal to youth audiences (Thorpe and Wheaton, 2011a). The star performers like Tony Hawk (skater), Shaun White (snowboarder) and Kelly Slater (surfer) have become celebrities who, like other global sport celebrities, transcend their subcultures and inhabit and apprise national and transnational space (Andrews and Cole, 2002).

The allure and excitement of lifestyle sport has been appropriated to sell every kind of product and service imaginable. Indeed, from a commercial perspective, 'extreme' has become a means for corporations and advertisers to tap the lucrative 'affluent, young male' demographic. Surfing, for example, has been used to market regions as diverse as parts of Australia, South Africa, the USA (California and Hawaii in particular) and the English surf-hub, Cornwall. In the UK, like many other countries, lifestyle sports are being promoted to new and previously peripheral audiences. Recent examples of the ever-expanding commercial possibilities of the surfing experiences and lifestyles in the UK include the proposed indoor surf dome in London (Bowes, 2007) and the construction of a million-pound surfing reef in Bournemouth as part of a wider process of urban renewal and tourism. The surfing 'experience' is being marketed to an expanding range of niche groups, such as 'tween' girls (e.g. *Roxy*'s[3] latest target) and hen parties, and as a focus for UK celebrity chef Jamie Oliver's enterprise, *Fifteen Cornwall*, located on the prominent and now gentrified surfing beach Watergate Bay in Cornwall.

Mediated sources range from the self-defined and still-expanding 'worldwide leader' in action sports, ESPN's X Games (Rinehart, 2008: 175), to a proliferation of internet-based sites. The ways in which consumers can experience lifestyle sports is also ever-expanding and diversifying. There are, for example, those who play video games, buy clothing and accessories, devour the vast array of media products (from social media and internet-based products to more traditional forms, such as DVDs, films and television shows) and experience activities through adventure tourism or as spectators. An array of action-sport-inspired video games has been produced, including platforms where the participants have to actually ride a board (e.g. Wii and PlayStation PS3 Move). In a seemingly bizarre twist to the 'authentic' adventure experience, luxury cruise ships now offer a surfing wave pool and climbing wall as 'on-board' entertainment. As van Bottenburg and Salome (2010) suggest, activities that have been characterised as self-directed, conducted outdoors and in 'nature' are increasingly being repackaged as more directed, indoor leisure experiences, a process they describe as 'indoorisation'. While these consumers represent increasingly important and significant sectors in understanding the cultural popularity and signification of action/'extreme' sports, they are not the prime focus of this book.

Given this increasing cultural visibility, it is unsurprising that in the twenty-first century, lifestyle sports are also attracting an ever-increasing body of participants, from increasingly diverse global geographical settings (Rinehart and Sydor, 2003; Wheaton, 2004a; Booth and Thorpe, 2007b; Comer, 2010). While the outdoor, non-association-based and itinerant nature of these activities makes it hard to accurately measure participation levels, it is clear from the available sources, such as sales of equipment, market research surveys (see in Tomlinson *et al.*, 2005) and wide-ranging media commentaries, that participation in many types of lifestyle sports continues to grow rapidly, outpacing the expansion of most traditional sports in many Western nations. L'Aoustet and Griffet (2001) claim that in France any observable increase in sport participation can be attributed to non-institutionalised informal sport activities, with surveys showing that 45–60 per cent of the French population now practise informal sports like skateboarding. Sport England's *Active People Survey* (2006, 2007) also points to the increasing popularity of more informal and individualistic sports and lifestyle sports specifically (see also Gilchrist and Wheaton, 2011).

Accompanying this rapid expansion has been cultural fragmentation, with enthusiasts engaging in a wide variety of participation styles which, in the (post-Fordist) capitalist economy, support new and profitable niche markets (Thorpe and Wheaton, 2011a). It is also evident that this expansion in participation includes not only the traditional consumer market of teenage boys, but increasingly older men, women and girls. These participants have a broad range of interests and experiences. They range from occasional participants, perhaps taking part via the array of 'taster' activities being marketed through the adventure sport and travel industries, to the 'hard-core' committed practitioners who are fully familiarised to the lifestyle, argot, fashion and technical skill of their activity(ies), and spend considerable time, energy and often money doing it.

Lifestyle sport, neoliberal ideologies and late modernity

Lifestyle sports provide interesting and useful cultural forms to map the ways in which sport and leisure cultures, experiences and identities are shifting in the transition from modernity to postmodernity.[4] In these activities, we can see some of the broader cultural developments, changing social terrain and paradoxes of advanced capitalist or late-modern societies. For example, expressions of self-identity are increasingly fragmented, mobile, multiple, personal, self-reflexive and subject to change and innovation, alongside a decline in collective and community values and a concurrent focus on the (self-fulfilled, hedonistic) self that Beck (1992) describes as a social surge of *individualisation*. 'The complexities of late modernity are experienced through the (potentially) emancipatory aspects of reflexive life projects, identity management and lifestyle' (Carrington, 2007: 51). That is, people have become compelled to make themselves the centre of conduct of life, taking on multiple and mutable subjectivities. Identity has become seen as a site for self-actualisation *and* political struggle (ibid.: 50), such as exemplified in Giddens' (1991) idea of the 'life politics' that emerge from new social movements, and their concerns with individual and collective self-actualisation.

Yet this dismantling of traditional social bonds, state–citizen relationships and communities has also provoked uncertainty, including an increased awareness of risk as a product of human action rather than fate. The need to *manage* risk reflexively is an important feature of late modern societies (Giddens, 1991; Beck, 1992), reflected in the discourses of risk-taking and risk-management that proliferate in lifestyle sports. Yet in neoliberal political contexts, risk has become closely linked to reflexivity, accountability and responsibility; neoliberal ideologies discourage state reliance or support, and inspire – even require – individuals to take personal responsibility for their actions (West and Allin, 2010). As a number of commentators have begun to explore, the turn to, and economic, political and cultural appropriation of, lifestyle sports in North America, Western Europe and Australasia is connected to the diffusion of wider neoliberal ideologies in sport, health and leisure cultures. The values promoted by and associated with lifestyle sports, such as individualism, risk-taking and management, the pursuit of human potential, self-responsibility, taking control of one's life, an engagement with one's environment and a DIY ethos (to name but a few), are certainly widely cited as the values promoted by neoliberalism as a cultural ideology (Harvey, 2005). For example, Spowart *et al.* (2010) outline how government-sanctioned physical activity imperatives, fuelled by the twin problems of 'the obesity epidemic' and an increasingly ageing demographic, have led to a range of policy initiatives aimed at producing trimmer and healthier populations. These normalising and disciplinary practices encourage – even require – citizens to behave in ways that encourage self-discipline and self-responsibility. Lifestyle sports, with their focus on individual rather than state or institutionally-provided 'solutions' to achieving these various health and well-being objectives, serve to establish normative notions of what a 'good', 'healthy' citizen comprises (Young and Atkinson, 2008; Spowart *et al.*, 2010; Erickson, 2011). Also recognising the ways action sports have been singled out as providing values seen to be desirable for the global economy, Heywood (2007, 2008) argues that the 'surfing girl' is an important iconic figure in the new global economy, embodying and representing neoliberal ideologies of flexibility, DIY subjectivity and possibility for all (see Ch. 4). The promotion of lifestyle sports employs discourses that fashion self-reliant, self-monitoring, individualistic and flexible consumers, values at the core of the new global economy, so furthering neoliberalism as a cultural and economic movement (Giroux, 2004). These perceptive analyses illustrate the importance of contextualising the meaning of lifestyle sports within these broader political and economic agendas, and recognising and exemplifying how discourses of lifestyle sports dovetail with ideologies of the neoliberal consumer and body. Yet, while it is undeniable that lifestyle sports are being mobilised by a range of agencies to suit their agendas, as case studies in this book illustrate, the process is not without contestation, and concurrently individual and collective experiences of identity and difference are also shifting.

Why *this* book, why *now*?

Academic interest in lifestyle sports has proliferated, producing numerous interesting and theoretically informing case studies of individual lifestyle/action/extreme sports (e.g. Ford and Brown, 2005; Robinson, 2008; Stranger, 2011;

Thorpe, 2011). However, less has been written that explores the empirical and theoretical connections between activities. For example, Ford and Brown's (2005) timely overview of *Surfing and Social Theory* covers an impressive range of issues relating to the surfing culture, as well as its ontology and philosophy. There are, however, many aspects of their study that can also inform our understanding of activities that share cultural spaces, forms of motion and industries such as windsurfing and kite-surfing. Illuminating the *differences* between surfing and other board sports, such as snowboarding and skateboarding, helps to reveal the cultural specificities of lifestyle sports and how and why they differ from – or indeed are increasingly similar to – more traditional sporting activities, as well as other cultural practices such as performance arts and/or various expressions of play. Edited collections such as Rinehart and Sydor (2003), Ormrod and Wheaton (2009), McNamee (2006) and Wheaton (2004c, 2010) have provided admirable syntheses and been extremely valuable in bringing together research across contexts and activities. Yet edited collections are always constrained by the scope and nature of the chapters, making it difficult to illustrate the connections between these activities. An exception is Booth and Thorpe's (2007a) encyclopaedia, which explores a comprehensive range of important theoretical themes and considers the contextual issues underpinning the popularity of these activities and their shifting collective significance and meaning (see also Laviolette, 2010).

Despite this proliferation of research in different contexts and locales, much has continued to focus on concerns such as gender and exclusion, commercialisation and professionalisation (albeit adopting more innovative theoretical lenses). These are undoubtedly important areas, but my broad aim here is to give more detailed attention to aspects of their cultural politics that have, to date, received little attention, particularly the racialisation of lifestyle sports and the development of lifestyle sports outside of the Global North. As Carrington (2007: 55) advises, sport scholars need to 'address the multiply-constitutive characters of a diversity of axes of power, inequality and identity on a global scale'. Centrally, we need to consider if lifestyle sports can be more than 'a metaphor for Western or affluent sporting cultures and places' (Jarvie, 2006: 272). Do these 'reflexive life projects', forms of identity management and lifestyles surrounding these cultures 'hold potentially emancipatory potential' (cf. Carrington, 2007: 51); that is, can they offer alternative identities and spaces that challenge the dominant ideologies of sport, and the broader politics of identity, in the twenty-first century? The broad aim of this book, then, is to exemplify and conceptualise these issues around the *cultural politics of lifestyle spor*t, teasing out the ways in which particular discourses about lifestyle sports are mobilised and circulated, but focusing on understanding the lived experiences, how these discourses are made meaningful by people. I argue that there are limitations with approaches to understanding the meaning and significance of lifestyle sport that do not *also* engage with individual and groups of people's contradictory and shifting experiences of it.

In the remainder of this chapter, I discuss the key theoretical and methodological issues that frame my research. First, I outline my understanding of cultural politics and how it frames my work. I then describe the structure of the book, suggesting how I intend the book to be read and used. In the final section of this chapter, I examine my methodological approach and outline the empirical case studies that inform the book.

Towards an understanding of cultural politics

Cultural politics is a vague term which has a range of varied meanings (see, for example, discussion in Giardina and Denzin, 2011). In an attempt to delineate its meaning and sphere, the editors of the journal *Cultural Politics* suggest its aim is to 'explore what is *cultural* about politics and what is *political* about culture' (Armitage *et al.*, 2005: 1). As an academic field, it encompasses not only cultural studies but also work across the humanities and social sciences. 'Cultural Politics embraces the study of local, national and transnational cultural identities and processes in addition to the analysis of political problems as well as examining the character and agency of cultural and political explanations' (ibid.: 2). Identity, however, remains a contested and confused term. Outlining the 'genealogical trajectories' of identity and identity politics within cultural studies, Carrington challenges the idea that identity is a 'barrier to understanding and challenging wider forms of social inequality' (2007: 50), persuasively arguing that identity is a 'precondition' for the development of an 'effective oppositional politics' (ibid.: 49). Centring questions of cultural identity, he argues, helps 'to reveal the play of power and the complex articulations of dominant ideologies while simultaneously recognizing the joy, creativity, and moments of resistance and, occasionally, transformation that popular culture and sport provides us with' (ibid.: 62). Furthermore, as Sugden and Tomlinson argue, it is inadequate for social scientists to simply *identify* power relations. 'They must also learn to understand what that power relations means to those engaged with it' (Sugden and Tomlinson, 2002: 9). They illustrate that the 'on-going narrative' of modern sports is a 'narrative of *struggle* that blends individual and collective action or agency with political, economic and cultural flows and forces' (ibid.: 8), highlighting that our analyses must be aware of the different 'forms of resistance that can be expressed' (ibid.: 19).

While both cultural studies and the critical sociology of sport have influenced my understanding of cultural politics, research emerging in the context of youth subcultures 'post' the Birmingham Centre for Contemporary Cultural Studies (CCCS), broadly referred to as post-CCCS subcultural work, has been a particularly important influence in understanding the relationship between identity, power and oppositional politics (see discussion in Ch. 2), and in developing a sensitivity to the contradictory nature of resistance in contemporary culture (see Wheaton, 2007a). In summary, analyses of the cultural politics of lifestyle sport cultures need to explore:

> the homogeneity and heterogeneity of experiences *in* and *between* sport subcultures, revealing the multiple and often conflicting identities of individuals

and groups within the cultural formations. The experiences of *all* participants – young and old, marginal consumers as well as 'core,' of different
experiences, genders, sexualities, dis/abilities and ethnicities – need exploration, and critically the ways cultural power is reproduced and contested.
Studies of sporting sub-cultures should not be divorced from questions of
power.

(Wheaton, 2007a: 297)

My particular emphasis in this book is on how embodied (sub)cultural identities,
articulated in the inter-sectionality of gender, sexuality, race,[5] dis/ability and age
are (re)constructed, performed, contested and represented across lifestyle sporting spaces, places and discourses. This emphasis emerges from my initial
research on lifestyle sport cultures, where it was apparent that for *some* participants, these activities were experienced as more inclusive spaces than many traditional institutionalised sporting spaces – in particular, that they embraced a
broader range of sporting identities. However, like Lewis (1998: 65), there are
also other aspects of lifestyle sport's cultural politics that I have found particularly intriguing, which I have written about elsewhere, including their 'strategic
consumption', ambivalence to regulation and competition (e.g. Thorpe and
Wheaton, 2011a), forms of bodily pleasures and 'direct political activism as
expressed through environmental lobbying' (e.g. Wheaton, 2007b, 2008a).

A note on theoretical approaches, disciplinary boundaries and knowledge (re)production

While the previous section has outlined key theoretical influences in gaining an
understanding of cultural politics, there is, however, no overarching sociological
perspective or framework guiding this work; rather it takes its theoretical lead
from the empirical case studies, and how to make sense of the questions, themes
and power relationships they exemplify.[6] Such an approach, that uses theory as a
tool box, 'heuristic device' (e.g. Pearson, 1981) or framework for understanding
cultural phenomena, is an approach that some theorists find problematic.
However, being open to a diversity of theoretical interpretations, as well as
methodological approaches (see below), enables the researcher to provide a more
vivid picture of the complex and shifting cultural phenomenon under study. This
conceptual and theoretical eclecticism has been advocated across diverse cultural
fields, including the study of lifestyle sporting bodies. As Thorpe argues in her
inspection of the snowboarding body, 'strategically juxtaposing a selection of
conceptual perspectives from commensurate paradigms' is valuable because it
helps construct a 'multidimensional representation of the social, cultural, political, gendered, practised, lived and interacting body' (2011: 13).

Thorpe aligns her multidimensional methodology and theoretical approach
with what has been termed the 'Physical Cultural Studies' (PCS) enterprise
(Andrews, 2008; Andrews and Silk, 2011). She describes PCS as a synthesis of
'empirical, theoretical and methodological influences' drawing from fields

including sociology and 'history of sport and physical activity, cultural studies, and the sociology of the body' (Andrews, 2008: 55, cited in Thorpe, 2011; 5). While at this juncture, the 'PCS enterprise' is, as its protagonists Andrews and Silk (2011: 1) recognise, 'a fledgling enterprise' involving a 'loosely aggregated group' of scholars, and that, as yet, the label is neither a 'commonly accepted' nor 'widely recognised intellectual formation', it is certainly growing in what Bourdieu might call academic capital.

My own approach is sympathetic to, and indeed shares many of the theoretical and methodological aims of, the PCS agenda (see, for example, Friedman and van Ingen, 2011; Silk and Andrews, 2011). However, from my British-based (and eclectic) academic grounding, the PCS label seems somewhat North-American historicised and driven, at times without reference to, or consideration of, the wider sociology of the sport community. I, therefore, locate such an approach that is guided by a 'compendium of influences' (Andrews and Silk, 2011: 3), and broadens the narrow definition of sport adopted by some (North American) sport sociology scholars to examine various 'expressions of active physicality' (ibid.: 1), in the tradition and development of the socio-cultural analysis of sport *and* leisure that characterises many critical scholars of sport in the UK. In the UK, sport sociology (variously defined) has always been a broad church encompassing and encouraging inter- and multi-disciplinary approaches (embracing sociology, cultural studies, anthropology, history, politics, gender studies, geography) and involving tourism, physical education and dance. This broader conceptualisation of sport/leisure/play stems in part from the institutional coupling of sport *and* leisure in, for example, associations like the Leisure Studies Association (where sports sociologists are embraced) and in government research assessment panels.[7] This trend, and its historical roots, is exemplified in an interview published in *Leisure Studies*, in which David Andrews interviews Alan Tomlinson, a long-standing advocate and driver of this approach (Tomlinson, 2001, 2005), prompting him to review and assess the interrelationships between leisure studies, cultural studies and sport studies (Andrews, 2006). For Tomlinson, sport is a part of the 'popular cultural leisure landscape':

> I strongly believe that the study of sport outside the context of broader issues concerning political economy of leisure, the leisure economy, and the shifting significance of leisure cultures, is too cocooned. It is too easy to enthuse students about sport, and to encourage them to talk only about this fragmented chunk of social or cultural life: in that sense an emphasis on sport alone or sport above all other aspects of contemporary culture and leisure can be damaging for the field as a whole.
>
> (Ibid.: 262)

Gratton and Jones (2004) coined the term 'critical interpretavism' to describe this approach promulgated by Tomlinson and his Brighton colleagues. For Sugden and Tomlinson (2002: xiii), core elements of this critical 'Brighton approach' include: locating the cultural form or practice within the 'broader historical narrative as well as within the contemporary politics of global culture' (that is, contextualisation); 'a healthy disrespect for disciplinary boundaries; an adventurous cross-cultural curiosity; and a commitment to critical social scientific knowledge not beholden to patrons, agencies or sponsors' (ibid.: xii). My intention here, however, is not to debate the merits, or 'newness', of the PCS project, or how it intersects with this 'critical interpretavism'; rather it is to advocate the value of this approach for understanding lifestyle sport. Specifically, an approach that: is contextually grounded; conceptualises their cultures, economies and representations, within the broader 'popular cultural leisure landscape'; that centralises power relations; and adopts methodological reflexivity and theoretical eclecticism.

Also central to both the PCS agenda and critical sports sociology as advocated through 'Brighton' work (e.g. Hargreaves, 2000; McDonald, 2002; Sugden and Tomlinson, 2002; Sugden, 2004)[8] is the emphasis on political engagement and public intellectualism. That is, academics need to go beyond theoretical inspection, to 'intervene in the operation and experience of power and power relations' in the social world around us (Andrews, 2008: 58). In outlining their vision for a 'new performative cultural politics', Giardina and Denzin (2011: 322) advocate the importance of 'public conversations' and interventions, 'getting one's hands dirty', suggesting that at its core is a redefinition of the 'concept of civic participation and public citizenship'. Similarly, Sugden and Tomlinson have argued that the 'investigative ethnographic tradition' is a way to 'stimulate democratic reform' (1999: 386). While the ways in which this 'engagement with real utopias, democracy and social intervention' (Atkinson, 2011: 137) can best be achieved differs, and requires continued reflection and engagement, these are important and timely questions – questions that, for Atkinson, are the crux of the 'merit, hope and future' (ibid.: 137) for the longevity of PCS and the sociology of sport more widely.

Yet, despite the rhetoric, it is still the case that much of the discourse about this 'new politics of possibilities' (Giardina and Denzin, 2011: 322) remains rooted in the ivory towers of academia, not civic engagement. As Atkinson claims:

> At present, PCS runs the very real risk of routinely resting on its own intellectual laurels – emerging far too often as an exercise in the philosophical reading of physical culture, power within social formations, or hegemonic representations of moving bodies and identities, and too infrequently as a concerted and unapologetic ritual of transformative praxis.
>
> (2011: 140)

And this is also a valid critique of the research presented in this book. As I have described, a political impetus underlines this project, through revealing some of the hidden, subordinated or marginalised voices and experiences. I have offered critical theorising and reflection on (among other things) embodied inequalities, racisms, revealing the power relationship in knowledge production and providing a platform for marginalised voices. However, it is not the 'charged interventionist work' (Atkinson, 2011: 140) demanded by McDonald (2002), Atkinson (2011) and others that intervenes, challenges and disrupts power inequalities.

Nevertheless, I hope it offers some *possibilities* for research that is a 'lever of engaged praxis' (Atkinson, 2011: 140). To give some brief examples: my interest in parkour (see Ch. 5) emerged from involvement in a community-led youth project aiming to provide facilities and recognition for local parkour participants. The research we conducted engaged with parkour stakeholders, including policy makers and young people, and has subsequently impacted the provision of parkour in this locale and more widely. My research centred on the Black Surfing Association in California (Ch. 9) and was seen by some members of the community as an important part of black surfers' attempt to find a public voice and reclaim lost histories. Through my work on windsurfing, I engaged with the process of cultural change, for example, through fighting for and then editing/writing a monthly column for female windsurfers in a previously male-dominated, male-authored windsurfing magazine (Wheaton, 1997b). While none of these interventions could be considered to be the invested, interventionist and engaged role that McDonald outlines in his radical activism, it demonstrates that a focus on 'new social movement, and identity politics' (see Carrington, 2007; Atkinson, 2011) in itself does not preclude the possibility of engaged interventionist work; that in these sporting contexts, cultural identity can be 'a premise of political action rather than a substitute for it' (Gilroy, 1996: 238, cited in Carrington, 2007: 63).

The empirical case studies

The empirical case studies that inform this book are those I conducted between 2007 and 2010. They differ in scope and depth, ranging from brief 'ethnographic visits' (Sugden and Tomlinson, 2002) to qualitative research projects sustained over several years. My methodological approach is eclectic, utilising a range of data collection methods, including participant observation (in 'real' and virtual worlds, such as online chat rooms), in-depth interviews, informal conversations and analysis of magazines, newspaper articles, advertising materials and websites. While some of these projects are the focus of specific chapters, others inform different theoretical themes in this book. I give an overview of each of these research projects in the final section of this chapter. However, in addition to these formal studies, I draw on a wealth of less formal but nonetheless extremely valuable 'sources'. Over the past 20 years I have been a participant in many lifestyle and adventure sports, including windsurfing, kite-surfing, surfing, sailing, snowboarding, paddle-boarding, kayaking, mountain-biking and skateboarding. My involvement in these has ranged from very occasional to avid enthusiast, and my embodied experiences evoked excitement, terror, pleasure and pain, at times all in the same day. I have also taken an active 'outsider' interest in activities as an educationalist, including supervising students on an outdoor-education module (including surfing, windsurfing, climbing and kayaking), and critically through my partner's still-obsessive addiction to kite-surfing and my children's nascent involvement as grommets. These multiple perspectives (as researcher, participant, supervisor and editor) and ever-changing experiences through *my* life course have given me a longitudinal perspective. This has allowed me to reflect on the sports' local and global character, temporal continuity and change, the complexities of identities, and specificities and differences between – and within – lifestyle sports.

The structure of the book

The remainder of the book consists of nine chapters, divided into two parts. Part I consists of three conceptual chapters that describe and theorise aspects of the lifestyle sportspace. Part II constitutes five chapters, each based on a different empirical case study or theme, followed by some brief conclusions. The book is designed either to be read in a linear fashion or to allow the reader to dip into the case studies. For this reason, the theoretical and conceptual issues outlined in Part I are drawn on and cross-referenced in each case study in Part II.

The research – a methodological journey

My initial foray into ethnographic research on lifestyle sport was during my doctoral work, which focused on the windsurfing culture (Wheaton, 1997a). This involved a two-year ethnographic project, including an extended period of participant observation focused around one beach community on the South Coast of England. Additionally, in-depth interviews with selected members of the windsurfing community were conducted, including female windsurfers and those on the periphery, such as 'windsurfing widows' (Wheaton and Tomlinson, 1998). As I have discussed in detail elsewhere, the field-role I negotiated was based on being a proficient coastal windsurfer competing in national contests, involved with the windsurfing industry and media, and as a journalist writing monthly features for British windsurfing magazines (Wheaton, 1997b, 2002). This role gave me the opportunity to travel extensively, both around the UK and internationally. My analysis was therefore informed by this 'glocal' (Robertson, 1992) perspective, particularly the time spent in the windsurfing Mecca of Hawaii, as well as Australia and the Caribbean.

This research took as its starting point an orthodox 'post-positivistic' ethnographic approach, somewhere in between the extremes of postmodern cultural relativism and positivistic realism – that is, 'the usual canons of good science' are retained, but 'require redefinition in order to fit the realities of qualitative research' (Strauss and Corbin, 1990: 250). This was reflected in the generic 'Grounded Theory' approach (Strauss and Corbin, 1994) I adopted in my research, which reproduces a naturalistic approach to ethnography but one that is nonetheless premised on the post-positivist approach. For example, I used analytic induction, negative case testing and other means to 'validate' my emergent themes and to ensure my account was rigorous and had theoretical and inductive generalisability (see Wheaton, 2002). As I wrote, 'my feeling at the time, was that a "good story was not enough" it needed the "appropriate" methodological legitimation of (post)positivistic language to make it "good ethnography" ' (ibid.: 247).

Through and after the process, however, my position shifted to one that rejected the assumption that a 'tangible, knowable, cause-and-effect reality exists and that research descriptions' can accurately portray that reality (Kincheloe and McLaren, 2005: 151); I worked towards a reflexive approach to ethnography that denied a single interpretative truth or reality, seeing validity as a process shaped by culture, ideology, gender and language (Lincoln and Denzin, 1994: 481). As I outlined:

> the central issue is to elevate the importance of the political and personal dimensions of ethnography such as: reflexivity, responsivity, a rejection of the hierarchical exploitative relationship between researcher and researched (in method and representation), and to foster an experiential, eclectic approach, one that is sensitive to, and engages with, gender and other (multiple) forms of oppression and difference in the research process.
>
> (Wheaton, 2002: 252)

Shifting sands: ethnographic approaches in transition

Subsequent projects have grappled with a number of these methodological dilemmas that have emerged in the context of my own developing understanding of the 'problem' of methodology and methodological reflexivity (see Wheaton, 2002). Additionally I have been influenced by broader shifts in our understanding of 'culture' across many academic disciplines that have challenged existing ideas of bounded definable research objects like the local subculture (Denzin and Lincoln, 1994; Marcus, 1994; Clifford, 1997). I will briefly sketch out the methodological issues particularly pertinent to the case studies discussed in this book.

First, it became increasingly evident that lifestyle sports were rapidly changing, largely in response to global economic processes. To understand participants' experiences at the local level needed a more sustained engagement with the discursive shifts in the meanings of lifestyle sports and the historical, sociocultural and economic, political contexts in which those discourses are embedded. As Saukko argues, 'How can one do justice to the lived experience of people, when at the same time, critically analyze discourse, which form the very stuff out of which experiences are made' (Saukko, 2003: 3). This tension between the 'microcosmos of individual experience' and 'macrocosmos of global, economic power structures' (ibid.: 6) runs through these case studies and informs the interpretations made throughout the book. So rather than thinking about lifestyle sport participation as an intensely personal activity, it recognises how embodied experience is highly mediated by a range of popular, mediated (and increasingly healthiest) discourses (see Spowart *et al.*, 2010) that are themselves intertwined with broader social, economic and global processes (especially the onslaught of neoliberal capitalism). To understand this complex, shifting relationship, a broader range of methodological approaches and forms of 'data' is required that, once combined, will help provide a more complete (yet always partial) picture of the phenomena.

Second, while my early research recognised the global flows in the windsurfing culture, more recent empirical work has considered more systematically the impact of the transnational flows in commodities, media, images and people, in understanding what lifestyle sports are, the processes of local and glocal identity production and how we can study them. As noted above, the traditional anthropological idea of a discrete local site for ethnographic inquiry has been called into question, as has cross-cultural or cross-national comparison. Instead, proponents of what has been variously termed 'transnational' or 'global ethnography' and the 'mobilities paradigm' (Buscher and Urry, 2009) explore the impact of global flows on, between and within 'local' subcultures, and their media and industries illustrating the (dis)connections between the sites and 'scapes' (Appadurai, 1996) and their contingent and shifting character. While the project on lifestyle sport in South Africa (Ch. 6) specifically examines how globalisation processes impact on local identity production in a locale that is geographically and economically distant from the global core, these methodological sensibilities inform much of this empirical work.

A third methodological focus is rooted in the problematic of positionality, particularly as conceptualised around insider/outsider relations. Insider research raises a number of theoretical *and* methodological debates, but particularly about the *nature* and *validity* of the insider (Wheaton, 2002). While debates about being a cultural insider are prolific in many subcultural fields, in sporting contexts they have taken a particular flavour, with accounts from those who have experienced the activities through their physical bodies seem to have a privileged and more 'authentic' view. It is argued that non-participant observers/ enthusiasts often misunderstand, or ignore, what the sport culture means to its participants – they do not explain or understand the embodied subjective experiences, such as pleasure, pain, fear and excitement, that make their lifestyles meaningful. While ethnographers have grappled with more innovative ways of researching and representing such embodied experiences (see, e.g. Sparkes, 2009), it is still the case that, in the context of lifestyle sport cultures, such as surfing, some still argue that participation in the activity is a prerequisite to understanding the sports' meaning and aesthetic.

However, as I argue in Wheaton (2002), the distinction between 'insider' and 'outsider' is a misleading binary opposition rooted in an essentialist and fixed understanding of identities, one that fails to recognise the multiple ways in which difference or 'otherness' is marked and measured. It masks the more fluid and contingent nature of the researcher's role and identity. As Song and Parker argue, 'dichotomised rubrics' such as insider–outsider 'put too much emphasis on difference, rather than on partial and simultaneous commonality and difference between the researcher and interviewees' (1995: 249).[9]

Furthermore, despite sport sociology's widespread acknowledgement of the *importance* of post-structuralist feminist theory, and increasingly postcolonial and black feminists' critiques of the universalised and essentialised white male Western subject, it has not always led to an *engagement* with its implications in ethnographic practice. While these debates have encouraged (white Western male) ethnographers to reflect on their 'otherness', and decentre their authority, 'gender blind' accounts (Bell *et al.*, 1993) still dominate ethnographic work in many fields. Sporting ethnographies, especially conducted by male researchers, often fail to acknowledge, investigate and make visible the 'self' as gendered and racialised subject (see, however, Free and Hughson, 2003; Carrington, 2008). In the context of lifestyle sport cultures, researchers have been proactive in revealing the experiences of some identities excluded or subordinated from the dominant discourses, especially female participants (see Ch. 4). In so doing they have challenged the idea that white, young men are the normative and/or only subcultural identity. Yet it is still often the case that researchers fail to make their own whiteness and (hetero)sexuality visible, nor do they consider how it has shaped knowledge production. My own research has helped me to recognise how as researchers we often fail to 'see' the parts of our 'selves' that are most personal and most obvious. The autobiographical voice can be used to question 'the relation of the self to experience, researchers to researched and the production of knowledge itself' (Probyn, 1993: 105), through experiencing and grappling with the constant and multiple tensions between 'self' and 'other' (Atkinson, 1990). As critical ethnographers, we need to aspire to 'create a space for minor voices and visions', particularly those voices that have been historically silenced or marginalised (Cole, 1991: 34). While my initial ethnographic work attempted to map a range of (sub)cultural experiences and identities – for example, targeting the experiences of female windsurfers and those on the periphery, such as older and more marginal participants and 'windsurfing widows' – these often became marginal voices in the publications that followed. Hence a central focus in this book is the marginal, subordinated and silenced voices and experiences; specifically of non-white participants, older participants and those outside of the Global North.

From the pavement to the beach: the empirical case studies

Windsurfing and kite-surfing

Over the decade since I completed my Ph.D. on windsurfing (1997), I have continued my involvement in the sport, albeit as a much more marginal (and older) participant. Additionally, I was involved with setting up the BWA (British Windsurfing Association), which ran wave-sailing contests, and subsequently sat on the RYA's (Royal Yachting Association) windsurfing committee. These experiences contributed to my understanding of different scenes and experiences and shifts in the culture and industry since the late 1990s. During this period, I also witnessed the emergence and rapid growth and development of kite-surfing, experiencing first-hand some of the conflicts over space and safety characterising the emergence of this sport (see Ch. 3). There has also been considerable cross-over in participation, with many windsurfers taking up kite-surfing in conjunction with, or instead of, windsurfing.

Surfing

The initial focus of my Ph.D. included surfing as well as windsurfing (however, I soon realised this was not a realistic task). Nonetheless, I collated several months of field-notes focused on self-reflection about my gendered experiences as a novice surfer. Subsequently, I continued to observe the surfing culture at the beaches and locales where windsurfing and surfing coexist in close proximity, such as in Maui, Hawaii. Since 2000, I have continued in my journey learning to surf, and these experiences – including surfing through pregnancy, then renegotiating my involvement as a mother – form the back-drop to several focused projects on surfing. Most recently, watching and helping my (and other) children learning to surf in both formal and informal settings has given me insights into the changing surfing industry, its professionalisation and the ways in which children and women are being targeted. In this context, I have conducted interviews with surf school providers in the UK and California (*Surf Diva*, San Diego, 2009). I also conducted research focused on surfing and environmentalism, involving a case study of the Cornish-based organisation Surfers Against Sewage (SAS; Wheaton, 2007b).

Most recently (2009–present), my interest shifted to 'silver surfers', focusing on how surfing activity, culture and identity changes through the life course, and the ways in which older female surfers challenge normative ideas about embodiment, risk and ageing. To date this has involved analysing a range of mass media texts focused on ageing surfers, and interviews with male and female surfers aged between 40 and 80 in England (South Coast, Devon and Cornwall) and California. This on-going research informs the discussion of ageing in Chapter 4. Also focusing on surfing, but shifting the attention to the experiences of ethnic minority participants, I examined the history and contemporary experiences of a small group of black surfers in California. This research forms the basis of Chapters 7–9, and its rationale and methodology are discussed below.

Lifestyle sport in South Africa

Lifestyle sport in South Africa is the basis of Chapter 6. Since the 1970s, Durban has been considered a surfing mecca and has produced a stream of successful professional white surfers (Thompson, 2001: 192). Given the previous political context of apartheid when, until the late 1980s, beaches were segregated, it is not surprising that surfing in South Africa has been, and largely remains, a white sport (see Booth, 1998). So when I read about a charitable project taking place at Durban's popular North Beach that introduced street children to surfing,[10] I was somewhat incredulous. In my search for evidence of this project (run by *Umthombo*, an organisation run by ex-street children in Durban in partnership with a UK charity, the Amos-Trust), I also came across a skateboarding park linked to some interesting participation initiatives. These involved promoting skateboarding to street children and rural Zulu youth.

In 2007, I got the opportunity to visit Durban, and this skate park, the municipal North Beach Skate Park, became my main research focus during my brief visit. I visited the North Beach Park over the period of a week, and interviewed Dallas Oberholzer, who ran the park, Jason,[11] a student who worked at the skate shop, and some of the children who skated there. Interviews with the street children who skated posed practical difficulties. I had very limited time to build a rapport with them and many spoke Zulu as their first language. As a consequence, in my analysis (presented in Ch. 6), the voices of the organisers are dominant. This brief 'ethnographic visit' (Sugden and Tomlinson, 2002) was supplemented with subsequent email correspondences and discussions with other researchers who had spent time with these street children in Durban and South African academics, as well as secondary research.[12]

Board sports, their audiences and industries

While traditional ethnographic work involved focusing on local, bounded (sub) cultural spaces, contemporary approaches recognise the importance of the global flows in images and discourses as well as people (Appadurai, 1996) and therefore as tools in fieldwork. In this context, my interpretations are informed by various projects exploring subcultural/niche media texts and audiences, and insights working as a freelance journalist for a range of board sport and outdoor activity magazines. In particular, with Becky Beal, I examined the consumption of subcultural media in the sports of windsurfing and skateboarding, exploring participants' readings of magazine advertising images and their discourses about 'authentic' identity and status in their subcultures, particularly through their complex and 'creative' readings of the meanings of images and brands (Wheaton, 2003a; Wheaton and Beal, 2003a, 2003b). More recently (2008a), a small project examined how different female audiences (self-identified surfers and beginners/non-surfers) read the Hollywood blockbuster *Blue Crush*, a film that showcases female surfers and has been widely attributed with contributing to the female surfing boom (see Ch. 4). Lastly, in collaboration with Holly Thorpe, I investigated the incorporation of lifestyle sports into the Olympic movement, based on case studies of snowboarding, windsurfing and BMX (see Ch. 3; Thorpe and Wheaton, 2011a, 2011b).

Parkour

My research on the emergence, institutionalisation and governance of parkour/free-running in the UK was conducted from 2009 to 2012 with Brighton colleague Paul Gilchrist. The research emerged in the context of a community-focused and funded[13] project that explored the reactions by various stakeholders to the emergence of parkour and plans to build a community-funded parkour training area in East Sussex. Our initial aim to understand this local policy intervention was then broadened to explore parkour's emergence across social policy initiatives in East Sussex and England more widely. We wanted to begin to understand the activity, its meaning and particularly its perceived social value (see Gilchrist and Wheaton, 2011). Additionally, following earlier policy work with which we were involved (Tomlinson *et al.*, 2005), we recognised the importance of documenting the various forms of governance structures emerging in this rapidly evolving activity.

Our empirical research involved interviews with stakeholders, including parkour participants, parkour teachers/coaches/promoters, police, community officers, P.E. teachers, sport and art development officers and representatives of local councils. We also examined key organisations involved with the institutionalisation and teaching provision of parkour/free-running in the UK more widely, and explored how parkour has been used in other social inclusion and regeneration initiatives, and in school PE provision. The initial research was conducted between September 2008 and October 2009, consisting of more than 20 in-depth qualitative interviews. We also used web-based research, including parkour chat-sites and media reports about parkour. We were also involved in running a workshop introducing parkour to trainee PE students. My analysis is informed by subsequent and on-going discussions with parkour practitioners, educators and policy makers, both in the UK and internationally, including at a British Academy funded workshop on *The Politics of Parkour* at the University of Brighton (October 2010) involving participants and academics from Europe, North and South America.

In contrast to all the other activities discussed in this book, I have no experience of *doing* parkour; I am an outsider to the culture and experience, which has presented numerous challenges, including initial difficulties gaining access to, and trust from, participants. I also witnessed resistance from insiders to academic non-practitioners like myself, whom they saw as unable to understand the activity (see debate in Wheaton, 2002).

Surfing and race: developing a research agenda

The racialisation of surfing has received surprisingly little academic attention – an absence that has fuelled the empirical research that is the basis of four chapters in this book. First, in Chapter 6, I explore beach cultures in Durban, South Africa; then in Chapters 7–9, I draw on a project examining the histories and experiences of a group of African-American surfers in California conducted during 2009 and 2010. California holds particular significance as in popular consciousness it is attributed with the birth of surfing culture (Booth, 2001: 91). Indeed, recognising the significance of California in many lifestyle sports' histories, and their global diffusion, Bourdieu called them *les sport Californiene* (1984). Thus, the California beach has particular significance both in the global diffusion of surfing (Comer, 2010) and in the reconstruction of surfing as a white sport.

My research was centred on the Los Angeles area. I interviewed five individuals – three men and two women – all aged between 30 and 60 and all self-defined as black surfers. I followed these interviews up with email corre-spondences, including with other black surfers and commentators on black surfing. I subsequently did extensive internet-based research, including using British Surfing Association (BSA) web materials and chat pages. While the interviews and correspondences I present constitute a very small, localised and highly-selective sample, given that their voices are marginalised in most (medi-ated) discourses of surfing, their experiences are salient. It is also likely that some of the processes and factors that affect black surfers in California have wider resonance. My analysis was informed by my observations of, and parti-cipation in, surf culture for the past 25 years, including in Europe, Hawaii, the Pacific islands, Australasia and the Caribbean, where (in 2010) I conducted a formal interview with a black Bajan surfer/windsurfer.

Race, gender and being an insider revisited

There are many methodological issues that my research raises, but particularly rel-evant is the 'epistemological and ontological dynamics entailed' in such 'race writing' (Nayak, 2006: 427) – that is, questions about 'what is legitimate to study', 'who knows about whom, and how this knowledge is legitimated' (ibid.). While these complex debates cannot be given attention here, it is nonetheless important to recognise that some advocate that only 'black people' can speak about race (e.g. see debate in Burdsey, 2010; Carrington, 2008). As Nayak warns, 'early race eth-nographies' were often produced 'through and against a standard of white nor-malcy', leading to 'pathological perceptions of racialized Others' (Nayak, 2006: 413). While mindful of this problematic, my approach here has been to adopt a 'critical epistemological standpoint' (Carrington, 2007: 57) that shows 'reflexivity about our positions in the various fields of study'. Thus, my location as a white, female, heterosexual, European person *who surfs* (but not a 'surfer') is central, recognising that 'many stratified positions of sameness and difference' structure such qualitative research (Nayak, 2006: 413). Yet, as Burdsey explores in recon-ciling his privileged position as a white non-Muslim academic researching Muslim communities, while 'empathetic and partial attempts at understanding are important [...] it is imperative to recognize that trying to provide a platform for the counter-narratives of marginalized, minority ethnic groups is not nearly as straightforward as white academics often believe' (Burdsey, 2010: 322). Ulti-mately, however, my research strategy was led by pragmatic rather than epistemo-logical concerns, that historically such 'subaltern voices' have been heard neither in the academy, nor, until very recently, in popular accounts of surfing. Indeed some respondents saw that I could give them 'a voice'.[14] Most interviewees requested that they were named, not anonymous. For example:

> As far as my quotes, please attribute them to my name. I need to be the one who is responsible for the things that I say.... And I am tremendously grate-ful that the world is listening. Thank you for your part.
>
> (email correspondence)

LIVERPOOL JOHN MOORES UNIVERSITY
LEARNING SERVICES

Mindful of feminist-led concerns about how power dynamics operate through the research processes (Wheaton, 2002), I therefore offered transcriptions of our interviews and the opportunity, for some, to comment on ideas. Nonetheless the geographical distance between myself and those I interviewed made sustaining a non-hierarchical power relationship difficult.

As the research developed, the complex dynamics of identity, inclusion and exclusion, particularly in the context of discourses about *being* a 'real surfer', surfaced. As I discuss in Chapter 3, self-identified 'core members' often employ authenticity discourses to 'aggrandise and legitimise' themselves, while marginalising other participants (Donnelly, 2006: 220), and such insider–outsider dynamics are often underpinned by race and gender (see Wheaton, 2002). In this research, some fascinating commentaries emerged about whose voice was (allowed to be) included and excluded, although in defining 'authentic' surfer status, race was not the central factor. Some participants did not want to be involved with my research unless they felt *all* the respondents were *real* (sic) committed surfers. This caused some tensions and subsequent difficulties in terms of my access to some potential voices. In part, this was because of the increasing media interest in their stories, and the recognition that, as one interviewee argued, 'history is being written right now and for the most part surfers aren't being talked to … we are trying to make ourselves visible and with that comes the politics of others … our voices are slowly being co-opted'.[15] In this context, my position as a white British female who surfed – but not *a surfer* – became increasingly problematic. These dynamics and how they impacted on the (often essentialised and misleading) notions of researcher positionality – for example, as an insider vs. outsider – require greater reflection.[16] In terms of the genesis of this research, my lens as academic interpreter, and the need to distance the research from the voice of individual participants, led me to make interviewees anonymous.[17] When considering issues around identity and community, although the researcher is central in framing the study, s/he needs to be able to 'adapt, reframe and listen to respondents in order to gain some insight into their emotions and feelings' (Clarke and Garner, 2010: 180).

It is possible – indeed likely – that other African-American surfers in California, and elsewhere, have different experiences of surfing, race and racism from the participants in my research. Such research, based on a small sample with limited exposure to their life-worlds, and constructed through my lens of multiple differences, is partial and contingent. However, I hope that this provides a starting point for analyses of how surfing reproduces white privilege, and for the subaltern voice in surfing to be heard.

Some caveats

Given the range of ever-changing, boundary-shifting activities one might conceptualise as lifestyle sports, and the highly selective and partial picture presented here, a number of caveats are necessary. Clearly this book does not, and could not, purport to give a comprehensive overview of current research. Nor, as

I have outlined, does it offer exhaustive theoretical explanations of the meaning and significance of lifestyle sports, nor of how lifestyle sports contribute to our understanding of social theory. In summary, then, the book represents empirical case studies conducted between 2008 and 2011, supplemented with selected examples from broader experiences and existing literature to illustrate selected theoretical themes within the cultural politics of lifestyle sports. Attributes that have received detailed coverage elsewhere, such as the commercialisation of lifestyle sport and gender power relations, will only be given brief discussion. Many important and interesting aspects will not be addressed at all, including the philosophical and socio-psychological aspects. The empirical case studies, as detailed below, are also not representative of all lifestyle sports; there is an over-emphasis on water-based board sports, especially surfing, and they are all indi-vidual activities. Nonetheless, as I illustrate in the discussion that ensues, the processes – if not the outcomes – appear to be more widely applicable across a broader range of lifestyle sport cultures and contexts.

Part I
The lifestyle sportscape

Conceptual and theoretical issues

2 Understanding lifestyle sport revisited

What's in a name: re-thinking 'lifestyle sport'

In the introduction to *Understanding Lifestyle Sports* (Wheaton, 2004a), I outlined that a wide range of labels were used to characterise these sports, including: extreme, alternative, lifestyle, whiz, action, panic, postmodern, post-industrial and new sports. I noted that, while these terms were used synonymously by some commentators, there are differences which signal distinct emphases or expressions of the activities. For example, Rinehart (2000: 506) suggested that alternative sports are activities that 'either ideologically or practically provide alternatives to mainstream sports and to mainstream sport values'. Thus forms of alternative sport can be very diverse, ranging from indigenous folk games and ultimate fighting to jet skiing, scuba diving and ultra-marathoning (ibid.: 505): indeed, pretty much anything that does not fit under the Western 'achievement sport' (Eichberg, 1998) rubric. Extreme, on the other hand, is a media-driven, all-embracing moniker that quickly became prevalent in media and consumer discourse fuelled by the emergence of ESPN's Extreme Games (later renamed the X Games) and widely adopted to signify these exciting, youthful activities (Rinehart, 2000). As Kusz outlines, extreme sport was initially 'decried' by sports fans and pundits, who saw them as made-for-TV pseudo-sports created solely to market products to the much-coveted teen male demographic (2004: 198). It is a term that many participants of the activities continue to reject, seeing it as an unashamed and cynical attempt to capitalise on and appropriate what were seen as alternative and oppositional sport forms (Rinehart, 2000: 508). Furthermore, while some 'extreme' sport activities such as BASE and tomb stoning[1] clearly involve great physical risk (and in some contexts are illegal), the majority of participants in lifestyle sports activities practise in safe and controlled ways. Indeed, many activities labelled 'extreme' are actually relatively safe (Booth and Thorpe, 2007c: 173) and, according to statistical evidence, cause fewer injuries and deaths than sports like rugby and boxing (Clemmitt, 2009: 297). Yet, as Chapter 3 explores, the perception of risk pervades, fuelled by the antics of the minority that make the headlines, driving debates about risk and irresponsibility.

Other categorisations that have at times been used synonymously with extreme sport include adventure sport (e.g. McNamee, 2006; Ormrod, 2009), hazardous sport (Laviolette, 2007) and edgework (Lyng, 1990, 2005, 2008). Edgework embraces a diverse range of high-risk activities, not exclusively sport, and has been appropriated to understand high-risk sports such as sky diving (e.g. Laurendeau, 2008). Some commentators have questioned whether these activities are more appropriately (or usefully) conceptualised as forms of play rather than sports (Stranger, 1999; Howe, 2003) and have highlighted the importance of their artistic sensibility (Rinehart, 2000; Booth, 2003) and spirituality (Stranger, 1999; Humberstone, 2011).

My preference for the term lifestyle sport was informed by these broad concerns about the labels of alternative and extreme initially in the context of understanding windsurfing. My predilection for lifestyle sports was because it was the descriptor that emerged in my empirical research; many of the participants described their activities as *lifestyles* rather than as *sports*. While it emerged in the windsurfing culture, it was used widely across other board sports. For example, in a radio interview, Jake Burton, the founder of Burton snowboards, claimed that:

> It doesn't have to be an extreme sport at all. There are a lot of people that, you know, snowboard in a fairly conservative manner. But I think what's a better moniker is maybe that it's a *lifestyle sport*, and a lot of the kids and people that are doing it are just completely living it all the time, and that's what distinguishes snowboarding from a lot of other sports.
>
> (Burton, 2002, cited in Wheaton, 2004a: 4)

Despite concerns that, as a sociological concept, lifestyle lacks theoretical clarity,[2] I used it in the sense proposed by Chaney (1996) and Miles (2000), signalling that, in late capitalism, lifestyle is intrinsically linked with patterns of consumption (see also Featherstone, 1991). Lifestyle helped encapsulate the ways in which participants and, increasingly, consumers of the activities sought out a particular *style of life* that was central to the meaning and experience of participation in the sport and that gave them a particular and exclusive social identity (Wheaton, 2004a: 4). As Miles (2000: 18) argues, lifestyle 'actively addresses the duality of structure and agency'. It illustrates the ways in which youth in Western societies creates identities through consumption, while also recognising that lifestyles are 'manifestations of the ways young people negotiate with structural constraints in their everyday lives' (ibid.: 35). It is in this sense that we can start to understand the significance of lifestyle in these sporting cultures. Their consumption is a socially and culturally constructed act, underpinned by determinants of choice such as age, class, gender, sexuality and ethnicity, and which cannot be understood simply in terms of market dynamics, nor in terms of a 'position which seeks to preserve the field of lifestyles and consumption, or at least a particular aspect of it (such as lifestyle sport), as an autonomous playful space beyond determination' (Featherstone, 1991: 84). While this is particularly evident and well-documented in academic and popular literature on board sports, researchers have charted the importance of lifestyle across a range of activities, including climbing (e.g. Kiewa, 2002; Lewis, 2004; Robinson, 2008), adventure racing (Kay and Laberge, 2004), skateboarding (Beal and Weidman, 2003), snowboarding (Thorpe, 2011), surfing (Ford and Brown, 2005), ultimate frisbee (Thornton, 2004) and parkour (Atkinson, 2009). Furthermore, there are similarities with other 'alternative lifestyle' groupings that have emerged from the counter culture, which involve locally situated identity politics rooted in lifestyle practices (Hetherington, 1998a: 3). Nonetheless, many activities I have labelled as lifestyle sports are also alternative sports, and aspects of them are clearly extreme (Dant and Wheaton, 2007).

Debate over the terms to describe these sports continues. It is noticeable that action sport, a term coined in the North American sports industry, has gained in currency and is now widely used by corporations and media. Lifestyle sport too has been adopted more widely, by practitioners, media commentators, academics and policy makers. Extreme sport, however, retains significance, particularly as a media and economic phenomenon (Booth and Thorpe, 2007c). As detailed in Thorpe and Booth's comprehensive *Encyclopaedia of extreme sport*, the long list of activities and sports characterised as extreme is ever growing, as is interest by spectators, media and corporations (Booth and Thorpe, 2007b: ix). In adopting the extreme label, however, they recognise that 'extreme sports do not constitute a single category of physical activity' and it 'defies ready classification' (ibid.). In empirical contexts too, such as Robinson's research on masculinity in the sport of climbing (2008: 2), the extreme label is advocated. For Robinson, it serves both as a descriptive category to describe the (relatively) high-risk forms of climbing (e.g. rock-climbing and mountaineering) on which her research focuses and as an analytical concept which she develops to help understand mundane and extreme experiences of masculinity and sport (Robinson, 2008). Nonetheless, Robinson recognises that not all the participants in her research use the term extreme. Some prefer to see it as a lifestyle and others began climbing long before the extreme moniker was in existence. Thus, rather than 'overstating the difference' in terminologies (and following Wheaton, 2004a), she emphasises that differences in nomenclature can obscure that it is the *meaning* of the terms, rather than the terms themselves, that matter. That is, to understand their *meaning*, we need to move beyond simplistic and constraining dichotomies such as traditional versus new, mainstream versus emergent or other related binaries, such as sport versus art. Lifestyle sport, and so-called 'mainstream' sport, can have elements of – to use Raymond Williams' (1977) categorisation – the residual, emergent and 'dominant' sport culture[3] (Rinehart 2000: 506). As Rinehart suggests, the difference between, and within, these sport forms is best highlighted by a range of debates, concerning their meanings, values, statuses, identities and forms.

Furthermore, it is questionable if the dichotomy between extreme and traditional sport is as 'rigid' as some theorists have claimed (Booth and Thorpe, 2007b; Robinson, 2008). In focusing on differences and the alternative nature of extreme/lifestyle sport, we have obscured many of the similarities. Michael Atkinson's (2010) exploration of the increasingly fluid nature of contemporary sporting cultures suggests that the boundaries between traditional and lifestyle sports are radically opened up. Adopting Pronger's (1998) notion of 'post-sport', he considers how fell running and yoga might be considered as spaces where participants move towards what he terms 'post-sport lifestyles':

> Fell running and yoga are forms of self and social boundary crossing, wherein modernity and techno-capitalist ways of forging athleticism as sport are placed *sous nature*. Here, the cultural associations between sport and dominant late modernist logics and identities (and all of their related trappings) are dislodged from the primary idea of athleticism.
>
> (Atkinson, 2010: 1265)

Although these are not activities one might expect to be labelled as alternative/lifestyle sports, Atkinson demonstrates that, while appearing to take the guise of mainstream sports forms, their 'individual and collective engagement' and experiences bear little similarities to their 'mainstream forms'. He suggested, therefore, that it is not the 'form and context' of sport practices but 'the orientation to and use of athletic movement in these post-sport spaces that creates fundamental differences' (ibid.). These practices help to clarify and extend our understanding of the boundaries of contemporary lifestyle sports, reminding us that our understanding of what lifestyle sports are (and might become), their boundaries and their characterisations needs to be continually reviewed in the light of emerging research. Research on parkour, in particular, which is variously described as a sport, art and discipline, has led me to a re-evaluation of some characteristics and indeed to question whether parkour can usefully be described as a lifestyle sport (see Ch. 5). Research on capoeira as a lifestyle sport has revealed similar boundary transgressions (Wisse, 2009).

To help delineate lifestyle sports and how they differ from other (traditional *and* extreme or alternative) sporting activities, I (2004a: 11–12) suggested that the defining characteristics of lifestyle sport could be summarised in a list of nine features. I did not intend this list to form the basis of an ideal type, which might falsely suggest that these activities are homogenous, fixed and unchanging. Rather my intention was to illustrate that, while each lifestyle sport has its own specificity, history, (politics of) identities and development patterns, there are also commonalities in their ethos, ideologies, forms of motion, cultural spaces and the (trans)national consumer industries that underpin their cultures. In summary, I illustrated defining features that I hoped would be refined, or indeed refuted, by subsequent research in different sports and contexts. A list of these features that incorporates more recent research is detailed below:

- The activities tend to be historically recent phenomena: activities that have emerged since the early 1960s, involving either the creation of new activities – such as kite-surfing, ultimate frisbee and snowboarding – or the adaptation of older 'residual' cultural forms, such as the (re-)emergence of paddle-surfing, or sport-climbing in rock-climbing. As Bourdieu (1984) noted, many of these sports originated in North America in the late 1960s and were then imported to Europe by American entrepreneurs.[4] With their roots in the counter-cultural social movements of the 1960s and 1970s, many retain characteristics that are different to the traditional rule-bound, competitive, institutionalised, Western 'achievement' sport cultures.[5]

- The sports are based around the consumption of new objects (boards, bikes, etc.), often involving new technologies, yet embracing change and innovation. Improvements to technologies have resulted in rapid advances in many lifestyle sports, often resulting in the fragmentation and diversification of the culture and its forms of identity (see Ch. 3).
- There is a commitment in resources, such as time and/or money, and a style of life and forms of collective expression, styles, bodily dispositions and attitudes, which they design into a distinctive lifestyle and a particular social *identity.*
- Although participants invest heavily in their lifestyles and identities, this commitment is to the feeling of being 'stoked', variously characterised as the 'buzz', being 'at one' with the environment, the standing still of time and the 'intense awareness of the moment' (Stranger, 1999: 269), through which the individual loses him/herself in 'transcendence of the self' (ibid.).[6] Participants embrace risk and danger, but in most cases as a means to provide the thrill or 'stoke' that characterises the experience.
- Lifestyle sport participants emphasise the creative, aesthetic and performative expressions of their activities. Rinehart (1998) has termed these activities 'expressive sport' (in contrast to the reward-driven 'spectacle' sports) as they are rarely conducted solely for spectators or exclusively for competitive practice. Nevertheless, practitioners are self-consciously aware of 'being seen', and presentation of self to others – whether in lived settings or in mediated forms – seems to be a part of the experience (Rinehart, 2000).
- Although in most lifestyle sports commercialisation and popularity have led to the erosion of their oppositional character, some participants still denounce regulation and institutionalisation and have an ambiguous relationship with forms of traditional competition (see Ch. 3). ESPN and other media transnationals have attempted to promote competitive forms of alternative sport, and some have subsequently been accepted as Olympic sports (Thorpe and Wheaton, 2011a, 2011b).
- Participant composition is predominantly middle-class, white and Western. However, despite being associated with 'youth', many activities have wider-based age ranges and, in some spaces, are less gender-differentiated than institutionalised sports. Unlike more traditional sports, subcultural affiliation tends not to be based around 'national' attachments, but operates more transnationally (Wheaton, 2005), often connecting with other 'alternative lifestyle' groupings, such as those found in art, fashion and music. Some practitioners refer to their activities as art.
- Activities are predominantly, but not exclusively, individualistic in form and/or attitude. Ultimate frisbee and adventure racing are two interesting

exceptions (see Kay and Laberge, 2002a; Thornton, 2004). The body is used in non-aggressive ways[7], mostly without bodily contact, focusing predominantly on personal challenges and goals.

• The locations in which these sports are practised are often new or re-appropriated (urban and/or rural) spaces, without fixed or delineated boundaries. Many occur in non-urban environments and are 'cultural spaces' in which one 'blends with' or 'becomes one with' the sea/mountain (Midol and Broyer, 1995). Non-urban lifestyle sport participants often express nostalgia for an imaginary past rural life, and a sense of nature as 'something mysterious and spiritual' (Hetherington, 1998b: 338) to be revered, protected and nurtured. However, paradoxically, some of the industries underpinning lifestyle sports (e.g. mountain resort tourism, surfboard manufacturing) contribute to rural degradation and operate in ways distant from the eco-friendly credentials espoused by environmental activist groups like Surfers Against Sewage (Wheaton, 2007b; Laviolette, 2010). Urban-based activities like skateboarding, parkour and BASE jumping from buildings adapt and redefine urban city spaces (see Ch. 5).

While most of these characteristics continue to exemplify lifestyle sport activities, as this book will illustrate, they are not fixed temporally or spatially and will need continued analytical revision. Research on parkour in particular has led to a re-evaluation of some features (see Ch. 5). Furthermore, despite these shared characteristics, lifestyle sports take multiple and increasingly fragmented forms, drawing on a vast array of narratives that are saturated with ambiguities and contradictions, reflecting the multiple configurations of identity or boundary-crossing practices characteristic of cultural processes in late modernity.

The conceptual tools for understanding lifestyle sport cultures

Sport researchers have adopted a range of sociological concepts and theoretical approaches for examining and conceptualising sporting-based collectivities and their identities. I draw attention to those I have found useful for conceptualising and mapping the cultures of lifestyle sport, and particularly the construction and performance of group identities.

Various conceptualisations of subculture have historically been, and still remain, influential in the study of lifestyle sports (e.g. Beal, 1995; Humphreys, 2003; Atkinson and Young, 2008). Other useful conceptual tools include: *subworld* (e.g. Crosset, 1995), Bourdieu's ideas *of field* and *distinction* (e.g. Wacquant, 1995; Kay and Laberge, 2002a; see below) and *serious leisure*, coined by the Canadian sociologist Robert Stebbins (1992, 2007). Serious leisure has informed my own and other studies of lifestyle sport (e.g. Dilley and Scraton, 2010), and is the foundation for Crouch and Tomlinson's (1994) concept of a *culture of commitment*, which I appropriated to describe the commitment and self-generated culture associated with lifestyle sport (Wheaton, 2003b).

However, (re)conceptualisations of 'subculture' or *subcultural formations* (Muggleton and Weinzierl, 2003b) emerging from what has been termed post-CCCS youth studies have been the central influence in my research.

Subcultural formations

Since the late 1990s, subcultural scholarship in the context of youth and style has undergone substantial revision, largely in response to criticisms of previous research, particularly that from or inspired by the Birmingham Centre for Contemporary Cultural Studies (CCCS) (see Muggleton and Weinzierl, 2003a; Bennett and Kahn-Harris, 2004). This body of work has received extensive airing in the sociological and cultural studies literature and is the basis for an extensive discussion in Wheaton (2007a). Therefore, here I highlight key points for understanding lifestyle sport cultures to ground my subsequent discussion of identity and status.

First, the limitations of the term *subculture* in many contemporary youth contexts needs to be recognised; a critique embedded in claims that more temporary, transient gatherings or 'postmodern tribes' (Featherstone, 1991: 111) characterised by 'fluid boundaries and floating memberships' (Bennett, 1999: 600) have replaced subcultural communities, particularly in style-based contexts. I have nonetheless argued that we can still usefully think about lifestyle sports as subcultures. Unlike Muggelton's style-based subculturalists who resisted 'interpellation into named subcultural identities' (2000: 93), many lifestyle sport participants demonstrate more stable, shared and uniform notions of their subcultures and forms of status and identity (Kiewa, 2002; Beal and Wilson, 2003, 2004). As Hodkinson's (2002) assessment of the contemporary Goth scene concluded, the 'bounded form' taken by the group did not fit with the postmodern emphasis on cultural fluidity, but could be conceptualised as a re-working of subculture. He documented 'group distinctiveness, identity, commitment and autonomy' (Hodkinson, 2004: 136), which he called 'cultural substance'. The Goths, like the windsurfers I studied (Wheaton, 2003b), were characterised by a 'particularly strong consciousness of group identity, and one that tended to cut across any perceived internal differences and subgroups' (Hodkinson, 2004: 144).

Second, 'post-subcultural studies' have the potential for understanding the *politics of incorporation* in lifestyle sports (Wheaton, 2007a; Thorpe and Wheaton, 2011a) and their internal status hierarchies (discussed below). Much of the early research on the institutionalisation and commercialisation of lifestyle sports focused on the negative effects of these processes, seeing incorporation as a process that undermined the 'authentic' oppositional or resistant character of 'alternative' sports (Wheaton and Beal, 2003a) and typically conceptualised commercialisation as 'a top-down process of corporate exploitation and commodification' (Edwards and Corte, 2010: 1137). As Giulianotti (2005: 56) suggests, the CCCS approach was insufficient for 'explaining "resistant" subcultures that actively embrace commodification, to function as niche businesses within

the sport industry'. The role of media and commerce in youths' cultural formations was not given systematic attention, nor was an explanation provided for
what occurs after the subculture becomes public or 'mainstream'. In contrast,
post-CCCS approaches attempt to understand and explain the complex and shifting power relations involved in the commercialisation of youth cultures before,
during and after the group becomes incorporated into the mainstream. They
recognise that the CCCS's concept of resistance – as a struggle with dominant
hegemonic culture – was often romanticised and misused; youthful leisure was
over-politicised and 'the subtle relations of power play within it' were largely
ignored (Thornton, 1995: 7). They, therefore, adopt various post-structuralist
conceptions of power, such as advocated by Foucault, along with theoretical
insights from Bourdieu, Maffesoli and Lefevre (see Muggleton and Weinzierl,
2003b).[8] As I have outlined (Wheaton, 2007a), this research alerts us to the
'contradictory nature of resistance in postmodern times' (Atkinson and Wilson,
2002: 381); provoking us to ask questions such as 'who is the subculture resisting, where is the resistance cited, under what circumstances is resistance taking
place, and in what forms is it manifest?' (cf. Barker, 2000, in Wheaton, 2007a).

Third, while recognising the importance of (and dominant focus on) 'micro-
political dimensions', in analyses of (lifestyle sport) subcultures, there has been
a concurrent de-politicisation of youth subcultures, particularly a failure to attend
to their 'macro-political context' (Martin, 2002: 79). Somewhat paradoxically
then, at a historic conjuncture when youth protest activities, such as the anti-
globalisation movement, have burgeoned, post-subculturalists have tended to
under-politicise youth formations (Muggleton and Weinzierl, 2003a). As argued
in Chapter 1, subcultural research must attend to *both* the micro-political – the
politics of everyday life – and the macro-political, particularly enduring questions of political economy and social stratification.

Identity and status: theoretical and conceptual issues

The lifestyle sport participant's group identity is marked by a range of symbolic
markers, extending from the specialist equipment used and clothing worn,
extending from the specialist equipment used and clothing worn, to musical taste
and the vehicles driven (such as the long-term status of the VW kombi van in
surf culture). There are also less 'visible' aspects that contribute to the social
construction, performance and regulation of embodied identity, including argot,
'attitude', forms of physical competence and prowess, and the use of space. As
research across a range of different (street-, mountain- and water-based) lifestyle
sports has detailed, although taste and style play an important part in constructing a distinctive sporting identity, members cannot 'buy their way into' the core
of the culture (e.g. Wheaton, 2000; Ford and Brown, 2005; Thorpe, 2011).
Rather, for core participants, 'authentic' identity tends to be constructed around
the embodied performance of the activity, around 'doing it' (Wheaton and Beal,
2003a). It is not my intention here to revisit these debates, but to discuss how
subcultural identities can be conceptualised theoretically, highlighting the

importance of recognising the constructed, shifting, fluid nature of these processes.

My own conceptualisation of (sub)cultural identity and how it is constructed, contested and (re)made has been rooted in cultural studies and post-CCCS approaches to youth subcultures. Identity, from this perspective, is a dynamic process undergoing constant transformation, about 'becoming' as well as being (Hall, 1990). Drawing on Butler's (1990, 1993) work on gender as a 'performative enactment', Muggleton (2000: 154) suggests that subcultural identity can usefully be seen as a performance that is never fixed or determinate, but is in a state of flux and change. Central to these identity performances, however, are the ways in which we perceive others as locating us and what differentiates us. As the plethora of empirical research on youth in the cultural studies tradition has demonstrated, claims to authenticity are central to the internal and 'external' status hierarchies in youth subcultures; 'authenticity is something sought, fought over and reinvented' (Brunner, 1989, cited in Rinehart and Sydor, 2003: 9).

Power hierarchies within a subculture

In trying to understand and map these processes, I found Sarah Thornton's conceptualisation of subculture as 'taste cultures' (Thornton, 1995: 8), emerging from her research on dance cultures in the 1990s, particularly useful. Through both her engagement with the subcultural sociology of the Chicago school (notions of status) and her appropriation of Bourdieu's (1984) work in *Distinction* (particularly the idea of cultural capital), she coined the term *subcultural capital*. While Bourdieu's work focused on the ways each class faction has distinctive preferences or tastes for leisure consumption, Thornton illustrates how taste can also be a marker of social identity that functions to classify other social groupings, including the social and cultural distinctions or hierarchies *within* popular culture. Subcultural capital involves a series of *distinctions*, or *authenticity claims*, within the culture (such as the authentic versus the phoney, the hip versus the mainstream and the underground versus the media). However, it is underpinned by *structural* differences in gender, sexuality, race, class and age (Thornton, 1995), contributing to gendered and racialised power hierarchies and exclusion processes. Despite its limitations (see Carrington and Wilson, 2004),[9] her approach recognises that a politics of authenticity underpins subcultural statuses, which in lifestyle sport is fought symbolically, through embodied attributes, materially and spatially. It also highlights the importance of mapping the internal power hierarchies, or differential statuses, *within* as well as *between* subcultures.

The negotiation of space for the expression of community and subcultural identities has long been a thread in youth subcultures, which can be traced back to both the CCCS and the Chicago school traditions. However, more recently, the 'spatial' turn in the social sciences (Warf and Arias, 2009) – particularly through the influence of cultural geography – has alerted researchers to the ways in which power inequalities are played out and reproduced through space

(Skelton and Valentine, 1998; Van Ingen, 2003; Caudwell and Browne, 2011). The impact of spatiality in lifestyle sporting spaces is also growing (see Ch. 5), emerging from Borden's work on skateboarding (2001) exploring the competing uses of social space and how 'different social groups appropriate and mark out social spaces within a particular place' (Bennett, 2000: 53).

Distinction and taste: the turn to Bourdieu

While a range of theoretical approaches offer productive ways of understanding the contested power relations within and between subcultural space and identities, another productive trend has been the implementation of Bourdieu's concepts of field, habitus, capital, style and taste, to 'facilitate insights' into sporting bodies 'as possessors of power, and the struggle over the legitimate use and meaning of the body' (Thorpe, 2011: 121). This is an approach championed by Joanne Kay in her revealing study of the adventure racing field (Kay and Laberge, 2002a, 2004) and subsequently adopted across a number of studies, including snowboarding (Thorpe, 2011), skateboarding (Atencio *et al.*, 2009) and climbing (Beedie, 2007).

Following Bourdieu (1984), we can conceptualise specific lifestyle sports as social *fields* that are 'characterised by the movement of the different types of *capital*' – cultural, physical and social capital – that are central to identity construction (Beedie, 2007: 25). The concept of field allows for the 'structured systems of social positions occupied' by individuals or groups of individuals engaged in the same activity (Thorpe, 2011: 116). Thus, as Kay and Laberge demonstrate (2004: 156), field and capital are useful not just for the study of social class, but of 'all unequal power relations', including those 'anchored in gender' (see Ch. 4). Kay and Laberge illustrate how these concepts help to understand the social dynamics and power relationships 'fuelling the sports evolution' (2004: 157) and the 'internal and external' power relationships (ibid.).

Despite their different theoretical roots, there are clear similarities between post-CCCS and Bourdieu-derived approaches, particularly in the questions they provoke the researchers to examine. For example, Thornton (1995) adopts *taste* as a key signifier or marker of social identity and in the accumulation of subcultural capital. Likewise, Thorpe (2011) explores how style and clothing is an important (but shifting) marker of the 'inter-group divisions' between snowboarders and skiers that share the same space, and between different snowboarding styles. In their analysis of the distinction of risk in forms of skateboarding, Atencio *et al.* (2009) explore how certain *styles* of skating (e.g. street skating) gain greater symbolic and material capital, while others (e.g. park skating) become devalued. They argue that 'the ways in which individuals come to be valued', both within a particular social field and across the range of social fields, is 'determined by the recognition of their embodied attributes' (ibid.: 1). Bourdieu's theoretical schema, therefore, highlights the ways in which the body itself is a site of distinction, 'how distinctions among snowboarders are expressed as differences between "embodied taste and styles" that are used to practise, perform and regulate in snowboarding spaces within the alpine snow field' (Thorpe, 2011: 17).

Despite different theoretical trajectories, these perspectives all point to the importance of examining the different and competing collective spaces and identities *within* lifestyle sport subcultures, and the power relationships that underpin them. That is, to be sensitive to the multiple voices, subjectivities and experiences *within* the subcultural group – including the marginalised[10] – and to expose the ways in which forms of subcultural capital underpin these power relations.[11]

Internal status hierarchies: fragmentation and de-differentiation

Facilitated by commercialisation processes, many lifestyle sport subcultures have fragmented into multiple scenes, each with their own styles of participation, such as the street and ramp skateboarders discussed by Atencio *et al.* (2009). However, we need to explore how these subgroups differentiate themselves, (re)constructing boundaries and (re)making claims to subcultural space, authenticity and status. In the windsurfing culture, a range of participation scenes emerged, based on different types of windsurfing activity, including longboarding, funboards/freeriding, speed sailing, freestyle and wave-sailing, each with a different style of participation (Wheaton, 2000). The wave-sailors tended to gain most 'respect' (status) due to the activity being the hardest to learn (requiring most commitment in time) and the most hazardous or risky form of the activity. Wave-sailors I interviewed had less 'respect' for speed or slalom sailors, who they characterised as being lower in skill, more 'into equipment' and more materialistic (ibid.). Such status hierarchies underpinned by authenticity claims were also apparent between subgroups of windsurfers, across types of windsurfing activities and across different geographical spaces. Similar authenticity claims are apparent in other lifestyle sports (Wheaton and Beal, 2003a). For example, Borden (2001) discusses the 'territorialisation of skate parks' in which 'locals' claim a skate park as their own, a process that is underpinned by spatially defined insider ('us') vs. outsider ('them') statuses. In Chapter 6, I explore these identity processes in parkour, in particular, contested ideas of parkour as sport or performance art.

Status differences are also played out *between* lifestyle sport cultures, particularly board sports. A hierarchy exists in which activities like surfing and skating are generally accepted as having greater subcultural capital (being 'hard core') than activities such as body boarding and windsurfing. For example, the surfing media use derogatory terms to describe windsurfers ('wind wankers') and body boarders ('spongers' and 'shark biscuits').[12]

However, there is some evidence to suggest the boundaries between activities are becoming increasingly blurred. Kiewa's (2002) study of Australian climbers suggests that the symbolic boundaries between what she terms 'real' (or traditional) and 'pretend' climbers are being blurred both in mediated discourse and in lived experiences. This process is evident between board sports that were previously quite oppositional. In an article on kite culture[13] in *Kiteworld* magazine, the author notes the 'dramatic break down of the boundaries between lifestyle sports'[14]:

> snowboarding magazines have interviewed freestyle skiers – long con-
> sidered the arch enemy – while tow-in surfing is gaining acceptance in titles
> as purist as *The Surfer's Path*. A dawning realisation has swept across many
> of us who pursue 'soul sports' – a recognition that perhaps we all share the
> same kind of stoke, independent of the unique experience our chosen sport
> gives us. Kite-boarding owes a lot to this new cross-over culture, and its
> explosive growth is in part down to the ways it has embraced and accepted
> so many influences from such a diverse range of sports.
>
> (Orec, 2003: 96)

Clearly then, our conceptualisation of subcultural identities must be attentive to this subcultural mobility and movement – the way status and identities shift and change and how individuals carve their own paths through subcultural spaces (Donnelly and Young, 1988). Commercialisation, as the next chapter explores, is driving many of these processes.

3   Mapping the lifestyle sportscape

From counter-culture to co-option

The landscape of lifestyle sport is characterised by the presence of a range of increasingly transnational corporate forces. Lifestyle sports have been appropriated to sell a vast array of products, services and experiences. Commentators have, therefore, described extreme sport as a 'co-opted' sporting movement, increasingly associated with the global expansion and reproduction of consumer capitalism and controlled by multinational and transnational corporations and media organisations (cf. Wheaton, 2005). Nonetheless, more recent research across different sports and contexts has illuminated how consumer capitalism penetrates lifestyle sport cultures in complex and contradictory ways (e.g. Rinehart, 2008; Edwards and Corte, 2010; Stranger, 2010), illustrating that the media and consumer industries' roles are often more complex, contradictory and fluid than incorporation and co-option. Consumers and participants re-work the images and meanings circulated in and by global consumer culture. Research on institutionalisation and professionalisation processes, especially as expressed through attitudes to competition and regulation, also provides important insights into understanding how co-option has been contested, and is my focus here.

Regulation and sportisation

One of the defining features of lifestyle sports is their spontaneous nature, with participation predominantly taking place in informal settings, often with a lack of external regulation or institutionalisation. However, there is increasing pressure from both commercial operators and state-funded or sanctioned leisure and education providers to professionalise, institutionalise and regulate. These processes are occurring both at the elite/professional level – for example, to enable the activities to be incorporated in traditional forms of competition, such as the Olympic Games – and at the grass-roots, where conflicts around the use of space or concerns about safety are played out. This section examines some examples of these intertwined processes of professionalisation, sportisation, institutionalisation and regulation, processes which are then exemplified in Chapter 5 in the context of the emergence of parkour.

Lifestyle sports are increasingly global in influence; international sporting rules and organisations have been established and, in some cases, competition between 'national teams' has evolved and grown. In some ways, then, the historical development pattern of lifestyle sports, particularly at the elite level, mirrors the 'sportisation phases' suggested by Maguire (following Elias) in his discussion of the globalisation of more traditional 'achievement sports' (Maguire, 1999). Elias described 'sportisation' as the process by which play-like activities become more regulated and organised (Elias and Dunning, 1986). Yet in many lifestyle sports, clubs and organisations tend to be formed only where required – for example, to assist in access to facilities or spaces. In windsurfing and kayaking, for example, clubs have been formed as a way to secure access to a particular beach or waterway (Wheaton, 1997a; Gilchrist and Ravenscroft, 2008).[1] Participants remain hostile to rules and regulations, especially those that are externally driven.

The Olympic paradox: incorporation and contestation[2]

The Olympics is the pinnacle in the careers of many athletes from traditional sports. However, as Thorpe and Wheaton (2011a, 2011b) explore, among many lifestyle sport athletes, events such as the X Games or athlete-organised competitions continue to hold more 'cultural authenticity' (Wheaton, 2005) and thus tend to be valued more highly within the lifestyle sports culture and industry. Practitioners have been wary of their incorporation in these traditional forms of competition, seeing it as a form of 'selling out' their 'alternative' values and ideologies. The cultural politics involved in lifestyle sports' incorporation was graphically illustrated by the transnational skateboarding communities' reactions to reports that 'skateboarding could make its Olympic debut at the 2012 London Games' (Peck and agencies, 2008). Thousands of skateboarders from across the world responded by signing an online petition (The Petition, 2010) titled *No Skateboarding in the Olympics* addressed to the IOC president:

> With due respect for Olympic Athletes, we the undersigned skateboarders and advocates strongly request that the IOC NOT RECOGNIZE SKATEBOARDING AS AN OLYMPIC SPORT, or use skateboarding to market the Olympics. Further, we ask that the IOC NOT recognize any individuals or groups claiming to be the IOC recognized governing body of skateboarding or provide funding to them. Skateboarding is not a 'sport' and we do not want skateboarding exploited and transformed to fit into the Olympic program. We feel that Olympic involvement will change the face of skateboarding and its individuality and freedoms forever. We feel it would not in any way support skateboarders or skate parks. We do not wish to be part of it and will not support the Olympics if skateboarding is added as an Olympic sport.
>
> (The Petition, 2010: para. 1)

In contrast to the ideology of achievement sport, attitudes to participating in organised competitions tend to stress more 'intrinsic' factors, such as challenging the self or the environment, even among elite and professional participants. When the first Olympic snowboard champion (1998), Ross Rebagliati, was stripped of his medal for allegedly smoking marijuana, he was celebrated by sections of the snowboarding subculture and media for having publicly re-established snowboarding's 'alternative' image (although his medal was later reinstated) (Humphreys, 2003; Thorpe, 2011). World champion Terje Haakonsen, who refused to participate in the 1998 Olympics, claimed to be protesting against snowboarders being turned into 'uniform-wearing, flag-bearing, walking logo[s]' (Mellgren, 1998: para. 8). Haakonsen revealed stronger identification with the global snowboarding culture and a transnational snowboarding company (Burton) than his nation:

> How can you have a sponsor for ten years and then you go to the Olympics and you can't even pack your own bags because the nation has sold you as a package? Norway is a great country to live, but it's never supported me like my sponsors. My flag should be Burton not Norway.
>
> (cited in Reed, 2005: 135)

For some committed lifestyle sports participants, not just snowboarders, a transnational sporting identity takes precedence over nationality (see also Wheaton, 2005), even at the Olympics (Thorpe and Wheaton, 2011b).

Re-assessing snowboarders' attitudes to Olympic incorporation a decade or more later, it is evident that contemporary snowboarding culture encompasses a range of subgroups, each embodying different values, styles of participation and contrasting viewpoints. In a context where Olympic and professional competitions have thrived, reflected in increasing professionalism at the elite level, many participants do not see the inclusion of their sports in the Olympic Games as a form of 'selling out' but, reflecting trends observed in other contemporary 'post-subcultural' youth and sport cultures (Beal and Wilson, 2004; Rinehart, 2008), they see it as offering further opportunities for participation and consumption within an already highly fragmented culture and industry. Nonetheless, most committed participants are aware that the Olympic Games are not the arena where the most progressive manoeuvres, innovative technologies and latest styles develop, and thus prefer alternative forums for performing, producing and consuming their sport. The marriage between the Olympic movement and snowboarding remains highly tenuous and based on compromise by both parties. Residual traces of snowboarding's counter-cultural past remain, which lead to 'cultural clashes' with the disciplinary, nationalistic Olympic regime (see examples in Thorpe and Wheaton, 2011a).

While snowboarding's inclusion in the Games (1998) has caused most debate, as Thorpe and Wheaton outline, contestation about the incorporation of other alternative sporting lifestyles has occurred, namely windsurfing[3] (Los Angeles 1984) and BMX (2008), which was introduced in the Beijing Games under the 'cycling' discipline[4] (see Thorpe and Wheaton, 2011a). However, despite the similarities in subcultural philosophies and ethos, the *particularities* of each activity need exploration (ibid.). The cultural politics *between* and *within* groups are unique, based on the distinctive history, ideologies, identities and development patterns of each lifestyle sport culture, and the specific historical juncture within which the incorporation processes occurred. In each case, the market-driven process of incorporation has led to complex but contextually specific power struggles between the IOC and governing bodies, media conglomerates and lifestyle sport cultures and their industries.

However, with the global economic downturn, some lifestyle sports industries are actively lobbying for the mainstreaming of their sports. The kite-surfing industry successfully petitioned the Brazil organising committee to be included in the 2016 Olympic sailing regatta (Sail-World, 2010) a decision that, following much controversy has since been revoked by the ISA (in 2013). Likewise, the International Surfing Association (ISA), with support from some of surfing's biggest stars, like Kelly Slater, has presented proposals to the IOC outlining the benefits of surfing's inclusion in the summer programme, even if this takes place in artificial wave pools (Aguerre, 2009).

This discussion of lifestyle sports' incorporation into the Olympics (reflecting the conclusions drawn by post-CCCS scholars) illustrates that inclusion does not follow a continuum from 'residual, emergent, to dominant' (Williams, 1977) or from 'oppositional to co-opted' (Rinehart, 2008). Rather, contemporary lifestyle sport cultures are highly fragmented and in a constant state of flux, such that myriad types of cultural contestation (as well as passive and reflexive consumption) are occurring, often simultaneously.

The X Games: commercialisation, professionalisation and shifting identities

The X Games – the self-defined 'worldwide leader' in action sports – is at the centre of many debates surrounding the commercialisation process (Rinehart, 2008: 175). The brainchild of the cable television network ESPN,[5] and backed by a range of transnational corporate sponsors, the X Games has played a central role in the global diffusion and expansion of the lifestyle sport industry and culture (Rinehart, 2000). In 1995, the inaugural summer X Games held in Rhode Island (US) featured 27 events in nine categories, ranging from bungee jumping to skateboarding. Following the success of the summer events, ESPN staged the first winter X Games in California in 1997, drawing 38,000 spectators and televised in 198 countries and territories in 21 different languages (Pedersen and Kelly, 2000). Blurring the boundaries between music festival and sporting event (Rinehart, 2008), the X Games have been hugely successful in capturing the imagination of the lucrative youth market. Sixty-three million people globally watched the 2002 X Games; in contrast to the ageing Olympic viewership, the average age of these viewers was 20 years (Thorpe and Wheaton, 2011a). While in the early years the X Games were all based in North America, they are now also held in Europe, Asia and South America (ESPN.go.com). In 2012, China hosted the KIA X Games Asia for the sixth consecutive year (ESPN.go.com). Audiences have also become increasingly global; the Winter X Games 13 was televised on ESPN's international networks to more than 122 countries, including Australia, New Zealand, Israel, Africa, Latin America, the Caribbean and the Middle East (Gorman, 2009).

The emergence of the X Games prompted heated debate among grass-roots practitioners who opposed ESPN's co-option of their lifestyle into television-tailored 'sports' (Rinehart, 2008). Beal described how, in the mid-1990s, skateboarders in Colorado, North America, who embraced competition and sponsorship were called 'rats' (Beal, 1995). However, ESPN has had a profound impact on defining skating, representing for a majority of world viewers how skateboarding can become a 'competition' (Rinehart and Sydor, 2003). Beal's more recent research in North America reveals skaters' changing attitudes to commercialisation, demonstrating they have become less critical of sponsorship and professionalism, seeing the benefits to the skating community (Beal and Weidman, 2003; Beal and Wilson, 2004). Many contemporary participants now recognise mass-mediated events such as the X Games as endemic to lifestyle sport in the twenty-first century and are embracing the new opportunities for increased media exposure, sponsorship and celebrity they offer (Beal and Wilson, 2004). The X Games have become the ultimate forum for setting records and performing ever-more technical and creative manoeuvres for international audiences. Nevertheless, as evident from the vociferous reaction to Olympic incorporation, many skateboarders continue to resist changes that will lead to increased regulation or a change in the ethos of skating, such as a creative/artistic sensibility, self-expression and an individualistic attitude (ibid.). They also continue to stress the importance of 'intrinsic motivation' – that is, incentives should be oriented to the act of skating, a commitment to the 'process' and not 'solely for money' or 'looking cool'. Beal concluded that skaters are not uniformly *against* the commercialisation process, but are concerned about how their activity is portrayed and the resultant impact that may have (ibid.). Like other lifestyle sport participants, skateboarders' assessment of commercialisation's impact is infused with ambiguity and contradiction (ibid.).

Increasing popularity has resulted in many lifestyle sports becoming fragmented. Within the current post-Fordist capitalist system, this fragmentation supports new niche markets essential for the continual economic growth of the industry. Lifestyle sports-related companies and media employ an array of creative production, marketing and design strategies to target market segments and accelerate turnover of fashions and styles (Humphreys, 1997; Wheaton and Beal, 2003a). Cultural fragmentation has also led to ideological differences among groups of participants, with various styles of participation, demonstrating philosophical, skill and commitment differences. In skateboarding, these range from park skating in relatively sanitised and controlled environments, to the more aggressive, unregulated and male-dominated street skating (Atencio *et al.*, 2009). Fragmentation continues to cause tensions and debate within these lifestyle sport cultures regarding processes of commercialisation and incorporation.

The professionalisation of surfing provides another revealing example of sub-cultural fragmentation, and what Thorpe and Wheaton (2011a) term the *intra-cultural* politics of lifestyle sports.

The professionalisation of surfing: counter-culture to Coca-Cola

Booth has written at length about tensions and conflicts in the history of the pro-fessionalisation and codification of modern surfing (Booth, 2001: 112). Initially, in the 1960s, the 'soul surfing' movement ('riding the waves for the good of one's soul') explicitly rejected materialism and competition, extolling 'creativity and self-expression within a co-operative environment' (ibid.: 113). Soul surfers interpreted their activity as an escape from bourgeois society, fusing surfing with the counter-culture. As surfing star Nat Young claimed, he was 'supporting the revolution' (ibid.). Writing in the late 1970s in Australia and early 1990s in the US, respectively, Pearson (1979) and Farmer (1992) observed a 'competitive taboo' in the surfing culture, arguing that competition against other individuals was not valued.

An interesting aspect of this professionalisation process was the ways in which the attempts – initially in the 1960s – to impose 'universal' international rules caused conflict between the main settings of California, Australia and Hawaii. Each wanted to preserve the 'authenticity' of its different surfing 'style', underpinned by divergent philosophies about 'mankind's (*sic*) relationship with nature' (Booth, 2001: 101). These styles reflected differing cultural values and masculine identities; the Hawaiians tended to 'dance' with the waves, whereas the Australians (and white South Africans) had developed a more aggressive and materialistic attitude reflective of Australian (sporting) masculinity. These dif-ferences and the consequences for the development of the sport, and Hawaiian culture more broadly in that period, are graphically illustrated in the documen-tary *Bustin' Down The Door* (Gosch, 2009), which outlines this key phase in the professionalisation of surfing. The film illustrates the ways in which white non-Hawaiian surfers in Hawaii in the mid-1970s actively professionalised their activity in an attempt to gain legitimacy as a 'sport' and to be able to sustain their lifestyle. However, for the Hawaiians this colonisation of surfing was seen as neo-colonialism; Europeans and North Americans, they believed, had stripped Polynesians of their culture and identity, and surfing was perceived as the last bastion, so they were not going to give up *their* meaning of surfing culture without a fight.

However, surfing has increasingly embraced capitalist culture via profession-alisation and, in the twenty-first century, professional surfers – including Poly-nesian Hawaiians – and surfing competitions (run under the auspices of the Association of Surfing Professionals) are a central element of global surf culture. But the impact of surfing's professionalisation on the *local* experiences of grass-roots surfing is geographically variable. In Australia, arguably where surfing's penetration of 'mainstream' sport is most advanced, surfing has become such a popular and widespread activity that it is part of the national psyche (Evers,

2009) and hard to conceptualise as different from other athletic pursuits. Surfing is part of the school PE curriculum, competitions at all levels (youth, masters, local, national, etc.) are prevalent and it has become an important aspect of sport policy provision. For example, Surfing Australia has aligned itself with Coca-Cola and The Australian Sports Commission in a partnership to promote safe surfing participation across the population (Kay, 2005).

In contrast, locales like the UK where the activity is less accessible (due to climate and geography) and has a much shorter history (see Mansfield, 2009), *being a surfer* still retains a degree of exclusivity. Here the professionalisation of elite surfing has had far less impact on the experiences of most participants, other than as a source of inspiration in surfing media or via consumption of products. Some are still wary of the 'popularity paradox', which they see as causing over-crowding. In the 1990s, the British Surfing Association actively dissociated itself from institutional control, claiming that it did not need government help or money (via Sport England) – the sport was already getting too popular and beaches too busy (personal interview with surf promoter/teacher). Of interest is whether, over time, surfing in previously 'non-core' places in parts of Europe, Asia and South America will mirror the Australian and North American 'sports' models. Or, conversely, will differentiation, fragmentation and the emergence of new styles continue to proliferate, such as the recent long-board revival, paddle-surfing resurgence and increasing acceptance of tow-in surfing.[6]

The changing values of surfing, and the surfing field, have also impacted on other activities that share space and participants, such as other craft to surf waves (e.g. body boarding, surf kayaking, windsurfing and kite-surfing). Windsurfing appropriated surfing's soul-surfing ethos, a style of participation which constructed the windsurfer as at one with 'nature', unfettered by materialism and appearing to be a rejoinder to competition and commercialism (Wheaton and Beal, 2003a). Nevertheless, simultaneously, elite windsurfing (driven by the industry) has embraced competition in any, and every, form it can, to bolster the waning windsurfing market. It is hard to imagine a less 'authentic' event than the made-for-TV spectacle of indoor windsurfing. These 'competitions' involved giant fans propelling windsurfers in slalom races and spectacular aerial antics off a jump-ramp, against a backdrop of loud music and a laser show. The prize money for these events matched that of the 'real' windsurfing competitions held in dangerous surf, and in the early twentieth century generated more subcultural media coverage than Olympic windsurfing. Thus, as Tomlinson *et al.* (2005) suggest, the forms of governance in lifestyle sports are particularly complex areas that require analysis. In windsurfing, the focus of the national governing body (NGB) is Olympic windsurfing, which is at odds with most other competitive and non-competitive forms of the sport.

While much of the discussion to date has focused on lifestyle sports that claim to have a special relationship with – even stewardship of – nature, as Chapter 5 explores, there are particular issues around the politics of space in urban-based lifestyle sports such as skateboarding and parkour.

Discourses of risk and irresponsibility

For many commentators on extreme/lifestyle sports, it is the element of risk inherent in these sports that provokes fascination. An increasing number of philosophical, sociological and socio-psychological theories have been proposed to examine the meaning and differing cultural constructions of voluntary risk-taking in these activities (see Thorpe, 2009b). Sociological theories have often understood risk-taking in sport as either cathartic or symptomatic of and rooted in the uncertainty inherent in a period of rapid social transformation (Giulianotti, 2009). Here risk-taking in lifestyle sport is seen as an escape from the over-rationalised and sanitised leisure experiences characteristic of late modernity, providing 'an antidote to our safety-first shrink-wrapped world' (Appleton, 2005, cited in Booth and Thorpe, 2007c: 192). For example, Le Breton proposes that dangerous sports are most prevalent in those societies that can provide their members with social and economic stability (2000), and Fletcher (2008) argues that risk-taking appeals more to a professional middle-class habitus. Stranger (1999), however, argues that the *embodied experiences* of high-risk sports practitioners require analysis. He offers a framework that explores thrill and risk-taking leisure (specifically surfing), linking it to the 'postmodern mode of aestheticisation'; risk-taking in surfing, he argues, is inherent in the search for an experience of 'self-transcendence' within the surfing aesthetic (ibid.). Laurendeau (2008, 2011) advocates the need to explore the gendered dimensions of voluntary risk (see also Robinson, 2004).

While theoretical interpretations of risk-taking is not a focus of this book, I make some observations about the discourse of risk promulgated by the media and explore how this has driven forms of regulation. It is important to recognise that accounts that overemphasise the risky and dangerous aspects of lifestyle sport are misleading. The actual risks in many extreme/lifestyle sports do not exceed, or are less than, those in traditional sports activities like football and swimming (Booth and Thorpe, 2007c; Dumas and Laforest, 2009). However for the majority of the population, the mass media are at the forefront of gaining information and knowledge about risk (Furedi, 1997; Davidson, 2008). As media theorists outline, the news media tend to frame events in particular ways, such as focusing on the relatively rare incident, accentuating negative events and the 'amplification and attenuation' of risk (Kasperson and Kasperson, 1996: 97, cited in Davidson, 2008: 4). The ways in which various youth subcultures have been 'stigmatised and romanticised in the popular media' and how the press has fuelled various 'moral panics about the troubled and troubling youth' (Wilson, 2008: 137) has been a long-standing theme in (British) research on subcultures. Nonetheless, as Davidson's analysis of the media's representation of a mountaineering disaster in New Zealand reveals, typically, a set of competing discourses are produced. They emphasise the negative outcome in outdoor adventures, while simultaneously promoting the heroic 'true adventurer' who accepts danger and the need to act in spite of uncertainty and even the possibility of death (Davidson, 2008).

Mediated discourses: risk and irresponsibility

These contradictory discourses of risk, (ir)responsibility and heroism infuse the dramatised media reporting of many lifestyle sports, and it is not unusual for the exploits of lifestyle sport participants to make news headlines. In November 2009, during a spate of storms that caused widespread flooding devastation, two British kite-surfers made the national news (in a momentary distraction from the widespread structural chaos inflicted by the gales). They attempted to jump 100 feet in the air over Worthing pier in winds gusting at more than 40 mph (BBC News, 2009).[7] The feat was subsequently taken up by a range of national media, including the *Daily Mail* (Derbyshire, 2009) and the *Sun,* and various recordings of the act were posted and then watched and discussed on YouTube, as well as across various online forums, including among kite-surfers. I argue that this moment – both the physical act and the wider commentary across the mass and niche media – characterises the public anxiety about young men engaged in irresponsible risk-taking through lifestyle sports, revealing how such risk-taking behaviour is simultaneously revered and admired.

There is of course nothing particularly new about such risk-taking behaviour; the historical development of mountaineering illustrates how similar concerns have been prevalent since the nineteenth century (Gilchrist, 2007). As Furedi (2006) outlines, the media's fixation on risk is symptomatic of the broader social process, not its cause (Davidson, 2008). Modernity is a risk culture, and an increased awareness of risk as a product of human action, rather than fate, and the need, therefore, to manage such risks are important features of late modern societies (Beck, 1992; Giddens, 1991). Risk-management has become a powerful form of discursive control (Furedi, 1997). However, this kite-surfing incident illustrates and reflects the contradictions inherent in mediated discourse and public perceptions about many of the more dangerous lifestyle sports activities, including aspects of climbing, parkour, bouldering, BASE jumping, gliding and surfing.[8]

Making sense of 'the jump'

> Two kite surfers from West Sussex took advantage of strong winds on the south coast to realise an ambition to jump over Worthing pier.
>
> (BBC News, 2009)

The mass media reporting of the act focused on and reinforced the spectacular (Celsi *et al.*, 1993), either via moving image clips or displaying large photographic images or sequences to show the enormity of the feat. According to YouTube statistical data, the clip had 70,000 hits in the first week, from around the world. The *Mail* described it as a 'death-defying stunt': 'the terrifying moment when death-defying kite-surfers took their lives into their hands' (Derbyshire, 2009). The photo caption also emphasised the 'adrenaline rush', while reinforcing that the kite-surfer was choosing this activity and in so doing taking control of his life and destiny: 'a kite surfer takes his life in his hands' (ibid.). While one of the duo described it as 'epic' ('It was everything I've lived for – amazing'), the pair (in their early twenties) were quick to add that 'the jump was quite hazardous and should not be attempted by amateurs' (BBC News, 2009). An interview with the kite-surfers (Lewis Crathern and Jake Scrace) on BBC South (16 November 2009) revealed that, far from being an impulsive act, they had been planning the stunt for several years and had aborted several previous attempts waiting for the 'perfect conditions'.

'Outsider' discourses

The act, predictably, provoked outrage from some commentators, who described the kite-surfers as irresponsible, and the act as dangerous. As one wrote: 'What a stupid stunt, totally irresponsible. These kite-surfers were not wearing helmets nor life jackets. Less experienced kiters will now try to emulate them and they will get seriously injured or die' (Mail Online comment, 17 November, on Derbyshire, 2009). The discourse of safety was a common thread, specifically the lack of safety equipment and the fact that others (impressionable, young) were likely to copy them. Others criticised the activity itself (or authorities that permit it), noting that kite-surfing is 'not at all cool' but a 'young', 'dangerous' and 'still largely unregulated sport'. In a similar vein, the validity of being a *professional* kite-surfer was in question, and these young men were characterised as layabouts, playing into long-standing discourses about surfers as slackers and 'dole blunders' (Law, 2001):

> Professional kite-surfers?? They should be sent to do community service.
> (Female, Mail Online comment, 19 November, in Derbyshire, 2009)

> 'Professional kite surfer'? So who pays him? ... Probably living off benefits, while the rest of us have to work so he can enjoy himself all day.
> (Male, Mail Online comment, 17 November, in Derbyshire, 2009)

These views only represent part of the picture; others admired their physical prowess and gave approval based on a discourse of individual rights and responsibilities:

> It's up to them what they do. If they love doing it leave them alone. Probably is irresponsible of them but who are they hurting, you only live once.
> (Male, Mail Online comment, 20 November, in Derbyshire, 2009)

> Absolutely awesome ... wish I had the skills and guts to do it.
> (Male, Mail Online comment, 17 November, in Derbyshire, 2009)

These men (for irrespective of their gender, they are depicted as male) who (annually) make national headlines battling the stormy seas on their windsurfers/

kite-surfers/surfboards are depicted as brave and fearless, playing into wider and historically based discourses of the white male imperial 'adventure-hero' (see Farley, 2005; also see Ch. 4).

Insider fears: increased regulation

Kite-surfers' responses tended to follow two threads: admiration of physical prowess, skill or guts; or, conversely, fear that the act will be perceived by outsiders as fool-hardly, fuelling perceptions of kiters as irresponsible, and so promoting calls for regulation of the sport:

> EXTREMELY STUPID! Yet another couple of idiots looking to give the sport of kiteboarding bad publicity. Now the next pair of idiots will eventually come along and try to go higher or jump further and DIE in the process, thus causing a ban on the sport. Yeah way to not think!
>
> (YouTube posting, November 2009)

Such fears were well grounded. Since kite-surfing's emergence in the UK in the late 1990s, fears have been expressed about the sport's dangerous nature, particularly from other beach users and the owners/managers of spaces where the sport is practised. Agencies with a duty of care, ranging from local councils to water regulatory bodies (like the Chichester Harbour Conservancy), have zoned, limited or banned kite-surfing activity. My observation of kite-surfing along the South Coast and conversations with participants around the country have revealed numerous attempts to regulate and control the sport, often following an incident where kite-surfing has made media headlines for being dangerous and the cause of injury.

While some of the dangers (to participants and onlookers) are specific to this activity, and particularly to the nature of the equipment (the kite), the patterns are more generic and reflect the development of numerous other lifestyle sports. In the early days of windsurfing, a sport that was *different* to the established activity of sailing and popular with young people, the public perception was that it was dangerous and participants were characterised as 'out of control' (see also the history of snowboarding in Humphreys, 1997 and Thorpe, 2011). Certainly one contributing factor is that, when a lifestyle sport is new, skill levels tend to be low and the equipment is unsophisticated. However, equipment and knowledge about how to use it develop and improve rapidly. Kite-surfing is a good example: rapid development in technology produced kites that are more stable across a broad wind range and have numerous safety features to gain better control and to depower them in emergencies. In summary, kites are undoubtedly much safer than ten years ago.

Nonetheless, regulation is often fuelled by perceptions of putative risk, not 'real' risk in any objective sense. As Dumas and Laforest (2009) argue, perceptions of lifestyle sports often remain tempered by the view of them having a high risk of injury. In skateboarding, these concerns have led to regulation of the activity and its participants (Borden, 2001; Dumas and Laforest, 2009), including: containing skaters in skate parks; enforcing rules about appropriate behaviour and protective clothing; and limiting street skating through legislation and modifications to the urban furniture (Borden, 2001). In the UK, local by-laws have been used (or adapted) to ban kite-surfing in venues where there were (potential) conflicts with other users (for example, pleasure boats or swimmers). In some locales, clubs were formed as a consequence of threats to ban the activity and have gone some way to appease the concerned authorities. Clubs serve to control the activity, requiring safety equipment and evidence of third-party insurance, and providing rules and regulations, such as who can kite at that locale and when they can kite. Often it is the members themselves who (unwillingly) police and enforce these rules, seeing it as an unwanted restriction. Nonetheless, some kite-surfers I observed continued to contravene these rules, flaunting regulations and ignoring bans, especially in venues where it was hard for authorities to police or enforce them. Such defiance is certainly not unique to kite-surfing, but characterises attitudes across lifestyle sports, although the most provocative examples of transgression come in sports such as BASE jumping, where the activity is often illegal, and part of the challenge is to evade police or security guards to gain access to the building and to escape after the ascent.

A narrative of blame in which accidents only happen to the foolhardy and inexperienced appears to be prevalent across lifestyle sport cultures (see e.g. Davidson, 2008; Booth and Thorpe, 2007c). Experienced kiters often blame beginners or the inexperienced for causing kiting incidents. Developing 'safe' and certified teaching establishments has therefore been seen as an important way of giving the sport credibility, and the British Kite Surfing Association (BKS) has seen this as one of its central roles. As Tomlinson *et al.* (1995) have suggested, while many so-called extreme sports transgress social norms and rules, they also establish sport rules and subcultural codes to ensure the safety of participants. This is particularly evident in mountaineering where the discourse of safe practice is linked to experience, skills, knowledge and information, such as measurements, grading systems, guide books, etc., representative of the 'cultural capital' of mountaineering (Beedie, 2007: 40). The fear that kite-surfing and many other lifestyle sports cause injury has led to increased regulation of the activity and its participants; however, as Chapter 5 illustrates, in parkour and skateboarding, because of their popularity among children, these fears and debates are intensified (see also Dumas and Laforest, 2009).

4   Lifestyle sport, identity and the politics of difference

In this chapter, I revisit assertions that, in lifestyle sport cultures, embodied sporting identities are less tied to the reproduction of white male power than in many traditional sports – that they can, and in some contexts do, challenge dominant discourses about gender, class, race,[1] sexuality and (able) body dominance in sport (cf. Anderson, 1999; Rinehart and Sydor, 2003; Wheaton, 2004b; Laurendeau and Sharara, 2008).

Gendered bodies and spaces

Early research on lifestyle sport, such as Pearson's seminal study of surfing subcultures in the 1970s, failed either to acknowledge or explore girls' and women's involvement. This reflected the 'male stream' (Scraton, 1994) scholarship dominant at the time. As feminist critiques of youth subcultures more widely illustrated, male 'opposition' to the dominant hegemonic culture tended to be celebrated, even when it was sexist and racist (see e.g. McRobbie, 1980, 1991). However, over the past three decades, the construction and representation of gender identity in lifestyle sport has attracted a wealth of studies across different activities and geographical contexts. Both male and female representations and subjectivities have been explored. Studies have demonstrated the complex and shifting ways in which different structural, material and ideological factors operate in excluding different groups of women and girls in these activities. Nevertheless, there are clear differences *between* activities, as well as spatial, temporal and cultural variations. As social constructionist and post-structuralist approaches to understanding gender remind us, we need to explore the multiple ways in which different women experience social oppression, and the significance of shared experiences and difference in understanding women's leisure worlds (Scraton, 1994: 258). The focus on detailed qualitative research adopted by many researchers has revealed the complex ways in which these various influences work to exclude women in different cultural milieu.

While social class has not been the focus of detailed research, as Bourdieu (1978, 1984) has illustrated, it remains of central importance in acquiring the 'taste' for lifestyle sporting practices and as the basis of their lifestyles. While research has illustrated some of the complex ways in which economic, cultural and physical capital operate in lifestyle sport cultures, and the differences between these and more institutionalised sports activities (e.g. Kay and Laberge, 2002b), in many – but not all – lifestyle sports, participants come from higher social economic groups (Tomlinson *et al.*, 2005; Fletcher, 2008).

For example, in my ethnographic research, almost all of the women who windsurfed were 'privileged' women: predominantly well-educated women between 20 and 40 in age, able-bodied, white and middle-class, many with their own income. Although some of these women found expenditure on equipment a financial drain, it was a lack of time that most restricted their participation, particularly for those who lived a considerable distance from the water, or who had children. Committed windsurfers needed flexibility in their lifestyles. The male institutionalised power evident in many traditional sports (such as in the ways in which men control organisations) was less evident in the predominantly informal windsurfing communities. Yet the sport's informal nature also created *barriers* for some women. For example, the lack of clubs often meant there were no changing rooms, showers, child-care facilities or safety services. Women, more than most men, lacked confidence in their own abilities; their need to be in control and feel safe (and a fear of failure) limited their windsurfing experiences.[2] Thus for those women who did have the economic resources and opportunities to windsurf, factors such as the British weather or perceptions of the sport (perpetuated in subcultural and mainstream media) as being very demanding, dangerous and requiring excessive strength contributed to their lack of interest or enthusiasm to persevere. In many lifestyle sports, exclusion often works in more subtle ways than in institutionalised sports. Lifestyle sports that, like skateboarding, require the least specialist equipment and are the cheapest and most geographically accessible are often the most male-dominated (Beal and Wilson, 2004), signalling that cultural and ideological factors underpin the reasons for women's lack of participation.

A female athletic revolution?

Over the past decade, there has been a boom in women's and girls' interest in lifestyle sporting cultures, both as consumers and as participants. This interest has included sports like surfing and skateboarding, previously seen as bastions of masculinity (Booth, 2004; Waitt, 2008). For example, media reports claimed that women constituted 60 per cent of learner surfers across wide-ranging geographical locations (Comer, 2004; Jarvie, 2006). In Britain, the media branded the popularity of surfing among women as a 'female surfing revolution' (BBC News, 2008), and the British Surfing Association (BSA) claimed that women showed a ten-fold increase (Barkham, 2006). This expansion has been reflected in surf shops, surf magazines, surf schools and surf tourism, all of which now produce female-specific products and services. Surfing has also expanded increasingly into more mainstream forms of popular culture, such as the Hollywood blockbuster *Blue Crush* and US reality TV show *Surf Curl*. Female surfers I spoke to in California described the 'huge difference' in the numbers of girls and women surfing, particularly since the turn of the century:

> It's changed a lot. Growing up there were two other girls besides my sisters that surfed at our school, our entire high school [...]. And now I see packs of little girls, teen girls, pre-teens on skateboards and bikes heading to the beach with their surfboards and it's the coolest thing.

Atencio *et al.* (2009) claim that the economic power of the (middle-class) female consumer is driving this growth; women and girls have become the new lucrative target niche market. Executives within the lifestyle sports industry identified women as being the crucial component in expanding their market (ibid.). The marketing manager of ski and snowboard manufacturer Salomon corroborates this view. He explains that: 'To be successful commercially you need women endorsing your brands' (Asthana, 2003: 20). This expansion has led to a flourishing market for a range of products and experiences. *Roxy*, Quiksilver's clothing and lifestyle brand for women, was reported to be growing at 35 per cent a year, whereas the male market had stabilised (Asthana, 2003). According to the owner of *Surf Diva* (in Southern California), the first company in the USA to organise women-only teaching and surf tourism, they teach 'thousands of women each year', ranging from young girls to grannies[3]: 'Some people that are visiting try it that one time; they just want to tell their grandkids that they surfed back in the day ... and some people absolutely stick to it' (personal interview, Tihanyi, surf shop owner and teacher, 2009). Tihanyi identified a range of factors driving this female surfing boom in California, including the growth of the female-marketed surf industry (clothing, travel, etc.), the impact of the Hollywood teen movie *Blue Crush* and shifting attitudes to leisure practices. These mirror the reasons identified by media and academic commentators more widely (see Comer, 2010). Tihanyi also suggested that in California around the millennium a range of 'mindful body practices' (Moore, 2011), such as yoga and surfing, had experienced a boom (see also Brown and Leledak, 2010). Surfing's increasing popularity, she argued, was related to this shift:

> A lot more people getting in touch with themselves spiritually, physically, emotionally [...] the whole materialistic thing was definitely coming to a complete close [...] women were looking for a lot more than just being super mum. Something more fulfilling.
>
> (Personal interview, Tihanyi, 2009)

Yet while the increasing numbers of young, white, middle-class women who surf, skate, climb, bike and snowboard are undeniable, then to suggest that 'gender is not an issue' – as some commentators do (Waitt, 2008: 77) – is somewhat premature. While female entry into previously male-dominated spaces offers possibilities for challenging gendered norms, in many lifestyle sports normative gender scripts are also reproduced (see e.g. Donnelly, 2008).

New times, new theories: shifting theoretical perspectives

Reflecting the development of feminism more widely, over the last two decades or so, sports feminism has been increasingly rooted in post-structuralist thinking, embracing complexity, examining multiple sources of power and emphasising both difference and diversity (e.g. Birrell and McDonald, 2000; Scraton *et al.*, 2005). Lifestyle sports have been seen as important arenas where feminist questions emerge and for exploring their potential to be politically transformative spaces in relation to gender (e.g. Laurendeau and Sharara, 2008), as well as age, sexuality and race. Empirical research includes an increasingly wide range of theoretical perspectives, including: hegemonic masculinity (Wheaton, 2004b; Robinson, 2008); various Bourdieusian insights (Kay and Laberge, 2004; Atencio *et al.*, 2009; Thorpe, 2010a); third-wave feminism (Heywood, 2008; Sisjord, 2009; Comer, 2010; Thorpe, 2011); and Foucaudian (Thorpe, 2008; Young and Dallaire, 2008; Spowart *et al.*, 2010) and Deleuzian-inspired post-structuralist approaches (Knijnik *et al.*, 2010; Roy, 2011).

Surfing, contemporary girlhood and third-wave feminism

In the USA, much of the recent research seeking to explain the global increase in participation among girls in surfing, and to a lesser extent skateboarding and snowboarding, has been inspired by debates about contemporary 'girlhood', particularly in what has been termed third-wave feminism.

Third-wave feminism is a contested and in-process political 'project' (see Gillis *et al.*, 2007), aptly described as 'more about *desire* than an already existing thing' (Pender, 2007: 225, emphasis added).[4] However, based in the context of the shifting and expanding opportunities for many privileged Western (white) women and girls, third-wave writing is often characterised by a concern with how women and girls engage with global popular culture, and with their different ways of 'doing' activism and feminism. Girlhood is seen as an important 'constitutive figure of the new global order' (Comer, 2010: 17). In the sporting context, third-wave proponents Heywood and Dworkins argue that 'athleticism can be an activist tool' (2003: 45), describing sport as the 'stealth feminism of the third wave' (ibid.: 25). Krista Comer (2004, 2010) and Lesley Heywood (2007, 2008) have examined various representations of female surfing in North America through a third-wave lens, suggesting contemporary women appear to be adopting a 'third-wave stealth feminist' subjectivity.

Comer sees the transformations in global surfing culture as a 'girl-friendly place', connected to the rhetoric of the North American girl-power movement, which, for her, represents a cultural and political shift from generation X to generation Y forms of female empowerment. The surfer girl who 'came of age during the age of an emergent and then consolidated neoliberal ideological transformation of the planet', she argues, has much to teach older (second-wave) feminists about the 'current condition of girlhood in the first world' (Comer, 2010: 28). Likewise, for Heywood (2008: 64):

The female surfer (and the female athlete more generally) reflects a representational nexus where the female body, instead of primarily signifying a dependent sexuality as in second-wave feminist analyses that spoke of 'the objectification of women', has come to signify an independent sexuality that reflects women's potential as 'self-determining' wage earners and consumers.

Neither Comer's nor Heywood's research is focused on the gendered *experiences* of surfing women; rather, their aim is to understand the global popularity of the surfer girl and the role surf girls are playing in the local, global and gendered politics of surfing (Comer, 2010). Comer's discussion (2004) includes analyses of the career of professional female surfer Lisa Anderson and of the Hollywood blockbuster *Blue Crush* (Stockwell, 2002), a film that charts the lives of three young female surfers living on the Hawaiian island of Oahu, widely claimed to have had a pivotal impact in promoting surfing to contemporary girls in the USA (see Comer, 2004) and further afield (Wheaton, 2008b)[5]:

It [*Blue Crush*] got so much media attention here [...] it was in the newspapers the magazines, the film premieres. We went to a bunch of them, packed with girls, little girls just ... you know ages eight to twenty. I know girls that watched it over and over. It's become like a cult classic.

(Personal interview, Tihanyi, 2009)

In the film, the heroine attempts to transcend her life as a hotel domestic through winning a premier surfing competition, allowing her to become a professional surfer. While there are multiple and competing discourses of femininity and masculinity produced in the film,[6] in contrast to most surfing and mainstream sports texts, the narrative and imagery foregrounds females as the 'sporting heroes'. The female protagonists are represented as strong and independent, evading dominant assumptions about masculinity and femininity (see Heywood and Dworkins, 2003).[7] It therefore disrupts aspects of the traditional relationship between sport and masculinity, and offers different embodied female subjectivities, reflective of what Lucia Stasia (2007) calls the 'post feminist (sporting) heros' – female protagonists who combine conventional white femininity with traditional male activities, so destabilising many female stereotypes (Comer, 2004).

Also fuelling the popularity of surfing as a 'girl-friendly space' and a space where 'heroines' are constructed is the story of iconic young blonde 'surfer girl' Bethany Hamilton, who aged 14 had her arm bitten off in a shark attack while surfing at her home in Hawaii. Hamilton's return to the sport just a month later, and her subsequent determination to become a professional surfer, has been the focus of numerous media commentaries, books, documentaries and a feature film (*Soul Surfer*, 2011).[8] Hamilton provides another interesting chapter in the visual economy of the 'global California girl' (Comer, 2010: 153), particularly how Hamilton's lithe, young, sexualised blonde-haired yet 'disabled' body has been claimed and (self)-marketed through intertwining discourses of empowerment and self-discovery, reliance and (dis)embodiment, consumerism and religious faith.

The third wave critiqued

There are, however, a number of broad concerns with such third-wave analyses (see Caudwell, 2011). Despite a desire to engage with difference, third-wave feminism has tended to focus solely on the concerns of white heterosexual, middle-class, Western women (Gillis *et al.*, 2007). This is a criticism that characterises most of the feminist work on lifestyle sports. Detailed considerations of how hetero-normativity[9] and race operate in these sport contexts, as well as their relationships to other aspects of identity, have been largely ignored (exceptions are discussed below). A central question is how these white heterosexual femininities are articulated and how they maintain a privileged position. In this respect, Comer's (2010) book is foundational, in that she identifies that surfing today as a global phenomenon is associated with 'privileged forms of whiteness'. She highlights some of the *racial* and national-based tensions that exist between the dominant 'California surfer girl' image and other discourses and experiences of surfing. For example, she explores the marketing of surfing to women in Indonesia (Bali), revealing the contradictory figure and experience of the 'Muslim surfer girl' (Comer, 2010: 228).[10] Her interviews with surfing women in Mexico reveal the tensions that surf tourism brings, particularly the environmental and cultural impact, which includes racism from visiting Americans. She also outlines the global surf industries' 'penchant for blondes' (ibid.: 153), a 'politics of blondness' (ibid.: 154), based on the visual economy of the global surf industry where the preferred female figure is the 'global California girl' (ibid.: 153). This politics, she argues, reinforces and adds another complicating layer to 'Mexico's own history of racial hierarchies' (ibid.).[11]

Another prevalent critique of third-wave feminist approaches is that the discourse of empowerment tends to be articulated as an individualised and personal act, located within the 'achievement' of conventional femininity through consumerism (Lucia Stasia, 2007: 246). As Lesley Heywood outlines, in this discourse of 1990s athletic girlhood, women's liberation has become a marketable commodity; images of female athletes 'make an implicit enforcement of neoliberalism and its attendant assumptions' (ibid.: 117). In her analysis of how female athletic bodies support a vast consumer/lifestyle industry based on the ideas of individual choice and self-determination, Heywood (2007, 2008) shows how surfing is constructed as a space where girls (who we can assume are predominantly middle-class, able-bodied, white and heterosexual) are encouraged to take control of, and responsibility for, their lives as DIY projects in self-making, caring for their bodies for health and success. In so doing they promote values which are at the core of, and fundamental to, the new global economy. Heywood (2008) points to *Roxy* adverts, which she argues target these girls as 'good consumers'. They depict lean, young, white women, who are happy, healthy and strong; they exemplify the image of uniqueness, strength and auto-nomy central to lifestyle sport. They also embody the ideals of girl power – taking responsibility for self, and a 'can-do-anything' attitude – in which individuals make their own choices. These images of female bodies, she sug-gests, do the cultural work of advertising equal opportunities, suggesting anyone can achieve this look if they just work hard enough:

> Girls thus become the ideal subjects of Empire, part of the new global economy that relies on individuals with flexibility that are trained to blame their inevitable 'failures' on themselves rather than on the system their lives are structured within.
>
> (Heywood, 2007: 104)

Heywood's perceptive analysis illustrates how the lifestyle sport industry marries the discourses of liberal feminism and neoliberalism with ideologies of the neoliberal consumer and body, masking the growing structural inequalities characteristic of the global economy (ibid.; see also Comer, 2010).

While these studies illustrate the value of contextualising the meaning of life-style sport within global agendas of neoliberal capitalism, they fail to reveal contradictory lived experiences of it.[12] In contrast, the studies of skateboarding emerging from North America, also informed by debates about shifting female subjectivities in contemporary girlhood (Porter, 2003; Pomerantz *et al.*, 2004; Kelly *et al.*, 2005, 2006), have revealed in greater depth these 'proliferating fem-ininities' (Atencio *et al.*, 2009: 17). Pomerantz *et al.* (2004) argue that female skaters have established a subculture that has the potential to challenge dominant attitudes to gender, space, risk and embodiment (see also Young and Dallaire, 2008). These skater girls saw themselves as actively constituting an 'alternative girlhood' that was 'oppositional to emphasised femininity' and resisted sexism (Kelly *et al.*, 2007: 123). These authors discuss the opening up of (traditionally male-dominated) media and industry spaces for girls and women,[13] in ways that challenge the dominant discourses of gender. Atencio *et al.* (2009) explore *All Girl Skate Jams*, and Porter (2003) examines the emergence of a wide range of internet forums, skate zines and all-girl competitions (see also MacKay and Dal-laire, 2013). Although corporate-supported, all-women skate spaces are often set to 'privilege a singular version of femininity', this was resisted by some women who participated in them (Atencio *et al.*, 2009: 16). These sites provided women with new cultural spaces to gain status and recognition, and challenge the 'dominant gender stereotypes associated' with the (male-dominated and defined) 'street skateboarding field' (ibid.: 14).

Foucault and beyond

In 1993, sport sociologist David Andrews made a cogent case and plea for researchers to explore the value of Michel Foucault's theoretical analysis in our study of the sporting body and of sport more widely (1993). Foucauldian

examinations of sport, exercise and the body have become increasingly prominent (Smith Maguire, 2002).[14] The first wave of studies focused on sport as a
'technology of domination' that disciplines women, producing docile bodies,
anchoring them 'into a normalising web of domination' (Markula, 2003: 88).
However, the focus soon shifted to incorporate Foucault's latter work, considering the local and embodied operation of power and exploring how individuals
can also challenge and change dominant discourses and 'the institutional use of
power in sport' (ibid.).[15] Foucault's concept of *technologies of self* was embraced
for understanding how individuals are actively engaged in producing their own
subjectivities, particularly those that challenge dominant discourses. Examples
of this approach include research on female skateboarders (e.g. Young and Dallaire, 2008) and snowboarders (Thorpe, 2008). Thorpe uses *technologies of self*
to examine the multiple discourses of femininity in the snowboarding media, and
ways in which the snowboarding media can be enabling as well as repressive
(ibid.: 200). Her analysis suggests that there are 'different discursive lenses'
through which male and female participants read sexualised media images, and
many read them through what she terms a 'third-wave feminist discourse', which
she argues 'embraces' rather than 'shuns' female sexuality (ibid.: 224).

In contrast to the prevalent focus on young women and girls, Spowart *et al.*
(2010) explore the experiences of surfing mothers in New Zealand. As Dilley
discusses in the context of her research on female climbers, motherhood – and
indeed parenthood – remains an important, but often restrictive, identity that
requires scrutiny in our post-structuralist analysis of leisure (see also Wheaton
and Tomlinson, 1998; Dilley and Scraton, 2010: 129). Spowart *et al.* are concerned with how surfing mums engage in 'practices of femininity' that at times
transgress dominant discourses of motherhood. Their starting point is the incompatibility of the subject position in the surfer/mother couplet; when, the 'surfer'
is represented as irresponsible, hedonistic and associated with freedom, and the
'mother' as caring, selfless and responsible. They explore the role that surfing
plays in these women's construction of self as women, mothers and physical
beings. They examine if surfing presents a way for women to devise and 'live'
alternative versions of motherhood, particularly the extent to which the 'dispositions' and 'practices' of surfing mums can be regarded as 'technologies of the
self' (Foucault, 1988) that create disruptive potentialities or spaces of freedom.
Spowart *et al.* suggest that 'contemporary individualist, healthist and familial
discourses afford a range of subject positions, providing opportunities for surfing
mums to occupy shifting positions of power and resistance, some of which
potentially transform and re-work traditional constructs of motherhood' (2010:
1186). Sports feminists have also turned to Deleuze for inspiration (Markula,
2006). Knijnik *et al.* (2010) examine the experiences of elite female surfers in
Brazil, one of the few national contexts outside of the Global North where lifestyle sports have historically had a significant cultural presence, and in contemporary times have become an important global player in surf culture and
industry. Their research focuses on the experience of the first generation of professional female surfers (Carrol, 2009). They explore whether, in a Brazilian

cultural context in which the female body is seen as an object of idolatry and consumption (they term a 'bikini-dictatorship'), surfing women can reject traditional Brazilian femininities. Is surfing a space where they can envisage their bodies and gender subjectivities differently? They adopt Markula's (2006) reading of Deleuze's *rhizomatic bodies* model, which, they argue, provides an insightful way of conceptualising feminine sporting bodies that does not perpetuate the dualism between thin, toned bodies (as oppressive) and strong bodies (as empowering).[16] Their research suggests that these women simultaneously reproduce and challenge the complex web of entrenched dominant discourses about gender attitudes prevailing in Brazilian society, and beach culture specifically.

Lastly, it would be remiss not to mention the ways in which Bourdieu's *masculine domination thesis* – theorising how male power is reproduced in sporting fields and the ways in which masculinity works as a form of symbolic violence – has usefully informed work on snowboarding (Sisjord, 2009; Thorpe, 2009a, 2010a) and skateboarding (Atencio *et al.*, 2009).

Spatiality, gender and race

Another productive trend in understanding how sporting spaces are gendered (classed and racialised) has been the impact of theoretical work on space and spatiality.[17] This body of work has highlighted that space is not just a physical and geographical phenomenon, but is socially created and sustained, reflecting the interests of dominant groups, and is central in the making and re-making of meanings and identities. As Van Ingen argues, 'research on sport and space cannot ignore the ways in which spaces are inexorably linked to the social construction of dominant ideologies and to the politics of identity' (2003: 210).

As Chapter 3 explores, lifestyle sports provide many revealing examples of the ways in which spaces – including beaches, mountains and city-scapes – have multiple and shifting meanings as places of sport and leisure production and consumption, in which space is used to transform and reproduce forms of social regulation.[18] However, often absent from analyses of spatial conflict (and the authenticity of discourses that underpin them) is consideration of the ways in which space is used to mask, reproduce and regulate these hierarchies of gender, race, age and sexuality. As Van Ingen (2003: 210) suggests, a central challenge for sport scholars is to 'develop more nuanced inquiries into the intersection of gender, sexuality, and race *in place*'. An exception is the discussion of *localism* (the conflict among surfers seeking to navigate space in the 'line up', and the ways non-locals are excluded), which has been well-documented and theorised (Ford and Brown, 2005; Waitt, 2008; Evers, 2009; Olivier, 2010).[19]

Research on short-board surfers in Southeast Australia by cultural geographer Gordon Waitt (Waitt, 2008; Waitt and Warren, 2008) provides a valuable example of this turn to spatiality. He connects spatial and embodied approaches to explore the interplay and 'changing relationships between space, gender and surfing bodies' (Waitt, 2008: 75). He conceptualises surf spaces as 'an outcome of a temporally, spatially and culturally specific set of social relationships that in turn, help to contour the gender subjectivities of surfers' (ibid.: 78).[20] Waitt analyses how the spatial can reconfigure gender relations between surfers (ibid.: 77). He argues that, although surf breaks are spaces with *possibilities* for reworking gender, these spaces are neither 'intrinsically oppressive nor liberatory' (ibid.). Rather, 'gender and space' are 'mutually constituted', with different surfing spaces offering different ways in which gender norms can be challenged, reworked and reshaped (ibid.). Recognising how embodied gender identities have 'local specificity' alerts us to map the differences in gender across local (mediated and virtual) spaces as well as across national contexts and different sports. Waitt's (2008) research also points to the reciprocal relationship between performative (Butler, 1990)[21] space and gender (e.g. Massey, 1994). In considering what Probyn (2003: 290) terms the 'spatial imperative of subjectivity', he argues that the way surfers experience subjectivities is not only multiple, fluid and often conflicting, but depends on the 'site and space of its production' (Waitt, 2008: 78). Similarly, Roy (2011) argues that, because surfing – and perhaps other lifestyle sports generally – are less spatially (and temporarily) bounded than most institutionalised sports, gendered power relationships are also less bounded. This 'opening up' of spaces allows alternative female subjectivities to emerge, which she terms 'spatial ruptures'. Roy proposes a more fluid conceptualisation of the ways in which masculine-defined activities are adopted by women and girls 'not as "one of the guys", or even as girl-powered "future girls" but as a part of the renegotiation of dynamic female subject hood' (Roy, 2011).

Masculinities, embodiment and the emotions

During the 1990s and 2000s, R.W. Connell's concept of 'hegemonic masculinity' (Connell, 1995) was widely adopted to determine how dominant versions of masculinity occupy and sustain their positions of power and dominance over other forms of masculinity, and over women. Research began to consider how different masculinit*ies* and femininit*ies* were constructed, reproduced and exhibited in various (sporting) cultural settings. Anderson (1999: 66) interviewed African-American, Latino, 'half-Asian' and white snowboarders, exploring how race as well as class and age intersected in 'complex and paradoxical' ways in the construction of snowboarding masculinity. Studies revealed the ways in which masculine identities differed both from more traditional sports and from other sites where masculine identity work is done, such as work, the family and other leisure cultures (ibid.; Ormrod, 2003; Wheaton, 2004b; Robinson, 2008). While the value of hegemonic masculinity has subsequently been re-assessed – particularly its roots in dualistic and over-simplistic thinking that can lead to differences being ignored (see e.g. McKay *et al.*, 2000)[22] – these studies nonetheless highlighted different and competing versions of masculinities within a particular sporting culture. They explored how these different masculine identities articulated with age, class and (hetero)sexuality across different work and leisure spaces, illustrating that some of these masculinities were more inclusive and pro-gressive than most traditional sporting masculinities (Wheaton, 2004b; Robin-son, 2008).

However, sporting spaces, including many lifestyle sports, are often policed by a masculine heterosexual gaze, particularly among younger men, where displays of heterosexual prowess are common-place (e.g. Laurendeau, 2004; Wheaton, 2004b). Evers (2006) asserts that homophobia is rife in Australian surfing cultures, and Wheaton (2004b) and Waitt (2008) document that British windsurfers and Australian male surfers, respectively, incite homophobia as a way to affirm normative ideas of masculinity. Among both groups of men, derogatory homophobic terms such as 'faggots', 'gay' or 'queer' were used to describe different, lower-status social groups using the surfing space, such as body boarders (see also Laurendeau, 2004; and Ch. 3). This hetero-normativity 'constrains rethinking points of contact between male surfers' (Waitt, 2008: 92).

While much of this research is *about* bodies, Evers – following Grosz (1994) – describes the surfing body as 'affective assemblage – affecting and being affected' (2009: 894). This includes considerations of all the different *sensory* ways through which bodies are experienced (see e.g. Shilling, 2005; Sparkes, 2009). His self-reflexive research about surfing masculinity highlights the importance of sensory *feelings* to men's sporting lives – the emotional and vis-ceral experiences of being a sporting participant, and how men 'come to under-stand themselves as masculine' (Evers, 2009: 894).

To date, it is researchers exploring climbing, surfing and parkour who have most systematically considered these emotional and visceral experiences of being a male lifestyle sporting participant,[23] and how emotions are integral to understanding gender (Evers, 2006, 2009). Unpacking men's 'sporting intimate inner lives' (Robinson, 2008: 96), and how they shift over the life course, is an important aspect of Robinson's analysis of masculinities articulated in and through climbing cultures, particularly how feelings of fear and trust are managed and controlled. She explores how issues of intimacy are dealt with in men's climbing friendships and in their 'everyday heterosexual relationships' (ibid.). Whereas studies of masculinity have often illustrated that men find it hard to 'do intimacy', male climbers in Robinson's research feel the 'closest and most intimate times with other men are forged at the rock face' (ibid.: 111).

Saville (2008) explores the central role of the emotions in parkour, and espe-cially fear, in participants' 'play with city space'.[24] In contrast to many other male-defined and dominated sports, in parkour, emotional engagement is encour-aged, not seen as a weakness. Guss (2011) explores how they saw fear not as an 'obstacle, or something to overcome', but as an 'aesthetic experience' (ibid.: 81). 'Traceurs', he argues, 'embrace fear as an intensification of awareness of their surroundings, an enhanced lucidity' (ibid.: 82). Waitt discusses feelings of praise, fear and shame which operate to make surfing participants aware of their bodily limitations and inadequate performance of masculinity (2008: 83).

Lifestyle sport research has helped to reveal how the ways in which men do masculinity, through both 'mind' and the 'body's sensual repertoire' (Evers,

2009), differ across sporting contexts, as well as in relation to other aspects of identity, such as age, class, nationality and sexuality (Wheaton, 2004b). In Australian surfing, 'male bodies are rooted in discourses that pass on expectations and enthusiasms that are about being assertive, hard, strong, bold, competitive, rough' (Evers, 2009: 901). Novice surfers have to earn the right to belong, and those who do not follow these informal rules are mocked and even disciplined (ibid.). While women's different movement styles, particularly their grace, balance and poise, are applauded by some, but not all surfers, it is nonetheless the case that the male-defined emphasis on power and aggression has dominated; male standards define *elite* surfing and demand the most respect.

In contrast, it appears that in some spaces different gender scripts operate. In parkour, competition is downplayed, and newcomers, outsiders and novices are welcomed (see Ch. 5). Our research revealed that the values of some parkour participants were less accepting of traditional sporting hegemonic masculinity, such as heroic displays of strength, speed and power. This was evident in the ways young men supported each other, and in the valuing of skills females tend to excel, such as with balance and agility, as well as the more traditionally male-defined attributes of risk-taking, speed and strength.[25] Although parkour is male-dominated, some elite practitioners believed there was a recognition of the value of *different* ways of moving to adapt to different physiques, including non-hegemonic ones, expressed here by one of them:

> There are routes, the routes are never set as in 'you must do this move', it's 'you must get from here to here' and you're given guidance and improvements on your route. But everyone does it in their own unique way ... there's as many ways to move as there are individuals so it doesn't really matter if you're male, female, tall, short, whatever, all that matters is that you're doing your best, and moving in your way, and trying hard. That's really what matters.

Ultimately, as the goal in parkour is for each person to challenge themselves, the hierarchies that have developed in other sports seem less likely to develop. Emotional engagement was encouraged, not seen as a weakness; learning parkour appeared to help boys and young men recognise, access and enjoy the more artistic, emotional aspects of their physicality and masculinity.

While recognising that younger men often forge their masculinities in different ways, places and spaces to older men (cf. Wheaton, 2004b; Robinson, 2008), the focus of sporting masculinity has focused largely on younger men.

Surfing through the third age: age and lifecycle

> Older surfers provide a great metaphor for how our society is struggling to redefine what it means to grow older [...]. The new attitude that is emerging – and supported by lots of medical and psycho-social research – is a view of our later years not dominated by sickness and decline. Rather, the later years

can be a very vital, satisfying and meaningful period of our lives. There is profound truth in the words of 71-year-old surfer Fred Van Dyke: 'If I'm getting old, I might as well dig it'. And there is wisdom in the enthusiasm of 93-year-old surf legend Doc Ball when he says that, 'Surfing helps me to stay stoked'.

(Roy Earnest, S*urfing for Life*; see Brown and Earnest, 2001)[26]

Popular representations of lifestyle sport have tended to be dominated by youth; a 'fact' corroborated by media reports and market research surveys that see interest in lifestyle sports as a narrow age and socio-demographic grouping: 15–24-year-olds, mainly men and those from higher socio-economic classifications (see sources in Tomlinson *et al.*, 2005; Thorpe and Wheaton, 2011b). However, there seems to be a shift in representation, with lifestyle sports being increasingly used to target older consumers, particularly in the context of health and well-being. Examples are evident across different forms of advertising. For example, an Age Concern supporter's newsletter titled 'Making more of life' depicts two older people – one man and one woman – sky diving. An advert for Health Span vitamin supplements (from a Saga magazine[27]) depicts an elderly white-haired man, wearing just Hawaiian-style surf shorts, riding a cruiser-style bicycle along the beach with a surfboard under his arm. The caption reads 'Live Younger!' The man, who is evidently about to go surfing, is lean and muscled, epitomising 'good health'. The small print tells us: '60 is the new 50s these days ... and we can all optimise the quality as well as the quantity of our lifespan to actively "live younger" – nutrition is the key to influencing a healthy lifespan'. These adverts need to be contextualised within wider socio-economic concerns about increasing numbers of ageing bodies in late modern societies, and political shifts in the discourses of ageing and health maintenance, from an institutional 'problem' to one of individual responsibility. In these adverts, neoliberal ideologies in which good consumer-citizens take personal responsibility for their health and well-being are evoked and promoted by taking exercise and being active, and through purchasing products from the health industry. Likewise, as Earnest writes in his *Surfing for Life* literature (Brown and Earnest, 2001), through the 'wellness movement' – of which he sees surfing as a part – we are 'empowered to take charge of our own health, and to become partners with our physicians and other health professionals rather than being passive recipients of their expertise'. The wellness movement promises individuals 'empowerment', perpetuating neoliberal ideologies where personal solutions are advocated to address broader collective, economic and political issues. These concerns about ageing and health have increasingly become a battleground for politicians and policy makers in advancing active lifestyles for an increasingly ageing social demographic.

It is not just representations of lifestyle sports that are shifting. My research on windsurfing in the 1990s revealed that many men, and some women, continued to be active participants well into their sixties. A windsurfing organisation called the Sea-Vets catered for women and men into their seventies (see Humberstone, 2011). The BSA (British Surfing Association) claimed in 2008 that older surfers had increased significantly in numbers during the previous five years, constituting ten per cent of beginners (cited in McWaters, 2008). With the (global) revival of long-board surfing, and most recently the emerging popularity of paddle-surfing,[28] surfing has remained popular with the generation who learnt over twenty years ago. This trend has been picked up and discussed in the mass and niche media (e.g. Warshaw, 2005; Britton, 2006; McWaters, 2008; Laing, 2008). At beaches on the South Coast of England, where I have been conducting research, older men and women now constitute a much higher proportion of water users, including surfers, kayakers and windsurfers. This appears to be a global trend (Comer, 2010). The owner of a surf school and travel business for women described (in 2010) how the female surfing demographic was shifting in California:

> I'm seeing a shift, just in the last two years, of more and more 'silver surfers' is what I call them.... And the baby boomers are now signing up and they are in great shape, and they do a lot of sports. They've taken great care of themselves and they've retired, and they have income. Despite the recession they want to have fun and they're bringing their daughters and granddaughters and they are surfing together. That used to be really unusual to see a mother, daughter, or a grandmother, granddaughter. And more and more I'm getting women 55 and up that are coming to surf, 55 to 75.... Even had 77 – probably the oldest that I've had ... and they'd never surfed before.

So, despite the image of youthfulness, healthy, middle-class participants are increasingly sampling and taking up many lifestyle sports much later in life, while for others interest is sustained across their life course, and in some activities well into retirement (Dilley and Scraton, 2010; Ormrod 2008; Robinson, 2008; Wheaton, 2004b). However, as Humberstone (2009: vi) warns, 'while the significance of active leisure to older people and society is now becoming more greatly appreciated, associated research and analysis has tended to remain functionalist in approach', ignoring 'socio-cultural dimensions' of ageing and the diverse perspectives of older people. In part, this is because much research around ageing and health has emerged from medical perspectives, which have largely pathologised what it is to age. However, a body of research on sport, embodiment and ageing is emerging (see Dionigi and O'Flynn, 2007; Tulle, 2008a, 2008b; Dionigi, 2009; Phoenix and Sparkes, 2009; Pike, 2010, 2011a, 2011b) that raises issues for the lifestyle sporting context. Key questions that need to be explored include: What are these participants' bodily and emotional experiences? What part does the sport play in their lifestyles and identities through the life course? How are lifestyle sports used as an identity resource in the extension of 'mid-life' (Featherstone, 1991) and in the process of negotiating (anxieties about) biological ageing (Tulle, 2008a, 2008b)?

Research exploring these questions is emerging in some lifestyle sporting contexts (e.g. Boyes, 2009). Robinson's (2008) research on climbing masculinities involved participants across the lifecycle, including older men. She illustrates the changing meaning of climbing identities through different life phases and significant moments, such as parenthood and retirement. While it is often assumed that men 'inhabit and perform masculinity in one space', such as the workplace, home or sporting realm, little attention is given to how 'men exist in different spaces' (ibid.: 37). Drawing on theoretical ideas about 'masculinities in transition' or 'mobile masculinities', she explores how men *do masculinity*, moving, for example, from being a father to being a climber, from a partner to a worker and back again 'over their embodied lives as bodies age, new relationships start, and (un)employment ceases' (ibid.). This shifting connection between age, masculinity and the sporting realm is graphically illustrated in the different ways older male climbers are viewed. For some, their continuing commitment and their refusal to define 'adulthood' in traditional ways (e.g. family and work) are admired, while for others (and mirroring attitudes to Wheaton's, 2004b, older windsurfers) the 'ageing Peter Pan figure was constructed as an object of pity' (Robinson, 2008: 117).[29] Certainly, as Earnest (Brown and Earnest, 2001) suggests, older participants are helping to challenge this negative view and the discursive construction of (lifestyle) sport and youthfulness:

> The surfers now over 60 are pioneers, showing us what is possible and prompting many of us to re-consider our own futures in a more hopeful way. Eventually, surfing and many other aspects of active living will lose their exclusive connection to youth. In their place will be a more expanded view of what it means to grow older.

Older female surfers, in particular, are challenging dominant discourses about physical activity, risk, age and embodiment. One of the life-long British female surfers I interviewed (2010), now aged 67, explained:

> When I was younger and fitter I'd take risks, but now I know my limitations and stay within them. I really don't know if I'll still be surfing at 80. I live for today as you never know what is around the corner. While I'm able, I'll carry on. If people comment that 'I'm too old to surf' then I really don't care. I do what I want to do. It's freedom, really. Surfing takes you away from the daily grind.

Understanding how and why these women and men adopt physically active lifestyles via participation in lifestyle sports, and their attitudes to embodied risk-taking, will contribute to our understandings of ageing bodies and how they are self-reflexively managed (Giddens, 1991) in late modern societies. However, despite the positive experiences of some men and women, not everyone can, or will, benefit from the so-called 'grey revolution'. We therefore need to locate such discourses in the broader political, economic and socio-cultural contexts of ageing, recognising the diversity of experiences and locations of older people (Humberstone, 2009). As the gap between the wealthy, who tend to have leisure time, financial resources and good health, and the 'have-nots' widens in many Western nations, important questions about what it really means to age, and about 'good practices for healthy ageing', remain (ibid.: vi) for different people across phases of the life course and particularly different stages of retirement.

Lifestyle sport and race

One of the central contentions underpinning this book is that most academic studies of lifestyle sports have persistently neglected to consider race or ethnicity in the analysis. In 1997, assessing the limitations of my doctoral work (1997a), I wrote, 'despite the almost exclusively white participation of British windsurfers, this empirical research has made little or no attempt to articulate race, or "ethnicity" other than observing that windsurfing is a "white space"'. At the time of writing, well over a decade later, despite a few notable exceptions explored below, this is a situation that has remained largely unchanged. Because of the whiteness of lifestyle sporting spaces, it is assumed that race does not matter.

Despite recognising the importance of these issues for some time, I have struggled with finding an empirical context in which to explore them. Although reading excellent work on researching whiteness such as Frankenberg's (1993) influential book and empirically based studies such as Byrne (2006) was useful, I still found studying white identities in essentially mono-white cultures like lifestyle sports in Western Europe and Australia extremely challenging. People's consciousness of their whiteness is often limited, and they may only 'feel white' when in the presence of a racialised other (Dolby, 2001; Wheaton, 2002). The naturalness of whiteness – both for research participants and for myself as researcher – made it hard to understand how 'acting white' was part of the everyday practices that constituted this 'imagined community of whiteness' (Chivers-Yochim, 2010: 104).

The turn to whiteness: white tribes re-imagined

Lifestyle sport, both in the increasingly ubiquitous appropriation of its imagery across media and public space and in terms of participants (in the West), is often constituted as a white space. As Kyle Kusz, drawing on the body of critical race literature focusing on whiteness (e.g. Frankenberg, 1993; Pfeil, 1995; Dyer, 1997; Bonnett, 2000), has argued for more than a decade, whiteness in lifestyle sport is often represented as a 'cultural space that is overwhelmingly white yet it is rarely ever imagined as a racially exclusive space' (Kusz, 2004: 207). It therefore acts as an invisible and unmarked 'norm' to most whites (Kusz, 2003, 2004, 2007).

Kusz's research foregrounds how mass media representations of extreme sport in North America became key cultural sites in the construction of whiteness. He argues that, in the late 1990s, extreme sports emerged as an important and politically powerful contemporary site of whiteness, used as part of a broader conservative cultural politics that sought to re-establish and secure the dominant positioning of white masculinity. He describes how the US media celebrated extreme sports as the 'symbol of a new American zeitgeist' (Kusz, 2004: 209). They promoted and revived traditional and specifically American values, including 'individualism, self-reliance, risk-taking, and progress' (ibid.). This masculinised and patriotic representation of extreme sports re-articulated and naturalised the link between whiteness and America, re-establishing the dominant cultural positioning of white masculinity in the American imagination. Kusz suggests, therefore, that extreme sports can be read as a symptom of and *imagined* solution to North America's perceived 'crisis of white masculinity' (ibid.: 199).

Mediated whiteness

Following Kusz's conceptual guidance, other informing studies of extreme/life-style sports and whiteness have followed (Erickson, 2003, 2005; Brayton, 2005; Chivers-Yochim, 2010). Most, however, have focused on the discursive con-struction of white identities in images, magazines and films (Beattie, 2001; Wheaton, 2003a; Comer, 2004; Frohlick, 2005; Smith and Beal, 2007; Ormrod, 2007; Stenger, 2008). Frohlick analyses constructions and readings of the white male 'adventure subject' (including world explorer, elite athlete and extreme adventurers) in mountain film festivals and how they re-inscribe the historically dominant version of the hegemonic male adventure hero as 'white, hetero-sexual, bourgeois, athletic, courageous, risk-taking, imperialist, and unmarked' (2005: 179). She points to the ways 'playful' white masculinity 'is recurrently represented in these mediated spaces, which serves to displace women and non-white men to the 'periphery of the adventure imaginary' (ibid.: 175; see also Farley, 2005).

The colonial imaginary informing the surf safari genre of discovery films like *The Endless Summer*, as well as magazine travelogues, has been noted by a number of commentators (Beattie, 2001; Comer, 2004; Ormrod, 2007)[30] and continues to infuse more contemporary mainstream Hollywood surf films.[31] Films such as *Point Break* and *Blue Juice*, produced in the 1990s, represented the female as 'culture and domesticity', who was 'marginalized on the borders of surf culture and space' (Ormrod, 2006: 12). These films were also exclusively white spaces. However, in more recent Hollywood productions like *Blue Crush* (Stockwell, 2002), aspects of the traditional relationship between sport and mas-culinity is disrupted (as noted above)[32] and ethnicity is also more nuanced than in previous surf films. However, the Polynesian *male* surfers are represented in bell hooks' (2004) terms as 'bad blacks': they are violent and living as surfing drop-outs (see also Wilson, 1997). As Comer suggests, the 'film makes a spec-tacle of black (athletic) bodies' (2004: 257) and mirrors the colonial imaginary informing previous surfing films.

A more progressive development is the emergence of art-house surfing docu-mentaries that have been appearing at film festivals around the world. In contrast to the plethora of commercially produced products emerging from the surf indus- try, they often focus on challenging dominant discourses about surfing space and identity. Recent examples include *Whitewash*, which explores 'the complexity of race in America through the struggle and triumph of the history of black surfers', and Mosley's *Verve* and *Surf Noir*.[33] Indeed, independent film-makers, rather than academics, appear to be more fully engaged with challenging the dominant histories and myths about the surfing culture and history (see Ch. 9), including representations of race and gender.[34]

Kusz (2005, 2007) explores the cultural politics of skateboarding in the widely acclaimed *Dogtown and Z-Boys* (Peralta, 2001), a film that traces the development of the urban skateboarding scene in Venice, California, in the late 1970s, and highlights the influence of the surfing short-board revolution on skateboarding's development (see Fisher, 2007). *Dogtown* refers to the beach- side strip of Santa Monica and adjacent Venice beach, which in the 1970s (before its gentrification in the 1990s) was known as a beachside slum and a rel- atively multicultural area of Southern California.[35] Directed by Stacy Peralta, a Dogtown resident and skateboard champion who went on to be a leading figure in the skate industry, the film is widely recognised as being influential in re- popularising skateboarding (Fisher, 2007). Yet, despite *Dogtown*'s critical acclaim, as Kusz contends, there remains a 'complete absence of commentary about racial aspects of the film' (2007: 111). He is 'astounded' that the antics of these predominantly white men[36] are read by film critics and (white) audiences not as deviant 'antisocial menaces', but as 'innocent youthful transgressions' of white teen rebellion (ibid.: 109). Kusz's analysis, which explores how whiteness articulated with gender *and* class, exposes skateboarding as a masculine and racialised space in which these white men are positioned as socially marginal- ised and economically underprivileged, which is foundational to their particular 'non mainstream' (Kusz, 2005) or 'outsider' (Beal, 1996; Atencio and Beal, 2011) white identity (see also Chivers-Yochim, 2010). He illustrates how such 'seemingly banal and apolitical cultural discourses and media stories' are playing a central role in 'reproducing and extending the power and privilege of white men, not only in sport, but in American culture and society in the new millen- nium' (Kusz, 2007: 187).

These analyses of representations of whiteness have been invaluable in high- lighting the normative assumptions of whiteness in lifestyle sports, and how identity politics contribute to contemporary cultural racism (Kusz, 2007). My interest here, however, is to explore how participants in these activities *experi- ence* such (racial) identities, and how race and ethnicity are related to exclusion processes in these subcultures. What are the structures and practices that main- tain whiteness's privileged position in lifestyle sport? As Byrne (2006) argues, showing how the practices, subject construction and identities of people posi- tioned as 'white' are racialised is central to the process of decentring whiteness. While marking whiteness does not counter racism, research that uncovers, chal- lenges and subverts forms of white privilege remains an essential task (Ahmed, 2004).

Furthermore, it is important not to essentialise whiteness. Despite its apparent ubiquity and privileged position (Dyer, 1997), whiteness, like other (racial) identities, is multiple, fluid and spatially contingent; therefore, the forms of whiteness that operate in different lifestyle sport contexts need articulating in order to explore if they are, in all cases, sites of domination, superiority and privilege (Kusz, 2004).[37] A number of commentators on surfing and Australian beach spaces have acknowledged, and begun to unpack, the whiteness of the 'quintessentially Australian surf space' (Waitt, 2008: 78), recognising that surfing's whiteness is rooted in, and associated with, the white-settler Australian identity.[38] McGloin (2005) documents that the 'racist histories, discourses and iconographies of surfing' are historically rooted in the Australian Surf Life Saving Association (SLSA) of the 1930s, which included the 'biological racism of eugenics' (cited in Waitt, 2008: 78). Surfing became an important way that white-settler Australians claimed sovereignty over the territories of the beach (McGloin, 2005). It remains an 'initiation of Anglo-Celtic Australian manhood' and a way of 'performing (white) Australianess' (Waitt, 2008: 78). The racialised geographies of the contemporary Australian surf-beach are evident in the punitive treatment of 'outsiders' documented in discussion of localism (see Ch. 3; Evers, 2008), which extends to anyone who is *different* – including non-heterosexuals and those racialised as non-white (Waitt, 2008). The power of contemporary discourses to exclude bodies racialised as non-white from surf spaces was graphically illustrated in the so-called 'race riots' at Cronulla Beach (11 December 2005; see Barclay and West, 2006; Evers, 2008; Waitt, 2008; Khamis, 2010).

Despite these important insights, detailed empirical research on the racialisation of surfing culture and space has received surprisingly little academic attention. As Evers reprimands, the 'vast majority' of scholarship on surf culture has failed to express the 'perspective of surfing's Others – women, ethnicities, sexualities' (2009: 895),[39] an absence I begin to address in the case studies in Part II of the book.

Skateboarding, identity and race

> It's [race] really no big deal. We just want to skate, you know?
>
> (Bradley, skater, age 15, in Chivers-Yochim, 2010: 104)

Skateboarding, with its home in inner-city contexts, appears to be one of the least middle-class and white-dominated lifestyle sports. This is certainly the view perpetuated by the sport's subcultural media, where it is often claimed that the values of skateboarding 'transcends' barriers of race, gender and class (Borden, 2001; Chivers-Yochim, 2010) and that the 'imagined community' of skateboarders is inclusive and racially diverse (Chivers-Yochim, 2010: 104). Billy Miller, interviewed in *Heckler* magazine, asserts that, 'There aren't the biases that exist in other areas of life. It's like we are our own *race*' (cited in Borden, 2001: 141). While there is some diversity in US skate parks and in skate niche media (Chivers-Yochim, 2010), as Kusz's (2005) analysis of *Dogtown* suggests, the discourses of race, inclusion and belonging in the North American skateboarding subculture are complex and inconsistent (see also Beal and Wilson, 2004; Wheaton and Beal, 2003a, 2003b).

Chivers-Yochim suggests that skateboarders' *claim* that their culture is 'tolerant', 'multicultural', 'open to all' and working 'hard to elide race', and that 'race doesn't matter – skateboarding does' (2010: 103). Yet in discussions about race, her interviewees still drew on the 'normativity of whiteness' (ibid.). She suggests that tolerance claims and rejection by skateboarders of the notion that their community might be 'exclusionary' (ibid.: 105) are rooted in their beliefs that it is the *practice* of skateboarding itself that is crucial to the ('authentic') culture, and not the performance of different lifestyles, such as 'appearing to be cool' or 'developing an exclusionary group' (ibid.: 103). Skaters believed they lived and operated *differently* from other adolescent groups and claimed a kind of 'outsider status'[40] (ibid.: 96; see also Atencio and Beal, 2011) which gave them a 'unique outlook on life' (ibid.). This outsider status frequently translated into 'assertions of cultural acceptance', diversity and multiculturalism (ibid.: 99). Similarly, in Beal's research (Wheaton and Beal, 2003a, 2003b), skaters were hesitant to discuss or acknowledge racial difference or exclusion; instead they wanted to discuss the 'generic' characteristics needed of a person to be accepted. On deeper inspection, however, their narratives were contradictory, and the 'generic' characteristics invariably reflected values associated with hegemonic white masculinity (Wheaton and Beal, 2003a). Like the Anne Arbor skaters (Chivers-Yochim, 2010), skaters in Beal's research claimed that they skated with a racially diverse group, but at the same time drew on stereotypes of race, such as describing African-American skaters as being able to 'Ollie' higher and Asian Americans excelling because they 'took it more seriously' and 'worked harder' (Wheaton and Beal, 2003a: 86). Beal concluded that black skaters in North America do gain subcultural status, but it is harder for them to gain respect than white skaters, and they are marked as different. The skateboarders' 'elision of race' alongside their 'continued reliance on individualised notions of identity and community' served to maintain the power of white, middle-class skateboarders (Chivers-Yochim, 2010: 105).[41]

Part II
The case studies

5 Risk-taking and regulation
Examining the sportisation of parkour

An introduction to parkour

According to its founders, parkour, which derives from the French *parcours*, meaning 'route' or 'course', is the 'art of moving fluidly from one part of the environment to another' (McLean *et al.*, 2006: 795). Other labels that have been used to describe this non-competitive physical training discipline include *art du deplacement*, the first name for the activity, which broadly translates in English as the *art of movement* (Parkour UK, 2011), and more recently *freerunning*. However, the name has never been as important as the 'methods and spirit of practise which remain at its core today' (ibid.). It is inspired by human movement which focuses on 'efficient motion' over, under, around or through obstacles. Each *traceur* – the name given to those who practise parkour seriously – moves from A to B under, over, and through obstacles, including walls, railings and roofs, by jumping, vaulting and climbing (Miller and Demoiny, 2008: 63). It is practised predominantly, but not exclusively, in urban areas using manmade or naturally occurring obstacles. While practitioners first learn a set of techniques, such as the *cat leap*,[1] parkour does not have a set of rules or objectives. It does not fit easily into existing categories, being described variously as sport, art and a 'discipline', with forms that intersect with other activities such as dance, martial arts and gymnastics.

Parkour in its current form emerged from the 'alienating' and multiracial Paris suburb or *banlieue* of Lisse in the 1980s (Mould, 2009), an urban space that over the past decade has been the focus of urban riots.[2] This environment is where David Belle, Sebastien Foucan and seven other friends began training and founded the *Yamakasi* group,[3] from which most of the parkour-inspired movements have originated (Parkour UK, 2011). While most subscribe to this version of parkour's recent appearance, many dedicated participants recognise that it has a longer history, rooted in the military system of physical training proposed by the French educational theorist Georges Hebert in the early 1900s (see Atkinson, 2009).[4] Elite participant and teacher Dan Edwardes explains that:

> Parkour comes from the term *Parkour de combatant* which is the core to the *training method naturale* and that term translates into English as 'assault

course' or 'obstacle course'. So what we're doing is not new. Parkour's not this new thing which has just suddenly come along. In its modern form it's almost 20 years old, but it goes back to 1906 and Georges Hebert.

(Personal interview, 2009)

Until recently, parkour was relatively unheard of; however, by the end of the 1990s, media across many Western industrial nations were documenting parkour's emergence. Since then, it has spread rapidly among young, urban, inner-city populations across Europe, North and South America, Australasia and Asia, through informal networks, internet forums and particularly its presence on sites such as YouTube. While parkour is a self-directed, individualistic practice, participants usually create small groups or teams to practise and train (each with their own team name, e.g. the *Yamakasi*), and periodically meet up with other traceurs, including at gatherings, or 'jams', promoted using social and electronic media (see Atkinson, 2009). Despite the individualistic nature of practice, traceurs have a strong sense of being part of a local and increasingly transnational collectivity, often referred to as 'the community', explained here by a teenage participant, Peter: 'The UK as a whole, this community is really tight. I mean pretty much everyone who is decent like and they know everyone. And you kind of say anyone's name and you'll kind of know who that is.' The nature of this collectivity appears to be less bounded or clearly defined than most traditional sporting subcultures, more akin to Mafessoli's description of a neo-tribe.[5] Guss also comments on the particular, and potentially unique, dynamic between the individual and group (2011: 74). He describes the parkour collectivity as 'integrated yet heterogeneous', combining 'singularity and collectivity' (ibid.). He suggests that it can be seen as a microcosm of Hart and Negri's concept of the *multitude*, which is 'an emerging subjectivity produced in the post-Fordist forms of labour organised around the exchange of information and the production of affects' (ibid.: 78). Guss argues that parkour shares the same conditions, develops according to the same process and logic, and creates a similar group dynamic as the *multitude* (ibid.: 80). For example, members, 'maintain their singularity, even as they are part of a larger unit as they communicate and collaborate across national boundaries' (ibid.: 74).[6] So in contrast to traditional forms of collective identity (such as nations) where group unity subsumes individual identity, the multitude maintains individual differences (ibid.: 78).

While the available evidence in terms of participation figures is still unclear (Gilchrist and Wheaton, 2011), online data sources (such as postings of personal videos on websites) suggest that participation stems from increasingly wide geographic settings, including those outside the Global North. The UK is now considered a centre for parkour; London seeing itself as the self-styled capital, the city being the base for many of the top traceurs and teams, such as *Parkour Generations*, which includes a number of the French second-generation 'masters' (see Angel, 2011b).

The parkour philosophy

According to Parkour UK's website (2011):

> Parkour is a discipline of self-improvement on all levels, an art that reveals to the practitioner his or her own physical and mental limits and simultaneously offers a method to surpass them. A practitioner of parkour aims to be self-reliant and physically capable; fit, strong and healthy; honest and sincere; disciplined; focussed; creative and always useful and helpful to others.

Parkour shares many characteristics with other informal lifestyle sports (see Ch. 2), including its spontaneous nature, the absence of bounded spaces for participation, a lack of person-to-person formal competition and an emphasis on self-expression and attitudes to freedom and to risk (Olivier, 2010; Robinson, 2004; Stranger, 1999). Nonetheless, the philosophy and meaning of parkour also differs from other lifestyle sports in important ways and, as detailed below, the parkour/free-running label embraces a range of often paradoxical and multifaceted activities and attitudes.

Anti-sports discourse

Practitioners claim that the activity is a form of art that uses many Eastern philosophies[7] requiring discipline, and serious participants often have martial arts[8] and/or gymnastic training (see Miller and Demoiny, 2008). While traceurs reject the label 'sport' because they are against formal competition, many aspects are 'sports-like', including their physically demanding 'training' regimes (see Atkinson, 2009). Devotees I interviewed were physically fit individuals who trained obsessively, often around 20 hours a week, and tended to adopt what is generally regarded as a 'healthy lifestyle', including abstaining from smoking, eating healthily and only drinking alcohol in moderation – or not at all.

Traceurs challenge themselves physically and mentally, but they do not – at least overtly – compete against others. As one teenage male participant explained, effort and attitude, not ability, is rewarded:

> There's no competitiveness between us, and the same value is put on me being able to do something very high and you being just able to get over a barrier, you know, the same emphasis and value is put on it.
>
> (Jake)

The prospect of competition was a source of debate among the community and on forums:[9] 'Inventing a parkour competition would be nonsense. That is why nobody has tried, because everyone that understands parkour knows that it would be pointless' (forum respondent). Nonetheless, quite nuanced views were voiced that recognised the difficulties of developing a non-competitive sporting practice

within a dominant culture infused by the values of competition. As one respondent put it:

> You can't be against competition in parkour and pro-competition in other
> activities. That would be self-contradictory. The goals of parkour are the
> goals of life. If your parkour goals aren't yet carried forward into all aspects
> of life then you need to think some more.
>
> (forum participant)

Indeed, as one teenage male acknowledged, in their training activities, his group
was sometimes competitive – for example, 'having a race to see who could
climb up an item the fastest' (Peter). He was adamant, however, that for parkour
in general 'competition – it's bad – full stop'.

> When you're training, we're not kind of training to be the best, we are train-
> ing to do parkour and then we are using our skills, which is quite fun. If you
> put competition to anything it just causes people to try and be the best in the
> competition and then you lose why you wanted to be good at it. Does that
> make sense?
>
> (Jake)

Traceurs also described their groups as 'non-hierarchical' and illustrated the
ways in which 'everyone will take responsibility for training everyone else in
what they know' (Jake). Traceurs had an *ethic of care* for the self, others and
the environment more broadly. Inclusivity and a sense of responsibility were
manifest in many ways, including attitudes to public space and the ways in
which beginners and 'outsiders' were embraced and supported, not derided,
as is often the case in other lifestyle sports, such as surfing and
skateboarding:

> I kind of find skate culture and BMX culture, they're kind of a bit 'we're
> BMXs, this is our place, no one else's'. Parkour's a bit more, it's got a dif-
> ferent kind of background and it's a lot more kind of 'everywhere is kind of
> yours'.
>
> (Jake)

Guss also claims that 'traceurs do not forge groups based on exclusion' (2011:
81). Paul, a parkour participant and teacher, explained, 'every technique is
underplayed with a philosophy and idea of responsibility, a responsibility about
the environment one practises parkour in, and the other users of that environment'. Academic studies have suggested that parkour has the potential to transgress bodily and spatial norms, bringing 'forth an aesthetic-spiritual reality of
the self' (Atkinson, 2009: 170).

Inclusivity discourses and difference: performing masculinity in parkour

One interesting manifestation of this ethic of care is the way in which identity and difference are constructed in relation to race and gender. Discursively, parkour's values appear not to embrace central aspects of hegemonic sporting masculinity, such as the win-at-all-cost ethos and the heroic displays of strength, speed and power prevalent in many traditional sports and some lifestyle sports (Wheaton, 2004b; Robinson, 2008). A posting on a parkour forum (2010) was typical in the way it promoted a discourse of gender inclusivity:

> The real point in parkour is not to be able to do incredible things, but rather to explore ourselves and to conquer our demons on our way to pure inner peace. I hope to see the female scene express itself and shine ever more among the parkour world. To all the *traceuses* [female participant] in the world, I give you my best wishes and hopes!

The rejection of aspects of traditional sporting masculinity was also evident in the ways young men supported rather than competed with each other for status and in the valuing of skills that females tend to excel in, such as balance and agility (in addition to the more traditionally male-defined attributes of risk-taking and strength). The lack of formal competition and the aesthetic and dance-like aspects of the performance were emphasised by many of the male participants:

> The difference between parkour, I guess, and other sports and disciplines is, there is no competition where you have to be the fastest [...] that's why, for example, in athletics, male stuff is always going to be there. Because it's the fastest a human can go or the furthest a human can jump. There's none of that in parkour. It doesn't really matter how far you can jump or anything like that, it doesn't make you a better practitioner.
>
> (Dan)

In contrast to many other male-defined and dominated sports, emotional engagement was encouraged, not seen as a weakness. Saville's (2008) interesting analysis of parkour explores the role of the emotions, especially fear, in traceurs' play with city space (see also Guss, 2011):[10]

> Parkour is bound to be emotional because it makes us face our own fears and weaknesses, it's like this for everyone, from the complete newbie to David Belle or others. Very few people have never shed tears because of parkour.
>
> (Couetdic, 2011)

Nonetheless, it was also certainly evident that, despite the *discourse* of anti-competition and of support, men *did* compete over status in similar performative ways to men in other 'non-competitive' lifestyle sporting contexts (Wheaton, 2004b). One revealing example was the (widely commented on) practice of men taking their tops off to display their 'chests and pecs', even in cold weather. As Paul described:

> There are loads of YouTube clips that start with a guy taking his shirt off slowly just to show the back, and then he starts to run and does stuff like that, and then starts looking into the distance, and then starts to do parkour. It's horrible.

Thus male traceurs' behaviour is contradictory; they perform hegemonic masculinity in ways that include engaging in risk-taking behaviour and displaying their muscular physiques, while simultaneously wanting to – and attempting to – encourage and promote the participation of men and women of all abilities. The traceurs we interviewed who were involved with the teaching and development of their sport were all conscious of, and proud of, having a positive attitude towards female participation.

In terms of ethnicity, too, parkour does not have the white imagery and participant-base associated with many other lifestyle sports, which can be a powerful cultural barrier for non-white participants (Kusz, 2004; Wheaton, 2009b). In contrast to most other lifestyle sports, black bodies are prevalent in parkour imagery.[11] Traceurs were, from the outset, an ethnically diverse group, including children of first-generation immigrants (Guss, 2011).[12] While demographic data on parkour is very limited, its continued popularity in inner-city contexts seems to suggest it has appeal across ethnic groups. In our research, it was evident, particularly in London, that parkour appealed to youth with a wide range of cultural and ethnic backgrounds.

Primark style

> Primark style [laughs]. Yeah, just basically cheap clothing.
>
> (Jake)

Another interesting difference between parkour and most other lifestyle sports is that parkour does not – as yet – have a recognisable subcultural style or even a 'look'. Participants wear comfortable and practical clothes for running, ranging from cheap sweats to high-tech athletics garments, depending on their budget and personal style. As one younger participant explained, 'You're probably going to rip your clothes and, I mean, a lot of young people don't have too much money.' Others expressed a preference for trainers that functioned well for parkour, rather than expensive brands. For example:

> Cheap shoes, these shoes I've got on now, they're ten pounds from a shop called Decathlon. And they're the best shoes for parkour you can get.
>
> (Peter)

Normally the best trainers are the cheaper running shoes. Definitely, the cheaper Nike, the cheapest Nike and the cheapest Adidas are the best for it (parkour).

(Sam)

Parkour was 'not about fashion' or consumption; the embodied forms of physical capital and the ethos of practice constituted a 'way of living' and were the essence of *being* a traceur.

For some of the parkour teachers, the parkour ethic involved care for 'the community'; and they saw it as their responsibility to promote ethical lifestyle practices, including (for some) encouraging ethical production and consumption practices. As Paul argued, he did not want to promote the expensive shoes produced by transnational shoe companies:

When we put the *Urban Playground* together we made a conscious decision to all wear Asics so that we didn't end up going into a school environment appearing to support Nike or Adidas or one of the big commercial companies, because we thought we're getting nothing from them, we don't want to give them anything by association. There's a philosophy there.

(Paul)

However, traceurs did not appear to adopt an aggressive 'anti-corporate ethos'. As one of them put it, 'It's not about *not* promoting big companies, it's a question of trying not to promote things that are damaging to an individual, promoting a healthy lifestyle, a kind of ethical lifestyle.' He cited alcohol, drugs and the energy drink Red Bull, which he described as 'a poison'. Nonetheless, reflecting the mainstream incorporation of most subcultural formations and alternative lifestyles, traceurs were very wary of outsiders trying to exploit the discipline for commercial gain. As one of the *Parkour Generations* team explained, they chose not to be sponsored by certain transnational shoe companies because they saw them trying to profit from parkour without giving 'anything back':

We don't need anyone's sponsorship and we don't really want anyone's sponsorship. A lot of groups ... they're just being, they're just sort of jumping on the bandwagon of these companies who want to largely exploit the discipline for promotion of their brand.

(Dan)

In contrast, traceurs accepted support or sponsorship from companies they believed wanted to 'support the discipline and help the discipline grow'. Like other lifestyle sports in the early phases of commercial incorporation, participants emphasised the importance of showing *commitment* to the lifestyle and ethos (see Wheaton, 2005). However, inevitably, transnational corporations like Nike are beginning to recognise the commercial potential of parkour, marketing clothing and shoes 'for free-running', and some participants admitted to being 'testers' for companies, receiving free shoes.

Parkour, the media and risk (mis)perception

A spate of media attention has contributed to parkour's growing cultural presence, including featuring in the BBC channel idents *Rush Hour*, starting founding traceur David Belle (see Mould, 2009), and in the blockbuster Bond film *Casino Royale* (2006), featuring a chase between Daniel Craig (as James Bond) and parkour expert Sebastien Foucan. According to our research participants, the Channel 4 documentaries *Jump Britain* (Christie, 2005) and *Jump London* (Christie, 2003) were widely attributed for bringing the activity to the nation's attention in the UK. The media depiction of parkour as a dangerous activity has contributed to widespread misinformation, particularly about the high degree of risk involved (McLean *et al.*, 2006): 'It's very simple, a lot of people just see what's in the media and they assume that's what they are going to be doing and it's just not the case' (Dave, sport development officer and parkour promoter). Many similarities can be drawn between the media reporting of parkour and the kite-surfing incident discussed in Chapter 3, including (moral) panics about irresponsible youth and a fear of copy-cat behaviour based on a small minority of 'extreme' incidents reported in the media (e.g. Sacramento News, 2008).

Hoodies on street-corners: perception of deviance

> I think unfortunately, these days, if an elderly person sees anybody in a hoody they perceive that as some sort of threat.
>
> (Community Police Officer, Sussex, UK)

It is not just in the UK where these views are held. Atkinson outlines how in Toronto, Canada, traceurs were the cause of several moral panics in local media (2004–2006), in which they were seen as 'disruptive', displaying 'aggressive tendencies' (Atkinson and Young, 2008: 68). City councillors and police officers alike decried their activities, seeing them as 'social junk' because of perceptions that their lifestyles were deviant and drug-related and that their activities lacked economic productivity, detracting from the 'normal' desirable productive use of the city space (ibid.). In the UK, too, fuelled by media-inspired fears about young people hanging around urban streets (characterised as 'hoodies'), there was a widespread perception that these (predominantly young) men doing parkour (or skateboarding, roller-blading, etc.) are 'deviant' bodies invading public space. Those involved with parkour as educators were acutely aware of these problems, recognising how films such as *Jump London* had contributed to the view that parkour encourages deviant behaviours, such as how to evade the police. As one sport development officer put it: 'You know, you get the same old analogies, "you are teaching the cat burglars of the future".'[13]

These prejudices were borne out in the parkour project that we examined in coastal East Sussex. In the first public consultation process in which the proposed parkour training area was rejected, one of the main reasons voiced was noise, and that it would encourage young people to hang around in the park. The local police confirmed that when parkour first emerged in the area they had 'constant' phone calls from (predominantly older) residents voicing concerns about the participants' safety, 'youths gathering' and 'damage to property'. The lads who were participating in the research project fuelled prejudices by, for example, choosing practice locales such as the street opposite a nursing home. However, the police and other community officials we interviewed recognised that there was little evidence of any real harm, such as damage to property:

> There were reports of damage being done and youths gathering together and jumping on fences and things like that [...] it wasn't so much damage – that they were jumping from one side to the other. I think people haven't really seen it for what they can do, you know, they've been seeing it initially as groups of youths hanging round.
>
> (Community police officer)

Despite no police evidence of damage, some members of the local police responded to complaints by asking the traceurs to 'move on'. From the participants' perspective, people 'in authority' generally saw them as a nuisance, and they were continually being 'moved on'. As Silk and Andrews (2008: 409) discuss in the context of a US city, the 'discursive constitution of a moral panic about youth' has led to new, pervasive and discriminatory forms of surveillance and regulation within the 'neoliberal city space, targeting those who have no legitimate, that is consumer-led, reason for being there'. Jake told me how he had once been stopped by police three times in a particular day. Another stated they were hassled 'every single day' by police, residents, security officers, in fact 'anyone who wants to'. When questioned about the reason given, Jake explained as follows:

> JAKE: We always ask 'why'. They use pretty weak excuses. Like for example, in Guildford, on the high street there was kind of a car park. And there was a brick wall going along, And we were being really safe, nothing high, nothing dangerous, not getting in people's way. And a police car pulled up, took all our details. 'Why?', we asked. 'What are we doing?'. 'Oh – you are being antisocial. Move on.'
> PETER: Yep, or 'this is private property'.

The philosophy of parkour requires traceurs to preserve and respect their environment and community (Bavinton, 2007; Atkinson, 2009), to use architecture in 'new and alternative ways', but 'never to disrupt, change or damage' (Mould, 2009: 743).

Insider values: safe practice

> They saw David Belle do a 20 m jump from one building to another and they saw Sebastien Foucan jump on HMS *Belfast* and they thought that was parkour. And it's not! It's stunt work.
>
> (Parkour teacher and promoter)

In contrast to media depictions, those who do parkour, or are involved via teaching the activity, reject the extreme or high-risk label, recognising the importance of 'being safe'. As one advocate explained, 'It's always broadcast as big, difficult moves', which 'seems to put the general public off enjoying it'; 'people don't realise that at a very basic level it's a safe activity' (Sport development officer). Likewise, the videos posted on YouTube and websites are misleading as they tend to show the most difficult and spectacular part of a participant's performance repertoire. Parkour practice involves slow-paced, repetition of manoeuvres, often close to the ground. Reflecting the safety narratives in other lifestyle sports (see Ch. 3), traceurs also claim that novices get hurt because they 'never learnt how to train properly' (Paul), whereas among 'real' traceurs injuries are rare. On several occasions, I was reminded that none of the originators had sustained serious injuries. This assertion is corroborated by academics studying injury rates, who claim that serious parkourists are 'tremendous athletes who practise their stunts in a controlled environment such as a gymnasium with mats, pads and foam pits' (Miller and Demoiny, 2008: 63). Serious injuries are rare and predominantly occur when novices, without proper training, attempt dangerous stunts (ibid.).

As discussed above, underpinning parkour is a wider philosophy, that advocates – even requires – discipline and 'safe training'. The importance of safety infused the conversations we had with traceurs. It was emphasised that 'safety is the *most* important aspect; every traceur should understand how to train safely' (Paul). Participants recognised that if the activity was not done safely, 'at your own speed', then it could be very dangerous. Participants required self-discipline, knowledge and responsibility to ensure they did not attempt overly difficult or risky manoeuvres. They believed it was *their* responsibility to impart this ethos and knowledge to other less-experienced participants:

> People are just copying what they see in videos and the internet and they have no idea of the training that goes on behind that; so they really don't understand what they are doing so they're just damaging their bodies. That's not the way it should be done at all, so that's not the point of parkour ... that's why we started teaching because so many kids are doing it wrong.
>
> (Dan)

This was also a central reason why competition, or any form of grading of manoeuvres (like belts in martial arts), was rejected. As one teenage male traceur explained, grading or belts pushed a person to try and progress faster, which in parkour could be dangerous and result in injury.

The institutionalisation of parkour in the UK

In this section, I consider the on-going professionalisation, institutionalisation and regulation of parkour. Building on the discussion of subcultural fragmentation in Chapter 2, I discuss the fragmentation of the parkour discipline into different styles of participation, including the activity characterised as free-running. Then I discuss initiatives to regulate and professionalise the sport, illustrating how safety concerns, as well as battles to control the parkour cultural field (Bourdieu, 1977), underpin these processes.

Free-running versus parkour: competing discourses of 'authenticity'

As is well-documented on parkour websites and in academic literature, an ideological split between two of the founding 'fathers' of the modern discipline, David Belle and Sebastien Foucan, led to the original crew (from Lisses, Paris) severing into factions (see Edwardes, 2007; Weigel, 2007; Atkinson, 2009). Like other lifestyle sports that have fragmented following intense media focus, different attitudes to commercialisation and competition drove this split, underpinned by competing notions of 'authentic' identity and status (see Wheaton, 2007a). David Belle led the Hébert-inspired version of parkour, for whom the philosophy of the activity, 'the spirituality behind the sport' (Dan) was seen as fundamental to parkour's meaning and credibility. As Atkinson outlines, Belle referred to parkour's depiction in the media as 'prostitution (and destruction) of the art' (2009: 172). Participants under this doctrine tend to emphasise efficient movement and discipline, seeing parkour as a 'non-competitive' discipline or art, underpinned by a philosophy that challenges the person's physical and mental abilities.

Foucan and his followers promoted a more all-embracing variety of the activity which combined acrobatic tricks and stunts, often characterised as free-running. As one proponent explained, it incorporated movements from other activities, including gymnastics, parkour and break-dancing, also termed *expressive parkour*: 'Free-running is very much a solid lifestyle sort of thing; it's around showcasing how good you are whereas parkour's more around the small things, the small developments, the developments you make as an individual' (Minogue, personal interview, 2009). However, according to Parkour UK:

> The term freerunning was the creation of Guillaume Pelletier, a representative of a group of French practitioners involved in the production of a Channel 4 documentary, Jump London (2003). This term was used in order to communicate this amazing new sport to an English-speaking audience.

To the outside observer, Foucan's own description of the 'art' of free-running does not appear to differ very much from traditional parkour, as he also stresses the centrality of the broader philosophy and spirituality (see also Weigel, 2007).[14] For example:

> Freerunning is an art that allows people to grow physically and spiritually according to their paths not society's [...]. My way is not about performing – it is simply the physical expression of being at one with your body and mind.
>
> (Foucan, 2008: 8–9)

However, many participants characterise Foucan and his followers as having embraced the commercial opportunities presented by parkour, such as stunt work, selling 'parkour to global audiences through television commercials, documentaries, movies, clothing lines, training schools, video games and even international parkour competitions' (Atkinson, 2009: 173). Describing the more global free-running movement, Atkinson suggests that competitive free-runners have become the 'largest demographic in the parkour global network' (ibid.), including marginal participants who prefer to align themselves to the free-running movement via consumption and those who prefer not to subscribe to the 'ideological commitment' of the practice (ibid.: 174). In the UK, too, parkour is already beginning to appear (re)packaged as a fitness activity taught in gyms and outside in parks.[15] A range of parkour-hybrid dance and performance activities are also emerging that use parkour as inspiration, such as Nike's *Dare to Dance*, incorporating street dance with parkour/free-running moves. In the performance arts, parkour has been incorporated into festivals, dance performances and art instillation. Famous performance groups like *Cirque du Soleil* and *Stomp* have incorporated parkour as artistic dance performance (Wisse, 2009).

For some participants we interviewed in the UK, the differences between parkour and the more freestyle aspects of free-running were significant. Parkour's differentiation was compared with cognate processes in the Afro-Brazilian martial art of capoeira (Joseph, 2009; Wisse, 2009). In both disciplines, fragmentation led to differentiation in scenes espousing competing discourses of 'display' (free-running) and 'utility' (parkour) (see Joseph, 2009; Wisse, 2009), with the more traditional, less-commercialised version claimed as the most 'authentic':[16]

> Parkour and free-running have got that same split, the same as Capoera, between the roots Angalero Capoera and the kind of high-jumping back-flip Capoera. And one of them you can use to defend yourself, and the other one not a hope in hell. It looks good but it's useless. And that's the problem with free-running. Parkour comes from this philosophy of I'm going to train myself to be useful, and if actually I train myself to look good in front of a group of girls because I can back-flip lots, then I've become useless.
>
> (Dan)

It was also suggested that free-running tended to attract younger men, for whom the more visible lifestyle aspects were particularly important, [those] 'who want the lifestyle, who like the tee-shirt, who like watching it, who like being on the internet and talking about it' (Sam). These narratives reinforcing the discourse of *display* versus *utility* clearly replicate the notions of (in)authentic identity and status espoused by core participants in many lifestyle sports, rooted in a distinction between an embodied identity doing/being/living versus consuming the sporting lifestyle via the media or subcultural style.

Yet it would be misleading to suggest that all participants saw the differences between free-running and parkour in such marked ways or that all participants subscribed to the views above. As one suggested, it was 'just around a different slant on a sport, that's all' (Peter). He suggested that the need to differentiate between the activities was fuelled by forums, those who spent their time 'talking about it, not doing it'. Most traceurs we interviewed were more concerned with their own practice than being critical of other people's interpretations of the discipline, recognising that the meaning of parkour is, and should remain, open to numerous interpretations.

In evaluating the local and global fractionalisation of parkour, based around his fieldwork in Toronto, Canada, Atkinson (2009: 173) identifies a third, but small contingent of participants which he describes as a self-labelled tribe of Natural Method traditionalists for whom, following 'Hébert's original woodland style is the only true method of practice'. These predominantly non-urban-based participants, who train 'in the wild', were not evident in our (limited) fieldwork in the UK, which focused on urban environments. However, it was evident that scenes were emerging based in rural settings that combined elements of parkour with other activities, such as bouldering.[17]

Distinctions between traceurs and free-runners are also characteristic of the various different groups promoting, teaching and claiming to represent parkour in the UK. A range of organisations in the UK subscribe to, and indeed police, the philosophy as espoused by Belle, including the *British Parkour Coaching Association* and *Girl Parkour*. However, the most prominent is *Parkour Generations*, based in London. It retains strong links with the French first- and second-generation traceurs, who are revered in a similar way to the masters in many martial arts disciplines (such as *mestres* in capoeira), where prolonged contact with the grand master is considered essential to learning the discipline properly (Wisse, 2009: 11). Likewise in parkour, educators expressed concern that many young people were not learning the discipline properly, but 'are approaching it as a new thing' rather than consulting with the originators (Dave). As one practitioner argued, it was 'not just tradition for tradition sake', but the *Yamakasi* in France who had been training for twenty years, so 'they know experientially what works' (Dan) to keep you safe, strong and alive. Intimate contact with a master gave the participant or organisation credibility or 'authenticity'. One educator claimed his organisation was 'better qualified to impact 'real' knowledge about parkour because of its involvement with, and 'seal of approval' from, a French master:

> I think that what sets us aside as a team from the other groups working in this country ... that we're working with two of the originators [...] with the two that went and got accredited to teach parkour before anyone else did.

And they are our teachers and they have taught us how to teach [...]. So we teach with their stamp of approval.

(Paul)

This view was widespread; indeed the websites of many organisations and per-formance groups advertised connections or meetings with French traceurs.

In contrast, and reflecting more global developments in the sport, the more commercialised, all-embracing and less disciplined activity of free-running had also gained momentum in the UK. *Urban FreeFlow*, another London-based organisation, was the main establishment for this movement in the UK.[18] Evi-dently some members of *Parkour Generations* (PG) and *Urban FreeFlow* (UFF) initially shared a vision, but disagreements over the sport's future led to the for-mation of PG:

Parkour Generations was born out of frustration by the original French traceurs with *Urban FreeFlow* and the direction they were taking the sport, i.e. for commercial gain. [...] Dan and Forrest along with many other ori-ginal founders and traceurs founded *Parkour Generation*s.

(Minogue, sport development manager and, from 2011, CE of Parkour UK)

A thread running through internet forums is the disdain for UFF expressed by those participants who see themselves as 'real', 'authentic' traceurs. They per-ceived that UFF was 'into exploitation and a desire for money above all else' (personal correspondence), also criticised for their lack of experience, without links to parkour's founders. Such anti-corporate attitudes have, in the early phases of their development, characterised most lifestyle sports, particularly being hostile to companies trying to appropriate or 'sell-out' the activity:[19] 'I don't think, I don't think they really care what they are doing depending on how much money they're making, they'll advertise anything that pays them' (James). Fuelling this view was the 1st World Freerun Championship held in London (in September 2008) organised and promoted by UFF, involving athletes from 18 countries. It was seen as a blatant attempt for media exposure and commercial gain. Critics vociferously condemned the event, arguing that competition was antithetical to the traceur philosophy, 'only worth watching as proof that com-petition is a bad idea' (forum posting). Regardless of various misgivings about the live event, the edited highlights that were available via YouTube for public consumption (and that made BBC News[20]) focused on injuries and 'death-defying leaps' (Aitch, 2008), fuelling concerns that parkour was being presented as a larrikin, Jackass-style activity, not a serious art form or discipline.

Sportisation

'Sportisation' (Elias and Dunning, 1986) is the process by which play-like activ-ities become more regulated and organised (see Ch. 2). In this section, I outline this sportisation process in parkour, exploring how different bodies were vying for control over parkour in the UK. Our research coincided with a number of attempts to regulate and institutionalise parkour and free-running, with proposals emerging from both within and outside the disciplines. We were well-positioned to track these developments, including parkour's use in school PE and the formation of a Sport England-sanctioned NGB. Of particular importance is exploring *who* was driving the institutionalisation process and *why*, mapping the similarities and differences in this process with other longer-established lifestyle sports. While the need to establish parameters of acceptable and safe practice was widely recognised, our respondents – including both insiders (participants, parkour teachers/promoters) and educators outside the discipline (e.g. PE teachers and sport/art development officers) – differed in their opinions about the bodies or organisations they believed would be best placed to lead these developments.

The battle for control: legitimacy through accreditation

In the absence of nationally recognised teaching and coaching qualifications, various different coaching qualifications offered by insider groups had proliferated. One interviewee described the situation as an 'accreditation bandwagon'. Those outside the discipline discussed that it was hard to assess their legitimacy or credibility. They were also concerned that young people without any teaching experience were being employed by councils, schools and sport centres. These were issues that, in an increasingly litigation-obsessed culture, concerned parkour providers, and (between 2008 and 2010) questions were being asked about who was doing the accreditation and under whose guidance and standards.[21]

While these are not questions that concern most traceurs, for a significant minority it had become an extremely important debate, which is likely to have a wide-ranging impact on the discipline. Centrally, the perceived need for professionalisation was about creating an environment where people no longer continually doubted the legitimacy of the activity or asked questions about it:

> Because nobody ever asks 'are we going to do rugby at school?', 'oh well, that's dangerous', you know, because there is, there is the assumption that there is safety standards, which there is. So if we do that for parkour it will just legitimise the sport for other people out there that are risk adverse.
>
> (Minogue)

Parkour Generations has been at the centre of a move to institutionalise the sport in England and more globally, in partnership with Eugene Minogue, then at the Westminster Sport Development Unit, which had been instrumental in generating parkour provision and support. Together, they have been instrumental in driving the formation of the NGB, Parkour UK, which came into being late in 2008, with legal status in July 2009 with support from Sport England.

The British Amateur Gymnastic Association (BAGA) was another body represented as vying for a piece of the parkour-pie by attempting to accredit a qualification in freestyle gymnastics. Minogue (a former gymnast) suggested this was an attempt to bolster gymnastics' waning popularity and status. He outlined how, in the early period of parkour, BAGA sent a directive to all their gymnastics clubs stating that they 'should not be using their facilities for any sort of parkour activity'.[22] Minogue argued this forced parkour away from gymnasiums and into community and student halls. However, once BAGA recognised the growth and thus commercial potential of parkour: 'They changed their stance, trying to include parkour and other acrobatic-type activities in gymnastics. British gymnastics have tied up a whole heap of other sports from trampolining to acrobatics under their umbrella' (Minogue). Traceurs and those in sport development and teaching recognised that freestyle gymnastics was not the same as parkour or free-running and was unlikely to have much impact on the activities. If parkour were to be incorporated into the gymnastic *club* location, with its sports-like focus, it was argued that it would inevitably lead to a change in parkour's meaning. Also, those qualified to do the coaching by British Gymnastics were high-level gymnastic coaches, but had no previous knowledge of the ethos or history of parkour. These aspects were seen by parkour's devotees as essential to teaching the discipline. It was also recognised that gymnastic settings were unlikely to attract the groups parkour appealed to, including youth who did not engage in traditional sports (see Gilchrist and Wheaton, 2011). In Minogue's view, therefore, this type of outsider seizure of the sport provided a strong rationale for the need for 'insider' accreditation and ultimately the development of a governing body:

> I would disagree with the legitimacy or the authenticity of that qualification and what it actually means. You know, there has been no dialogue with anybody from the parkour community around this qualification [...]. We need to tie up this sort of grey area around qualification. Parkour is very different from gymnastics, and somebody that comes from a gymnastics background is going to have pre-conceptions around moves, activities. So it all gets diluted again and this is the problem, and why we need to get a separate national governing body set up.
>
> (Minogue, personal interview, 2009)

Parkour UK: parkour becomes a sport

For the NGB Parkour UK, the issues of safety, insurance, accreditation of coaching, and teaching and instruction qualifications, as well as retaining insider control, were the key objectives. As Minogue (CE, Parkour UK) outlined, it has taken considerable time and work to get support (and ultimately funding) for parkour:

> We know how long it took to get us to this stage, and a lot of that was around the questions of qualifications, insurance, liability, and *is this sport safe*? [...] make sure they are meeting set criteria from people like the Youth

Sport Trust, afPE, Sport England [...]. It just sort of legitimises the sport and it mitigates all the sort of questions that are out there: 'is it dangerous?'.

(Minogue, personal interview, 2009)

One of the first initiatives was to accredit a national coaching training scheme and a graded certification process called ADAPT (Minogue, 2011).[23] In contrast to BAGA's qualifications, ADAPT integrates parkour's physical skills with an understanding of the broader ethos and lifestyle. The development had been a protracted process, in part as they consulted with prominent 'sporting' bodies, such as Sport England and the Association for Physical Education (afPE), to ensure it would be ratified and endorsed by the relevant coaching and teaching frameworks and bodies.

All those who pass the ADAPT qualification get public liability insurance specifically for parkour. Getting parkour-specific insurance was an extremely significant, lengthy and difficult process.[24] During our research, we spoke to individuals and groups who were involved with parkour-related provision in the arts, in schools (both in the PE curriculum and in after-school clubs), in the provision of parkour as a fitness-type activity in recreational exercise classes, and in various youth projects (funded by local authorities and the Arts Council). For all those bodies teaching in any sort of formal setting (whether in a gym, leisure centre, theatre or school, or out on the street), providing insurance cover and allaying safety concerns were central considerations.

That insiders to the culture should be the ones to drive regulation of the activity seems somewhat antithetical to the laissez-faire, rule-free nature of the activity. However, as discussed in Chapter 3 in the cases of surfing, mountaineering and kite-surfing, participants' aspirations to legitimise and protect their own sports have been instrumental in the processes of sportisation. In parkour, too, there is a desire to protect the discipline both from outsiders (e.g. BAGA) and from insiders (e.g. UFF) who the (self-appointed) leaders of the sportisation development did not believe had the 'right intentions'.[25] In contrast, PG saw itself as preserving parkour as a competition-free activity. Dan Edwardes told me how they had 'defended' the activity from approaches by ESPN's X Games to turn it into a competitive sport (instead negotiating for various performances – such as at the opening ceremony for London 2012 – that PG believed would showcase the activity in the 'right way').

All those involved with professionalisation of parkour discussed at great length how and why these measures were for the 'good of the sport'. Clearly cognisant of being seen as selling-out the art, they explained how the formation of an NGB benefited the broader community rather than themselves as individuals (or PG as an organisation) and that the need was driven by the (global) parkour community, of which they saw themselves as leaders:

This is also led by the parkour community itself saying this is what we want, this is where we want to go with the sport [...] this is not something we are forcing people to do, it's not something we are imposing on people.

(Minogue, personal correspondence, 2010)

Minogue recognised the importance of the parkour community being involved if the body was to retain credibility, and discussed that over time it needed to become a democratic body, run by the parkour community with elected officials, involving 'everyone': Dan Edwardes argued that, 'It has to be set up by someone but once it's set up it needs to be run by the community.'

While those with the responsibility of providing parkour in formal settings, such as educationalists and policy makers, undoubtedly welcomed these developments, it is still too early (in 2012) to tell if Parkour UK has the community 'buy-in' and support as its originators believe (in Bourdieu's, 1977, terms, whether it has legitimacy from those inside the parkour field). Based on the views of the handful of traceurs we spoke to, they were broadly ambivalent about the formation of the NGB, and trusted 'the community' to do the 'right thing'. Yet, as I've illustrated, despite the notion of 'community', it was in reality 'imagined' and fragmented.

Contested vision of parkour: discourses of art vs. sport

Many of the parkour initiatives we examined in Sussex were funded through the arts not sport.[26] In Crawley, for example, the local council had been involved with parkour-related provision for several years, initially using Arts Council funding to run a two-year project, *Jump Crawley*. Their broad remit was to engage young men with 'some sort of artistic notion of movement and physicality' using parkour (Dave, *Jump Crawley* project manager). Subsequently, an extreme sport manager was employed to work on the development of a parkour park, which opened in the summer of 2009. They saw the 'fusion between extreme sport and art' as extremely productive and non-contradictory, and chose a particular parkour group (UPG from Brighton) as consultants because of 'the way in which they engaged young people through their experience of other art forms' (Dave).

One experienced parkour teacher/provider we interviewed was particularly vociferous that the arts, not sport, was 'the most natural' place for parkour.[27] His background was in the arts as a physical theatre practitioner, and his parkour performance team was comprised predominantly of dancers, so the way he taught parkour was 'very connected' within an 'artistic discipline'. He expressed concern about the development of parkour in the UK and the moves to institutionalise it as a 'sport', which he believed would change the ethos of parkour:

> I think there's a big movement in the country to get parkour accredited as a sport and it will inevitably damage parkour to do that because parkour grew out of a physical training called 'method naturelle' [...] and the whole basis of it is that it is an autodidactic method of training that's non-competitive. [...] and one way you can describe parkour is 'environmental dance', certainly performance as parkour is environmental dance and animation of public space.
>
> (Paul)

It was also apparent that defining parkour as art provided a more secure anti-corporate location for those concerned with what they saw as the 'sell-out' being pursued by some groups:[28] 'Two of the original nine that, you know, established parkour in France, they felt very like "it's a sell-out", "no that's not what we're about". And then they've come round to, within an art setting, being comfortable with it' (Paul). For these advocates, parkour performances in festivals, or as street theatre, provided a way of publicising parkour in a more positive way.

For the proponents of parkour as art, the new sports-based NGB Parkour UK seemed incompatible with their vision, as accreditation was based on a standardised, sportised qualification with 'standards' and 'quality assurance' (Minogue) that contrasted with the broader discourse around parkour emphasising its creativity and fluidity.[29] As Paul put it, 'is it possible to accredit an artistic discipline without losing its creativity?'. 'We're certainly not against accreditation. Accreditation is fantastic [but] the only means of reinforcing that accreditation is by having the set curriculum model [...]. And the problem with that is that it's anti-self-expression' (Paul). He exemplified this argument using skateboarding, arguing that because of the competition-based focus on doing rotations, vert skating had become predictable and boring. The original skating 'art form' involving a variety of forms of self-expression had been reduced to 'who can spin the most', killing the 'creative urge which is in the people that get involved'. Those I spoke to at Parkour UK were certainly aware of, and concerned about, this criticism, arguing nonetheless that 'what we need to do is set some sort of framework for everybody to work in' (Minogue), and that it is a misconception that creativity and self-expression are not at the heart of their accreditation process.

Parkour, school provision and the PE profession: negotiating discourses of risk and safety

These developments are particularly relevant to, and visible in, the PE context, where intense and on-going debates about the role and use of parkour in school have taken place. Framing this debate in England was the wider framework of the new PE curriculum, which was introduced into secondary schools in 2009.[30] It shifted the emphasis from a focus on *activities* (such as team games) to *core skills* (such as balance and flight). It appears to have encouraged *some* teachers to adopt a wider range of activities, and some schools have expanded provision, incorporating a range of non-traditional sports, including skateboarding, ultimate frisbee, surfing, street surfing and parkour (interviews with PE teachers).

However, parkour has had a somewhat contested and contradictory reception within the PE profession, largely due to health and safety fears. A bulletin produced for afPE early in 2008 stated 'afPE cannot support an activity that appears to fly in the face of safe practice and acceptable risk on several counts. [...] In short, it is inappropriate, misguided and dangerous' (Glen Beaumont, afPE's health and safety officer, cited in Cornford, 2008). However, the interpretation of these recommendations appeared to be regionally variable; Westminster, for example, had provided parkour in PE for several years, while East Sussex County Council banned parkour in curriculum time (Bob Lake, PE and sport development service manager). Moreover, a few months later, afPE issued a second statement (in *Physical Education Matters*): [31] 'afPE believes parkour-related activity has the potential to offer young people an alternative movement experience that is both challenging and fulfilling in both its skill and aesthetic demands' (Beaumont, 2008). The PE and sport development professionals interviewed in this research recognised these concerns, but nonetheless pointed to inconsistencies in afPE's position, recognising that health and safety legislation often protects the teachers not the children:

> Well, our attitude is that ... parkour for me is another form of gymnastics. That's how I see it. I remember being taught to do gymnastics assessments, jumping off window sills in gymnasiums. That was part of our environment. That was the space that we were in. Use it. There are issues with health and safety, but you can't wrap kids up in cotton wool and the principles are the same, regardless if you are teaching them gymnastics, parkour, whatever.
>
> (PE head)

Even two years later (December 2011), I had reports that some local authorities would not allow parkour in schools, despite the existence of the NGB, largely because, somewhat paradoxically, it was still not recognised as a 'sport' by Sport England.[32] To be considered a legitimate sport, the activity needs to fulfil a range of criteria that are antithetical to the parkour lifestyle, including having a club structure with a competitive element to it and an anti-doping policy. This was a source of frustration for Parkour UK (Minogue). As Tomlinson *et al.* (2005) argue, there is a need to understand the governance structures of lifestyle sports, particularly the (impact of the) contradictory role of NGBs across different types of informal sports.

Regardless of these different views, it is hard to imagine that there will be much sustained resistance to the sportisation of parkour. It is likely that the qualifications Parkour UK endorse will be seen as useful for those traceurs wanting to teach and coach; and in so doing this standardised teaching method and framework will be rolled out across the UK, Europe and more widely. Yet, like other lifestyle sports experiencing mainstreaming through popularity, with increasing pressure to regulate (see Ch. 3) and become more like a traditional sport and less like a form of play or artistic practice, it is likely that the processes will be accompanied by continued fragmentation and shifts in the meanings, identities and cultures. In capoeira, where contestation over whether the activity is art or sport has occurred over decades, different types of organisations continue to coexist. Brazilian mestres lack consensus about formal organisations and, in common with parkour participants, those whose incomes depend on capoeira are keen for regulation, whereas professionalisation is 'mocked' by advocates of capoeira's free-for-all philosophy (Wisse, 2009: 23).

Cultural shifts: from deviant youth to active citizens

In the last section of this chapter, I consider how the growing popularity of parkour among those urban youth who policy makers and educators have labelled as *hard to reach* has led to a belief that parkour can be a potentially productive tool for policy makers (in sport, the arts and education). To understand this shift, a brief excursion into the literature on skateboarding and urban politics is required.

The context: street sport and urban politics

Scholars, particularly from fields including urban planning, architecture and cultural geography, have showed sustained interest in how street-based lifestyle sports, such as skateboarding, roller-blading and parkour/free-running, connect to the politics of public space; that is, how space is used, given meaning, contested and policed/governed (Silk and Andrews, 2008; Madden, 2010). As Silk and Andrews discuss, 'civic policy is a powerful means through which city space is controlled, regulated, and governed' (2006: 323).

Ian Borden's study of skateboarding was one of the first to explore relationships between street sport and urban politics. Borden drew on Lefebvre's theories of the production of space to conceptualise skateboarding as a critique of capitalist space. Street skaters, he argued, actively re-appropriate and redefine government, business and commercial space in the city, they critique ownership, refusing to consume architecture as pure image, using it as 'a material ground for action' (2001: 239). Borden, therefore, argued that the resurgence of urban (street) skateboarding in the 1990s was a performative critical practice that challenged the form and mechanics of urban life, confronting the social, spatial and temporal logic of capitalist space.

Borden's analysis inspired a spate of articles on skateboarding and urban politics examining the relationship between skateboarding and those who manage and control city space (see, for example, Jones and Graves, 2000; L'Aoustet and Griffet, 2001; Wooley and Johns, 2001; Stratford, 2002; Howell, 2008; Chiu, 2009; Vivoni, 2009). From this research, it is evident that, until fairly recently, there was a lack of provision for skateboarders, who were excluded from public spaces and marginalised in decision-making processes (Howell, 2008: 478). Ocean Howell, however, suggests that a shift in the relationship between skateboarding and the city has occurred in North America since the late 1990s. Howell claims that skateboarding was being 'reconfigured as an instrument of development' (2005), illustrating how once bohemian or counter-cultural lifestyles were becoming institutionalised as instruments of urban development in the gentrifying city. Howell (2008) explores the explosion in provision for skate parks in North America around the beginning of the twenty-first century and the motivation for 'urban managers' (the plethora of people involved in commercial and state-funded leisure provision) to provide new facilities. The financial muscle exercised by the $5.5 billion skate industry played an important role, providing skateboarders with resources to 'lobby municipalities for skate parks' and 'provide funding and technical assistance' (ibid.: 476). Subsequently, skate parks were developed into 'zones of economic activity' (Vivoni, 2009).

Nonetheless, Howell suggests that urban managers focused less on 'satisfying consumer demand' and more on the characteristic behaviour of skateboarders, which included 'refraining from bringing liability cases for injuries' (see Dumas and Laforest, 2009), informally policing the neighbourhoods surrounding the parks and showing 'personal responsibility, self-sufficiency and entrepreneurism' (Howell, 2008: 476). These characteristics are core to the neoliberal economy, servicing it as a cultural and economic movement (cf. Giroux, 2004), and therefore are highly prized.[33] Howell argues therefore that skate parks are one of the mechanisms through which neoliberal ideals are being promoted, especially in terms of the sought-after personal characteristics of young citizens (2008). Similarly, Banks (2008) explores how in Richard Florida's description of the 'creative class' – who for Florida and his followers are a pronounced characteristic of post-industrial societies – the pursuit of adventurous, creative leisure (such as found in lifestyle sports) is valued for their creative qualities. These qualities provide an 'expression of the radical individuality inherent to the new economy' (ibid.).[34] Indeed, Howell sees skateboarding park provision as part of a wider process of 'neoliberal governance reforms' by new public managers, encouraging 'public agencies to function as businesses' (2008: 477). In this process, the 'citizen–state relationship' shifts from 'entitlement' to one of contractionism (ibid.). While Howell's case studies are focused on the North American city, these political processes and their cultural and economic impacts have wider resonance in other neoliberal contexts, such as the UK.

Sociological research emerging from youth studies and cultural geography has also begun to challenge the negative public perceptions of street-based lifestyle sports, highlighting their social benefits (Jones and Graves, 2000; Wooley and Johns, 2001; Dumas and Laforest, 2009; Bradley, 2010). In a report on teenagers and public space, Wooley and Johns (2001) found that, although teenagers may be treated as antisocial, they often understand the needs of other users of outdoor spaces and are willing and able to accommodate other groups (cited in Travlou, 2003). Research has also examined the factors that contribute to successful skate parks, illustrating that the park can become an important social space in which young people – not just skaters – can gather, socialise and take responsibility to police, preserve and protect the park and wider locale, fostering a sense of 'responsibility, ownership and control' (Jones and Graves, 2000: 137). Skate parks that are successful in attracting both experienced skaters and novices (and thus reduce the antisocial behaviour and danger associated with street skating) have tended to be driven by participants themselves, with their input in the planning of the facility seen to be vital to their success (ibid.).

Parkour and the city

The increasing visibility of parkour/free-running via commercial media and films has also provoked a spate of academic research across a range of interdisciplinary areas (e.g. Geyh, 2006; Daskalaki *et al.*, 2008; Thompson, 2008; Atkinson, 2009; Guss, 2011; Rawlinson and Guaralda, 2011). Echoing the skateboarding research, researchers have examined how this form of movement provides a different way of interacting with the (urban) environment (Geyh, 2006; Daskalaki *et al.*, 2008; Saville, 2008; Thompson, 2008; Atkinson, 2009; Archer, 2010; Angel, 2011b; Guss, 2011). Parkour has been seen as an escape 'from the practices of power that govern our movement and regulate our behaviour' (Ortuzar, 2009: 55).

Guss argues that parkour is 'a subversive social or artistic way of living and imagining space that re-appropriates the dominated, planned spaces' (2011: 76). He sees parkour's emergence in France as a response to urban policy characterised by surveillance and containment. Parkour, however, goes 'beyond *contesting* conceived space' by reshaping space in the ways traceurs 'imagine and experience new possibilities for movement' (ibid.). Similarly, Daskalaki *et al.* (2008), following Borden, explore how parkour transgresses capitalist space, disrupting and destabilising capitalist meanings of the city's physical and social landscape. The examination of the activities and the philosophy that underpins them leads Daskalaki *et al.* to propose that parkour is a form of 'urban activism' that poses a challenge to 'fixed, sterile organisational behaviour, fixed models and ready-made answers' (2008: 61). They describe the practice as one that opposes the commodification and commercialisation of the body and of the institutional controls in city spaces. Michael Atkinson's ethnographic research with traceurs in Toronto (Atkinson and Young, 2008; Atkinson, 2009) illustrates how dominant social constructions of the urban environment as sanitised corporate spaces are challenged.[35] He describes these traceurs as innovative inventors of an 'anarchoenvironmental movement (Shepherd, 2000) who at once critique the political economic ethos underwriting the design of, and physical cultural movement within, urban cities [...] and who bring forth an aesthetic-spiritual reality of the self' (Atkinson, 2009: 170). There are many developments occurring in parkour that parallel those in skateboarding's development, such as the emergence of the provision of designated parkour training areas and the motivations of policy makers to use parkour as a tool of urban development (see Gilchrist and Wheaton, 2011). With Gilchrist, I give an overview of the key initiatives encountered during our research in Southern England to illustrate the different ways in which parkour is being utilised by policy makers in sport, art and education, and for cross-cutting community initiatives and partnerships drawing on several of these aspects.[36] Nonetheless, pervasive and disciplinary discourses about young people 'at risk', serving to find ways to produce normative, 'healthy' (McDermott, 2007) and productive neoliberal citizens (Silk and Andrews, 2008), have also fuelled these policy initiatives. For Guss (2011: 75), parkour's emergence in Paris was linked to French urban policy, which has (since the early 1980s) been characterised by 'surveillance and repression', leading to French suburbs that were 'isolated and racialised spaces'. Parkour, he argues, provided a means to 'escape claustrophobia' and 'take control of urban space' (ibid.: 76).

In some locales, urban managers have attempted to contain and regulate parkour using similar techniques to those adopted to deter street skateboarding, including signage banning the activity and adapting the urban furniture to make it difficult to skate (see Borden, 2001). For example, in the Paris suburbs where parkour originated, the civic authorities built fences on the edges of roofs, intended to be a deterrent, but, ironically, this merely provided new obstacles to climb: '"This is heaven for us, this is brilliant, keep adding obstacles, the more you do the better it gets", until the council realised and took it all down again because it was just making something even better' (Paul). Yet, as explained above, the parkour philosophy does not welcome this 'outsider' deviant image, but sees itself as promoting ethical and considerate behaviour that respects the environment. For example:

> If a cop tells you to move along or a security guard tells you to move along, don't argue or anything just say okay and move along to a different spot. Doing this will only help the kindness that follows with the discipline/philosophy which is parkour.
>
> (forum posting)[37]

Containment: the emergence of the parkour park

The provision of parkour training areas or parkour parks is a relatively new and uncharted development. In 2010, only a handful of parks were open (including Crawley, Surrey, Summer 2009) and Newhaven (2010).[38] Since then, there has been a proliferation, overseen by both parkour and free-running communities, including the world's largest in London, L.E.A.P. (London Experience of Art de Placement and Parkour), which was completed in 2011 and opened in January 2012.

Although parkour parks have been described as performance and 'play' spaces, as Howell reminds us: 'playgrounds were conceived of as places to contain young people who might otherwise be playing in the street, while simultaneously cultivating in those young people social values that advocates deemed desirable' (2008: 478). Clearly, the provision of the park could potentially lead to a containment of the activity, with street traceurs being marginalised and subject to increasingly stringent legislation. Yet park development has often been driven by the participants. In both Crawley and Telscombe, the parks grew out of the local councils seeing a need to provide physical activity provision, and in the case of Crawley to regenerate an area. Yet, in both cases, parkour was chosen by local youth as a priority in public consultation activities and/or following parkour sessions provided by local providers.

Nonetheless, traceurs we spoke to were certainly aware of the potential for parks to 'become a way of containing the discipline'. As one sport development officer suggested:

> If it's called a parkour *park* we're saying this is where you do parkour. If we call it a *parkour training area* then we are saying we accept that you will do parkour elsewhere. Because one of the big problems with the skateboard

parks in the past has been 'we've given you a park and now we're going to put no skateboarding signs everywhere else'. And it doesn't work. It doesn't stop people skateboarding. It just means that every skateboarder necessarily has to adopt a kind of two-fingers up attitude to authority in order to be a skateboarder, which is stupid.

The development of parkour facilities, and the rationale for providing them, is an on-going research interest in order to see who uses them and why, as well as their impact on the broader parkour field. Parks have already diversified to include managed as well as non-managed permanent spaces. At the Westminster park, where traceurs are required to become 'members', a small charge is being levied and rules imposed, such as wearing 'appropriate clothing' (in 2012). Some resistance has already been encountered, with reports of traceurs scaling the perimeter fence to gain unrestricted entry (facility manager).[39]

Parkour's adoption in social policy: 'cotton-wool-wrapped kids'

One of the reasons for the growing popularity of parkour is that urban-based young people can experience risk and adventure (Gilchrist and Wheaton, 2011). There is a widespread belief that young people have limited opportunities to challenge themselves and are living increasingly 'bubble-wrapped' (as well as sedentary) lives (Furedi, 1997, 2006).[40] For example, *The Royal Society for the Prevention of Accidents* publicly endorsed parkour. The society's safety education adviser said:

> Anything that encourages young people to be active and try new challenges in a supervised environment will help them learn to manage risk. Free running is like any other activity in that it tests their limits. It is better they learn it in schools than on the streets.
>
> (Dr Jenny McWhirter, cited in Johnson and Wroe, 2009)

Our interviewees recognised and espoused this benefit of parkour. Parkour is seen to provide a way of reintroducing some sort of risk into sport and play, to give young people in urban settings a sense of challenge and adventure and to enable them to learn to use risk safely. The nature of the activity makes it accessible and desirable for urban-based young men. Parkour clearly has few of the economic and cultural barriers that participants face in many traditional sports; it can be conducted alone or with friends, anywhere, at any time, without rules or restrictions. There are minimal costs involved, there are no fees for facilities or coaching and the clothing requirement/style is just cheap trainers. Knowledge about the activity is gained online, or through joining other participants in meetings or jams. The inclusive nature of the community encourages participants to welcome novices, and girls and women. Many gate-keepers (elite participants, parkour teachers, etc.) recognise the importance of being welcoming and inclusive for neophytes. As a result, participants develop informal but strong friendship and support networks.

There was a widespread belief across all the policy interventions we examined that parkour has a unique ability to engage groups that have resisted involvement in physical activity, including those who are anti-school PE in general and team games specifically (see Gilchrist and Wheaton, 2011).[41] Interviewees believed that the ethos and values of parkour, particularly its non-competitiveness and its values of support and inclusivity, were central to the ability of parkour to engage a wide range of participants. Through parkour, it was suggested that individuals viewed their relationship to self, others and their environment differently. In the school setting, this ability to bring together diverse social groups and networks appeared to translate across contexts. As the head teacher of one school observed, the friendships developed through parkour had led to 'the sorts of students who wouldn't naturally' mix 'working together in normal class-room activity': 'One of the benefits has been seeing people working together and learning from each other and supporting each other' (head teacher). Parkour, therefore, was widely seen as a way to engage young people not only in a form of 'sport' but in their communities more widely. There is nothing surprising or unique about sport being used in this way; at that time sport was central to the British government's (under New Labour) broad social inclusion agenda for improving communities' 'performance' in health, crime, employment and education (Coalter, 2007). However, historically it has tended to be traditional sports that have played this role, with extreme/lifestyle sports being characterised as dangerous and deviant. Yet in the UK, parkour – as well as a range of other extreme/lifestyle sports – was beginning to be valued for its perceived ability to contribute to physical health, well-being, and community and civic engagement.

This was particularly evident among the small group we were involved with at the parkour park in Sussex. Through their involvement – via Regen[42] – in fighting for and helping in the planning for the parkour park, teenage traceurs had been involved with forms of civic engagement. Parkour was credited by their teachers, community workers and indeed some participants as having developed the confidence and maturity of the boys involved. In a couple of cases, it was believed to have completely changed the attitudes and behaviours of pupils on the verge of being expelled from school. As a member of the Regen team commented, through the activity these teenagers learnt to think and behave in more 'creative' and 'productive' ways:

> They approached problems in a different way, it wasn't just A to B, but a bit of lateral thinking, a different way of looking at problems, which was really interesting. I just thought, it's absolutely amazing, it's outside and it's one of those things you've got to train to do and it's inexpensive and if it can help at school it takes credit.
>
> (Local councillor)

One of the teenage boys told me 'I used to be really unconfident before I did parkour. I think once you do parkour, it definitely changes you.' Like the skateboarders discussed in Howell's (2008) research, their maturity, resourceful-ness, self-direction and creativity positioned them, in the eyes of leisure provid-ers, as 'good', productive (neoliberal) citizens. While parkour in particular appears to have captured the zeitgeist, evidently other lifestyle sports previously characterised as deviant are also shifting in public perception. In Sussex, for example, a community police officer described the resourcefulness of the local BMXers who had 'been coming out with shovels and wheelbarrows making their own BMX track', challenging their preconceptions: 'Again, no criminal element involved, just you know, they want that area.'

In summary then, the on-going and rapid institutionalisation and sportisation of parkour provided a revealing case study to illustrate processes characterising the development of many lifestyle sports. The discourse of risk, and how it is managed by stakeholders, is increasingly influenced by discourses about popula-tions 'at risk', especially moral panics about youth (Silk and Andrews, 2008) fuelling disciplinary discourses about children 'at risk' (McDermott, 2007) and ways to produce healthy, productive, creative neoliberal citizens.

6 Globalisation, identity and race

Lifestyle sport in post-apartheid South Africa

The global diffusion of lifestyle sports

North America is undeniably the home of the extreme sport phenomenon (cf. Rinehart, 2008) and, as Bourdieu (1984) observed, the spiritual base of many lifestyle sports. There is, however, evidence of the increasing global reach of lifestyle sports, both as mediated events and as participatory experiences. In this chapter, I consider if, as Jarvie puts it, lifestyle sport is solely the 'lifestyle choice' of a privileged 'Western play-world'? (2006: 277).

As mediated experiences, lifestyle sports have spread rapidly around the world, driven by an increasing range of transnational corporate sponsors and commercial interests (see Ch. 3). For example, ESPN's X Games is at the centre of the global diffusion and expansion of lifestyle sport (Rinehart, 2008; Thorpe and Wheaton, 2011a). Together with Thorpe, I outline that the X Games are now beamed via ESPN's global networks to more than 122 countries, including those across Africa, Latin America, the Caribbean and the Middle East (ESPN Winter, 2009, cited in Thorpe and Wheaton, 2011a). Regional games are staged across North America, Latin America, Asia and Europe. Yet little is known about who the consumers are, other than their ages, which are considerably younger than those of most traditional sport audiences. Anecdotal evidence suggests that the X Games' impact on the broader sportscape varies; it is greater in Asia, for example, yet in Europe has failed to have much impact, despite claims of a global audience.[1] Surfing competitions illustrate the continued North American bias of the X Games. Despite surfing's popularity outside the USA – particularly in Australia and Brazil – most X Games have hosted teams of East Coast USA vs. West Coast USA. It was only in 2007 that the teams incorporated participants from *outside* the USA, and even then in the format Team USA vs. 'Rest of the World'.

In terms of participation, too, some lifestyle sports appear to be spreading into previously peripheral areas outside the Global North, fuelled by global flows of people, images and particularly transnational companies like Quiksilver seeking global markets. The 16 female BMX finalists at the Beijing 2008 Summer Olympics represented 13 countries, and the 16 male finalists represented 11 countries; at the Vancouver 2010 Winter Olympics, 188 snowboarders from 26 countries participated (Thorpe and Wheaton, 2011b). Pockets are emerging across South America (see e.g. Knijnik *et al.*, 2010) and Africa, and some Asian countries, including Japan, Korea and China (Booth and Thorpe, 2007a). For example, in China, lifestyle sports have an escalating status among the rapidly expanding middle-class youth (Booth and Thorpe, 2007a).

Empirical research that explores the global diffusion of lifestyle sports or the experiences of participants outside North American, Australasian and Western European contexts remains limited.[2] Global flows were a profound feature of late twentieth century sport and have continued to be significant in the twenty-first century, including the migration of elite talent, the movement of technology and the manufacturing of clothing and equipment (Maguire, 1999). Maguire suggests, however, that the emergence, diffusion and increasing popularity of 'alternative sports' (he cites snowboarding, hang-gliding and windsurfing) is evidence of the increased heterogeneity in the range and diversity of sport cultures in world sports, a 'creolisation of sport cultures' characteristic of the latest phase of 'global sportisation' (Maguire, 1999: 211). For Bale, such adventure activities are part of a green-wave that, along with other alternative body cultures, present a challenge to, and critique of, the Western sport model (Bale, 1994). Yet, while these globalising forces have fundamentally transformed the political, economic and social structures of contemporary culture, our understanding of how globalisation influences local cultural identity is still partial (Jackson, 2005; Andrews and Ritzer, 2007). Andrews and Ritzer (2007) argue that contemporary sport analyses often fail to adequately comprehend the interpenetration of the global – that is, how it shapes the practices, structures and experiences of the sporting 'local'.[3] However, as is clearly evident in the growing number of empirical studies of lifestyle sports in different national and local contexts, differences in their production, consumption and representation need articulating, and their relationship to the global media organisations and multi and transnational corporations driving their global expansion (Wheaton, 2005). As contemporary theorising about culture across disciplines suggests, adopting a global consciousness and seeing culture as a *circuit* rather than an object centred on *places* (Clifford, 1997) transforms our task as cultural analysts. Clifford (1997) suggests that local (sub)cultures no longer exist in isolation. Therefore, rather than examining local, geographically bound subcultures, or cross-cultural/national comparisons, our analysis needs to explore the impact of global flows on, between and within 'local' subcultures. We can then illustrate the connections between the sites and 'scapes' (Appadurai, 1996),[4] illustrating how identity shifts and is transformed. In this chapter, I contribute to these debates, drawing on case studies of surfing and skateboarding outside the Global North, specifically in Durban, South Africa.

My central objective was to explore some of the local (or what Robertson, 1992, describes as glocal) and trans-local differences in the representation and consumption of these sports and the ways in which Western assumptions about lifestyle sport as exclusively privileged, white male spaces were both challenged and reproduced. Put simply, was it possible to re-envisage lifestyle sport in ethnically diverse, non-Western contexts, and specifically post-apartheid South Africa? However, in my exploration of these issues, my research and subsequent discussion raised a range of other issues, particularly the use of lifestyle sports to engage non-privileged youth, and street children specifically. The more specific questions that framed my research were: first, how did participants construct race[5] (including whiteness[6]) as a location of subcultural identity? How was the marking of identity and difference in lifestyle sport related to exclusion processes and claims for subcultural authenticity? Second, what were the practices and structures that maintained white people's privileged position in lifestyle sport? Third, how was the Western commodity culture of lifestyle sport reworked and given meaning in the South African context? During apartheid, South Africa seemed distant from the global core, but now encounters an increasing range of transnational products and practices. For example, Dolby's (2001) research at a racially mixed school in Durban illustrates the importance of the global/local matrix as a framework for understanding how racial identity is articulated through popular culture. She illustrates that the commodities that engage Durban school children take specific racialised meanings, and that the 'global intimately shapes students' play with the local, lived reality of race' (ibid.: 11). She argues further that race is constituted and driven by a 'discourse of taste' (ibid.: 63) that positions identity within the commodity culture fostered through global popular culture and can dislocate other important sites where race is constructed, such as 'nation, culture or biology' (ibid.: 113).

(Lifestyle) sports in (post-apartheid) South Africa

Historians and sociologists have provided detailed and compelling accounts of the historic and contemporary role of various sports in South Africa, both during and post-apartheid (e.g. Nauright, 1997; Booth, 1998; Hargreaves, 2000; Booth and Nauright, 2003; Desai, 2010). A brief introduction to this literature will contextualise my case studies and highlight some of the issues underpinning the emergence of lifestyle sports.

Booth's book (1998) *The Race Game: Sport and politics in South Africa* details that sport has always played an important and complex role in the politics of race and national identity in South Africa. Historically, men's cricket and rugby union were the team sports that were most closely tied to white-colonial settlers (Nauright, 1997: 25). Yet, as a study of 144 sports in KwaZulu Natal in 1988 revealed, 'black participation reflected the racial compositions of the region in only 4 multiracial associations representing two sports – boxing and soccer' (Booth, 1998: 142). Moreover, blacks were absent in 40 sports and, in a further 78, blacks' participation constituted less than 8 per cent (ibid.). Since the ending of apartheid in South Africa in 1994, sport has been promoted as an important unifier for the new 'Rainbow nation' that is, at least on a discursive level, inclusive of all people (Nauright, 1997: 5). In the now infamous and dramatic moment when, following the 1995 Rugby World Cup victory in South Africa, Mandela chose to wear a Springbok jersey, 'signalling the acceptance of this decade-long symbol of oppression as a national emblem for the rugby team' (Desai, 2010: 1), Mandela's gesture was seen as an important catalyst for building a 'rainbow nation' predicated on a common identity (ibid.). For Mandela, sport was believed to have the potential to unite, 'because it speaks a language and has ideals beyond the reach of politicians' (Evening Standard, 27 October 1995, cited in Hargreaves, 2000: 15).

Sport has remained an important element of South Africa's social cohesion and nation-building agenda and became 'an arena of intense engagement and contestation' (Desai, 2010: 2). However, despite the rhetoric, in sport, as in most aspects of life, most people 'still live their lives with the legacy of colonialism and apartheid' (Hargreaves, 2000: 16), in which extremes of poverty and wealth remain (ibid.: 25). Football is one of the few sports that has been appropriated by black South African men across class divides (Pelak, 2005: 53). It is this complex and shifting postcolonial context that underpins the emergence and meaning of 'new(er)' sports like skateboarding and surfing.[7]

Skateboarding

The skateboard project that is my focus here was developed by Dallas Ober-holzer, a former professional, white South African skateboarder. He oversaw the operation of the municipal skate park situated on the North Beach seafront in Durban. He also ran the Indigo Skate Camp (subsequently the Indigo Founda-tion), situated in a rural village in the Valley of 1000 Hills, KwaZulu Natal (between Durban and Pietermaritzburg). The venue hosted skateboarding camps for more privileged South African youth, but had also introduced skateboarding to under-privileged rural Zulu communities.

Rural youth: the Indigo Skate Camp

The Indigo Camp ran residential courses for children aged 9–18, mostly boys from middle-to-upper-class backgrounds from around South Africa. These visi-tors skated alongside the local rural Zulu children who were introduced to skate-boarding. Rural life in South Africa was still very impoverished; unemployment was rife, education standards low and HIV a persistent problem (Pitcher, 2006). Leisure activities were very limited, and I was told that rural teenagers felt iso-lated from the (global focused) youth culture that seemed to be part of their urban contemporaries' lifestyles. There was a lack of trust in the state to provide and instead a culture of self-help and local (and charitable) initiatives dominated. As Dallas explained (in 2006):

> Look, I think everyone realises that when the government changed, everyone had these big ideas that everything was going to change. And the government ended up doing nothing really. Lifestyle in the Zulu village hasn't changed much in the last 10 years, 20 years. It is still very poor and

rural and very impoverished, so I think everyone looked out to see what they can do individually, to make it a better place. [...] And I just wanted to make it possible for a group of Zulu kids to skateboard.

In 2006, Dallas got funding from the Sport Trust to build the skate park. The project was also supported by the skate industry through equipment and scholarships.[8] The programme not only included skateboarding but also offered a range of experiences considered to complement the skateboarding lifestyle, ranging from 'traditional African living' to relaxation techniques. Dallas claimed that the skate park was embraced by the local community who helped build the ramp (and importantly he claims it was endorsed by the local Zulu chief). Facilities such as dormitory accommodation, flushable toilets and showers had improved the living and sanitation conditions for the local villagers. Local kids had been given skateboards and shoes to enable them to use the skateboarding facilities. The photographic evidence supports Dallas's claims that these children were involved and having fun. He also believed that the skaters were learning a number of life skills and that the camp was providing skills training, jobs and education for the community. Dallas was (in 2007) setting up a volunteer programme with other community-wide initiatives.

Durban skate parks, space and race: North Beach and Gateways

In 2007, North Beach Park was one of three public skate parks in the Durban city area (see Figure 6.1). It was situated on the seafront promenade, an area that was popular with tourists and accessible to many communities in Durban. The skate park was council-owned, but overseen by Dallas's team. Like many skate parks worldwide, there was a relative lack of adult supervision or regulation; anyone could turn up and skate, BMX, bike ride or hang-out (see Wooley and Johns, 2001; Stratford, 2002). On my weekday visits, the park was quite empty, except for a handful of the 'regulars' skating, painting graffiti on the colourful concrete walls of the park (but not on the urban furniture around it) or just hanging out. On one occasion, the routine was disrupted by some police who came to do a 'dope raid'. However, according to Jason, a student who worked there, most weekends around 80 kids from the Durban area frequented the park, and early on the Saturday morning I was there, around 20 kids had already turned up. Singh also observed that this skate park included a mixture of black, white, Indian and coloured boys and a few girls (Singh, 2007: 193).

In contrast, the other Durban skate park I visited was situated in the Gateways Theatre, a large shopping mall outside Durban. The mall was (in 2006) claimed to be the biggest mall in the Southern Hemisphere and housed a centre for lifestyle sports facilities called The Royal Palace of Youth Culture. This included a pristine, graffiti-free skate park designed by Tony Hawk, the Wave House Flow Rider Surfing Centre and, in the central atrium of the shopping centre, an indoor climbing wall. The venue also included bars and restaurants, and was a venue for live music events. The marketing literature described it as 'an awesome

Figure 6.1 The North Beach Skate Park.

fusion of all board sport cultures providing the ultimate place for the cool youth to hang out as well as being a great spot for a family day out'. However, contrasting with Durban's diverse ethnic mix, only white faces appeared in the marketing material. Indeed, the 'cool youth' who frequented this pristine, air-conditioned mall, a highly regulated leisure space, accessible only by car and patrolled by armed security police, appeared to be predominantly the white, urban middle-classes. This mall vividly illustrates how racialised social relations are spatially expressed; and that leisure spaces are important sites in illustrating the on-going racialisation of space (see also Ch. 7).

North Beach street children

The seafront skate park had become the home for a group of 10–12 homeless boys aged somewhere between 10 and 17 (Figure 6.2). Street children remain a widespread problem in urban South Africa, with Durban being dubbed the 'new Rio' (HOPE HIV, 2006). The Boy's Brigade UK (2006) estimated there were 15,000 street children in Durban; almost all are black and 81 per cent are male (HOPE HIV, 2006). Although UNICEF's categorisation of street children tended to mark them as a homogenous group, there were varying experiences and styles of life from those who lived exclusively on the street to those who spent only some time on the street (Baker, 1999). They tended to be children who were orphaned, many due to the AIDS epidemic, who had been forced to leave homes in townships because their extended families could not care for them or who had escaped abusive homes or sodomisation (Baker, 1999). As one boy at the skate park claimed: 'My father drinks, he abuses me. My mother takes drugs' (Thabo, cited in Singh, 2007: 194). They earned their living by stealing, selling drugs, prostitution and so on (Chetty, 1997; Baker, 1999; Ennew, 2003) and were commonly associated with 'poverty, crime, drugs and dirt'. They were seen as a *problem*, particularly where they came into contact with tourism (Singh, 2007: 193).[9]

This stretch of the Durban seafront was an ambiguous place; popular with, and marketed for tourists, but close to poor areas of the city, such as the no-torious Point district, which lies just a block behind the façade of Durban's five-star beachfront hotels. In the context of escalating crime in the city, and the congregation of white middle-class South Africans into the (white) suburbs, at night the beachfront was considered a no-go area for tourists. The North Beach street children slept in and around the huts on the back of the promenade (per-sonal interviews, see also Singh, 2007). Gaber (2009a) suggests that these boys, in contrast to many street children in other areas of Durban, spent most of their time in a very small section of the neighbourhood, and differentiated themselves from other, more violent street dwellers.

Figure 6.2 Some of the North Beach crew with Jason.

Typically groups of street children were well organised in terms of having a leader and setting rules for belonging. Likewise, these boys hung out together for security and camaraderie, providing 'emotional and material support networks' (Singh, 2007: 190). I watched them beg for food and coins. Despite this struggle for existence, they had (in 2006) been skating at the North Beach Park for 2–3 years. They hung out there all day most days. Dallas provided them with their own boards and shoes, which were stored at the shop overnight; not because he did not trust them, but because possessions of any kind made them a target for attack. Dallas claimed that 'skateboarding is providing these youth with purpose and keeping them off destructive drugs'. Glue sniffing, in particular, was a widespread problem among street children (Baker, 1999). Singh suggested that these particular boys also used drugs, including marijuana and glue, largely to alleviate hunger and deal with the stresses of street life (2007: 194). However, Gaber (2009b)[10] suggests that drug use among this group was not as prevalent as among most groups that constituted Durban youth street culture (which encompasses both street children and young men). She argued that these boys differentiated themselves as living a cleaner, more responsible lifestyle, identifying themselves as 'skaters' (Gaber, 2009a).

Skating was evidently the central thing in these boys' lives. As one boy explained, 'I sleep here, wake up, skate, sleep, wake up, skate.' They were very enthusiastic about skating and about being photographed displaying their skills (Figures 6.3 and 6.4). Gaber also observed that 'all the boys felt positive about,

Figure 6.3 Street kids skateboarding.

Figure 6.4 Street kids skateboarding.

and took pride in their ability' (2009b). I was told that one of the boys, Thalente, was very skilled – he had won local contests and said he 'hopes to become a pro'. Another said, 'Everyone tells me that skating can get me far. I think they are correct about that.' As Dallas suggested: 'Well, just the self-satisfaction of doing something. Look at their confidence, and it picks up their spirits. [...] Every push or every little turn of the skateboard is an achievement for them, and it motivates them.' As Singh discussed, despite stereotypes that these children are a 'menace' to society, she found them to be cheerful, 'positive and resourceful' (2007: 191) and, while not wanting to 'canonise them', was amazed by their camaraderie and care for each other (ibid.: 192).[11] I also found the boys to be surprisingly jovial and (as also described by Singh), when I distributed the goodies I had brought them, watched with surprise as the leader carefully shared out the food and then, despite the boys' evident hunger, also offered a chocolate bar to Dallas.

All those I spoke to recognised that what these kids needed was a stable environment and education. But, despite being compulsory, education in South Africa was not free. Jason (a student who worked there) also suggested that many lacked the confidence to go to school. The boys themselves seemed ambivalent; on one occasion, they told me they would like to go to school with their friends, but later said to (my co-researcher) Toni: 'The schools here aren't nice. They don't teach you anything, all the kids are cheeky and druggies. The teachers just do what they have to do' (Thalente). According to Morrell, such a view is not uncommon; indeed, he suggests that schools are often 'wracked with violence' and thus many do not see them as 'avenues to escape poverty' (2001: 7). While the North Beach Skate Park evidently provided the street boys with some temporary escape, Dallas's long-term hope was for them to move to the Indigo Camp to get away from the city, and to give them the chance to go to school. He hoped to set up a permanent street children's 'home' at the Indigo Camp. While not all those I spoke to shared Dallas's optimism about such a project, recognising that such forms of interventions can also present an array of issues (e.g. child monitoring, legal protection, etc.), there seemed to be a recognition that, despite being fraught with complications, skateboarding was providing 'massive potential for upward mobility' among this group (Gaber, 2009a).

Sport, of course, has a long history of being used by all kinds of agencies, from policy makers to missionaries, to help deal with the 'problems' of poverty and social exclusion. As has been widely discussed, sport-led initiatives have been important in re-building post-apartheid South Africa (e.g. Burnett, 2001; Gemmell, 2007). Projects generally address issues such as developing life skills, language and HIV education, and share similar aims (but often on much larger scales and in more organised ways than the very small-scale Skate Park initiative). But as Jennifer Hargreaves (2000: 34) has written about in relation to sport development and South African women specifically, 'the popular development model is one of "civilization"' and in these initiatives there is 'a risk of a neo-colonial discourse developing that essentialises the position of African women [and here youth], and represents them as uniformly backward, illiterate, and oppressed'. In the North Beach project, as in most models of sport for development, there are issues around cultural imperialism that need recognition and consideration (Coalter, 2007; Spaaij, 2009; Kay, 2009; Coalter, 2010). I certainly felt a sense of unease about the possibility of (re)producing a neo-colonial discourse, and essentialising these street children's problems and experiences (see also Ennew, 2003; Ataöv and Haider, 2006; Diversi, 2006). Indeed, Gaber's research highlights a number of important issues in relation to the boys' differential social positions and vulnerabilities, and that *within* the small group at North Beach there were key differences that significantly impacted each individual's lifestyle and life chance. She suggested that 'some felt bitterly about favouritism around the park', arguing that for some boys, commitment to skating also required (or was perceived to require) sacrificing other more conservative (and arguably more important) lifestyle goals, such as education and formal living arrangements. Clearly, further empirical research is required to assess these issues and the long-term impact of skating for these boys' life chances. However, in the context of this chapter, my focus is on exploring the specific role that skateboarding as a new, individualistic and unregulated lifestyle sport has played.

Skateboarding as a tool of integration?

Dallas claimed that skateboarding's 'newness' was an important factor in explaining why it was being appropriated by young, black South Africans. He argued that it represented a rejection of the traditional colonial sports of rugby and cricket:

> It is becoming popular among the blacks now because (of) lots of colonial sport with its connotations of whites only. And (it's) a new sport that everyone is developing and creating, and it is always progressing, so they like to be part of something that is progressive like that. And with the connotations of hip hop and street culture, they find it attractive.
>
> (Dallas)

Furthermore, aspects of skateboarding culture, such as the focus on the individual, self-direction and the lack of rules and infrastructure, suited the needs and aspirations of these young, black communities. Paradoxically, for those boys living on the street (or for those in the rural village near the Indigo Camp), some of the traditional barriers experienced by under-privileged young people, such as access to facilities and transportation, did not pose a problem. Other potential obstacles, like lack of equipment and tuition/coaching, were also overcome due to the philanthropy of the skate park team and other users (who donated old shoes and clothing), and their commercial supporters (who donated skateboards).

Dallas also argued that skateboarding was better suited to integrating communities than more traditional sports with a history in apartheid and colonialism. Given the widely recognised importance of football among black communities across South Africa (see Pelak, 2005; Desai, 2010), this claim is surprising. Nonetheless, as Dallas suggested, skateboarding, like football, had a simplicity. He explained that 'skating is also uncomplicated as you just need a skateboard and your own imagination to create and have fun'. The lack of regulations and competition were important factors for understanding skateboarding's popularity:

> Look at this skate park here [...] people that can come from all parts of the city, and interact. And especially because skateboarding is not competitive, so it is a sport where people encourage each other, not so much team against that team scenario [...] all encouraging each other to progress. And people can come from different backgrounds and instantly connect at the skate park or the skate camp.

In South Africa during and post-apartheid, traditional sports institutions and clubs played a key role in perpetuating ideologies of race and exclusion. Private sports clubs, which were the 'foundations' of South African sport, were 'notorious bastions of white exclusiveness' (Booth, 1998: 140); and while (throughout the

1980s) white sport administrators claimed their sports were striving for integration, they remained racially exclusive. Thus, in this context, the lack of regulation and (white) authority in public spaces like the municipal skate park takes on particular significance.

Nonetheless, Booth (1998) has highlighted some examples of the ways in which informal lifestyle sport also contributed to racial exclusion during apartheid. For example, during an international windsurfing competition held in Cape Town (in 1982), a newspaper reported that the City Council removed 'apartheid signs at the whites-only beach', replacing them again after the contest (ibid.: 142).

Importantly, the boys agreed with the claims Dallas made, that the simplicity and newness of skating appealed to them: 'Soccer is more competition, skating you can chill and do your own thing. And there's no rules to it or nothing' (street kid, name unknown). My observations at the skate park suggested that, in comparison to other leisure spaces I had been to around Durban (such as the malls, the beach, restaurants, leisure park and rugby stadium), a greater diversity of users was evident. The street kids had integrated with other local (male) skaters from a range of backgrounds (see also Singh, 2007; Gaber, 2009b). The street children said they liked the fact that you meet 'lots of different people', including from different countries at the park. Julian, a white teenage skater (age 15) who skated with the street children, claimed 'skating brings us all together'. He said that street kids were an 'accepted part of the park life' – all the kids hang out together and the street boys are 'popular with the pretty girls'. He told us that he and one of the street boys, Thalente, were 'good mates' and that he had asked Thalente to his house to stay; he had also taught him to surf. Similarly, another white boy claimed, 'Thabo gives me stuff; bearings for my skateboard. If Thabo needs help I will stay with him' (cited in Singh, 2007: 192).

Understanding 'race', identity and inclusion

The skaters' claims that the skate park had an integrated and non-excluding culture need further interrogation. As outlined in Chapter 4, there was an erroneous mythology perpetuated in the skateboarding culture and its subcultural media that claims that the values of skateboarding transcend barriers of race, gender and class (Borden, 2001; Chivers-Yochim, 2010). Yet on deeper inspection, skaters' narratives invariably reflected values associated with hegemonic white, heterosexual masculinity, serving to maintain the power of white, middle-class skateboarders (Wheaton and Beal, 2003b; Chivers-Yochim, 2010). As Beal highlighted, black skaters in California did gain subcultural status, but it was harder for them to gain respect than white skaters, and they were marked as different (Wheaton and Beal, 2003b).

This lack of status did not, however, appear to be the case in Durban. Gaber (2009a) suggests that the street children had become an accepted part of the social life of the park, and, perhaps reflecting their status as full-time committed participants, were *higher* in the 'pecking order' than the weekend skaters.[12]

Nonetheless, she recognised that the North Beach Park had a set of differentiated and hierarchical social relationships, and that the boys were marked as *different* in various ways. This variable social positioning was often perpetuated
by adults involved with the skate park. For example, not all the street children
found negotiating friendships with other skaters easy, and for those who had
low competency in spoken English it was harder to build cohesive relationships
(Gaber, 2009b). Gaber also explained that the vast social inequalities between
the skaters, and street children's lives became particularly pronounced when
they tried to pursue a career skating. Furthermore, although they were popular,
some had a reputation for being brattish and ungrateful. She saw this behaviour
as a consequence of their refusal to conform to the status of victim, and as a
way of handling the humiliation of begging or being given hand-outs (Gaber,
2009a).

Some stereotypes of race, particularly in terms of black physicality, were also
evident. For example, Dallas suggested, that the boys' 'culture' made them well-
suited to skating: 'One of the good things is that they are pretty fearless. And
that is Zulu culture, that they are quite strong and fearless. It helps when
skating.' Dallas's comments here are playing to stereotypes of the imperial
encounter both as the 'native entertainer' and as the physically gifted athlete and/
or body (Carrington and McDonald, 2001b).

In Singh's (2007) work, she also recognised and began to unpack the association of skateboarding and whiteness in Durban, and how the street-kid skateboarder boys understood and made sense of their otherness. First, she observed
that, despite the ethnic mix at the skate park (reflecting the black, white, Indian
and coloured communities in Durban), the street children referred to skaters as
'white boys'. She suggested whiteness was used as a general term of otherness,
emphasising how different the skaters at the park were (regardless of their ethnicity) from street children. Additionally, whiteness had a 'connotation of afflu-
ence', 'associated with commitment, ambition and getting on' (Singh, 2007:
193). Thus, as illustrated in the following conversation (cited in Singh, 2007:
193), by identifying with white skater boys, the black street children were 'constructing themselves as very different from caricatures of (black) street children
as lazy, lacking ambition and undisciplined' (ibid.):

THANO: You know what Miss? I am a white boy trapped in a black boy's body.
SHANTA: I don't understand what you mean Thabo?
THANO: I am like a white boy. I speak like them, the whole day I play with the
    white boys in the park. We are one (points to his white friends).

Singh illustrates that Thano's comments about whiteness emerged not in
response to a question about identity, but organically from a broader discussion
about hunger, suggesting he was particularly concerned about presenting himself
as being *different* from the normal 'bad' black street children that are the basis of
the stereotypes (Singh, 2007). As Gaber also discusses, these boys felt they lived
a cleaner, more committed and less violent lifestyle than many street dwellers;

they differentiated themselves from the violent and notorious personalities in the North Beach, and used their skater identity as a way to do this (2009b).

The glocalisation of skateboarding: 'African style'

In lifestyle sports, the availability of local and foreign subcultural media, commodities (such as clothing, equipment, etc.), and increased contact via internet-based forums and with foreign tourists, has facilitated access to global commodities, ideas and images (Wheaton, 2005). Subcultural networks and communities extend beyond geographically defined spaces. So, although actual mobility was very limited for the least privileged youth, like Durban street children, these participants still had access to global commodities (see Diversi, 2006).[13] Moreover, as research on youth across race and class divides in Durban has illustrated, popular culture is 'the raw material they draw on to think about themselves and their relations to others' and is where their identities are invested (Dolby, 2001: 115). The subcultural media, particularly magazines and videos, were an important influence for these Durban skaters, including the street children. The shop at North Beach was full of skating commodities, including South African and North American skating magazines and brands.[14]

Dallas suggested that, although South African skating was informed by North American culture, it took on its own specificity, a view informed by his experiences competing around the world as a professional skateboarder, including at the X Games: 'In many ways because we are isolated, [...] we don't look too much to the rest of the world to see what is going on.' He contended that the lack of visiting professional skaters had caused isolation and the development of their own style. He suggested that there was recognition – and a hope – that skateboarding in South Africa could be different: 'African style, because anything goes in this country, and everyone kind of gets looked out for, you know, does get kind of acknowledged in a certain way.' Another interesting aspect of the creolisation of skating was the appropriation of aspects of black street culture. The literature on skateboarding and snowboarding in the US has illustrated how street culture and especially the urban 'gangsta' image was co-opted by snowboarders and skaters to signify their distance from middle-class whiteness (Brayton, 2005; Atencio *et al.*, 2009). Affiliating themselves to 'streetwise' masculinity grounded in 'notions of an urban underclass' (Atencio *et al.*, 2009: 10) enabled street skaters in the USA to differentiate themselves from 'soft' and feminine versions of middle-class masculinity (ibid.).[15] These street kids were cognisant of, and discussed, gangsta style and its appropriation in skate culture: 'If you are a skater you have to look like a gansta.[16] You have to look stylish. If you don't look stylish, you're an idiot' [meaning 'you look like an idiot'] (Thalente). The black skaters at the park mixed indigenous vernacular forms of African culture with Western imports. For example, they combined stylistic elements of both hip hop and skate style, wearing gold jewellery, baseball caps and beanies. Gaber (2009b) suggested that adopting street style in this way was also prevalent among the older white skaters and BMXers in Durban. It was suggested that, for black African youth, the USA was a place of inspiration, a place where black people had success and power. As Dallas advised, 'Blacks here are aspiring to be "cool Americans" and a lot of them try speaking with an American accent and it's kind of weird.' As illustrated in Dolby's research (2001: 11), the 'global intimately' shaped young peoples' 'play with the local, lived reality of race'. Popular culture is increasingly important as 'the raw material' young people 'draw on to think about themselves and their relations to others' and is where their identities are invested (ibid.: 115), which can dislocate other constructions of race such as 'nation, culture or biology' (ibid.: 113).

However, it is not just Western commodities that were re-worked. These black skaters also adopted indigenous vernacular forms of African culture. During the interviews, the street kids all took their turn at rapping for me, using my tape recorder as a microphone. The rap was in Zulu, which I later discovered was called Kwaito, a Zulu breed of rapping which was seen as the musical voice of young, black, urban South Africa (Swartz, 2003). Supported by black youth, with less cross-over to white and coloured youth, the rap can be in any language but English. If white South Africans wanted to be part of this street culture, they had to learn an indigenous language (ibid.: 11), providing an interesting reversal of the cultural hegemony. Writers have discussed the similarities between Kwaito and hip hop for black men in the USA, that is, as a specifically black cultural expression that prioritises voices from the margins, and as a basis of affinity for a diverse population that shares a history of racist subordination and hybridisation (Swartz, 2003; Swink, 2003). Kwaito music was part of a wider movement among black South African youth to oppose imported music fads and style, so distancing themselves from the hegemony of American culture (Swartz, 2003). However, the South African skateboarders appeared to mix vernacular culture forms like Kwaito *with* North American cultural forms such as skateboarding, thus producing a variety of complex, competing cultural flows, and in so doing reconfiguring lifestyle sport cultures and identities.

The Durban beach

Positioned on the warm Indian Ocean, Durban – like many South African cities – has an abundance of beautiful beaches, which are important leisure resources for residents and tourists (Preston-Whyte, 2002: 312). Durban is a recognised surfing centre of the global surf industry (Thompson, 2001: 91). However, the heavy surf often makes sea-bathing dangerous, and unsuited for learning to swim (Hemson, 2001). Lifesavers – both professionals and volunteers – were present on all city beaches and therefore were an important feature of beach culture (ibid.).

As Durrheim and Dixon discuss, beach segregation was practised in South Africa throughout the twentieth century, but was intensified during apartheid based on the 'principles of racial hierarchy and non-contact' (2001: 436). In the 1970s, when apartheid was formally entrenched, the beaches along the Natal coastline were highly segregated and racial hierarchy underpinned their allocation. In the province of Natal, 90 per cent of the coastline was either a white group area or controlled by whites (ibid.).[17] Likewise, in Durban, not only did whites (constituting just 22 per cent of the population) control a completely disporportionate percentage of beach space, white beaches were the most accessible to the city, with better facilities. The black designated beaches were furthest away, most dangerous and often unsuitable for recreational use (ibid.).[18]

In the transition from apartheid to the 'new' South Africa, beaches remained 'contested and exclusive spaces' (Durrheim and Dixon, 2001: 439). While for whites the beaches were seen as apolitical recreational spaces, during the late 1980s, beaches became a site of powerful (yet largely peaceful) political struggle, 'championed by the Mass Democratic Movement under the banner of "All of God's beaches for all of God's people"' (ibid.: 438). In Durban, the first integrated beach was (controversially) implemented in 1982, and by the end of the 1980s all beaches were formally desegregated (ibid.: 435). Hemson (2001) discusses the rapid increase in numbers of black African people visiting Durban beaches during the 1990s.[19] However, a range of powerful ideological representations of race continued to underlie practices of segregation and exclusion. In the 1980s, blacks were depicted as 'corrupting family space through their political activity. Black conduct was depicted as agentic, purposeful and organised, and contrasted with the carefree 'fun-in-the-sun' essence of holiday time and beach space' (Durrheim and Dixon, 2001: 448). Then into the 1990s, the black presence on beaches was depicted as 'corrupting' (white) family space. Black beachgoers were represented as 'unmannered, uncivilised, chaotic and lacking in decency' (ibid.). Although a degree of integration now exists, it is still common to find beaches predominantly populated by the same ethnic groups that inhabited them during apartheid (ibid.).

These shifting racialised discourses about beach space and culture also impacted on the use of beaches for sports like surfing and surf lifesaving. In the next section, I explore whether surfing, historically a bastion of white privilege, also saw a discursive shift in its white identity, with a concomitant rise in participation among black participants.

Surfing masculinity and white privilege

Surfing in South Africa has received little academic attention, an exception being Glen Thompson's analysis of the development of surf culture and surfing masculinity, from its emergence among lifesavers in the late 1940s, to the late 1970s (Thompson, 2001).[20] His research, therefore, predates the ending of beach apartheid, but nonetheless aids understanding of the historical development of surfing as an expression of white, largely 'English-speaking privileged masculinity' (ibid.: 91). While numerous factors, and particularly lack of economic resources and beach apartheid, excluded many black South Africans from the sport, small pockets of black and coloured surfers existed, particularly outside of the city (ibid.).

Thompson's research explores the representation of surfing masculinity and culture in *ZigZag,* a South African surfing magazine that was set up in December

1976 (Thompson, 2001: 93) and is still (in 2012) in production. He outlines how the magazine focused on professional surfing masculinity as the dominant masculinity in South African surfing culture, subordinating all recreational, non-elite surfing, including, therefore, both women and black surfers (ibid.). 'By representing surfing as the sole sporting preserve of white society, *ZigZag* upheld white privilege and confirmed the existence of pervasive racial discrimination and inequality' (ibid.: 101). Nonetheless, he also describes some 'ambivalence to race' in the magazines, evident, for example, in the ways in which difference was marked, particularly among Hawaiian surfers. When a restaurant refused to serve an esteemed visiting Polynesian–Hawaiian surfer, the magazine condemned it for its racism. Thus, as Thompson argues, 'while the roots of racism on dry land were not challenged, the contest in the waves offered a refuge from which the "issue of equality" could be seemingly evaded and broached' (ibid.). Nonetheless, *ZigZag* largely ignored recreational black surfing, and evaded politics and social change, seeing the waves as an escape from 'the everyday anxiety of a privileged life within white society' (ibid.: 100). Nonetheless, Booth (1998) documents that some white surfers actively excluded non-white participants. He recounts how, during a surfing competition for Indians and coloureds on the Durban beachfront (1989), white surfers harassed the visiting surfers and refused to leave the water, forcing the cancellation of heats (ibid.: 142).

Contemporary surfing spaces

Since the end of formal beach apartheid, surfing in all its forms has become more popular among blacks.[21] While the black surfing experience in South Africa, as elsewhere (see Ch. 7), remains largely hidden in mediated and academic accounts, documentaries such as the *Zulu Surf Riders* are important resources in beginning to understand identity and exclusion in surfing. This documentary, produced and directed by three white South African surfers, claims to chart the 'roots of a black surfing community' for the first time. It focuses on the area around Umzumbe, South of Durban on the KwaZulu Natal coast. The director, a lifelong surfer, admits: 'Previously I had never seen black kids or adults venture past the shore break, let alone surfing in some of the most demanding conditions in SA!' (Nortje, 2008). The documentary looks at the life stories of these surfing pioneers, focusing on twins from Umzumbe, Sandile 'Cyril' and Mishak Mqadi, who, having become committed surfers, then inspired and taught a community of local youngsters (Cronje *et al.*, 2008). The writer, Brenen Nortje, claims that, despite numerous barriers and very few resources, 'Stoke[22] bred like wildfire through the community' (Nortje, 2008). The documentary points to some of the cultural, financial and physical barriers[23] for contemporary South African black surfers. Nortje highlights the 'huge taboos associated with the ocean', which, as Hemson (2001: 63) also notes, was seen by many Zulus as 'threatening and dangerous'. Like most surfing spaces, forms of exclusion operate targeting the less competent surfers (Waitt, 2008; Evers, 2009). As Preston-Whyte (2002) describes, those beaches considered the most exclusive surfing spaces (e.g. Dairy

Beach and North Beach) were also the least tolerant of low skill levels and historically also the most white beaches.

In the documentary, Cyril Mqadi discusses how, when he first tried surfing, he could not swim,[24] but managed to avoid drowning because he was attached to his board via the leash.[25] In South Africa, swimming has always been associated with white privilege (Booth and Nauright, 2003). South Africans rarely learn to swim in seawater as there is a lack of 'calm inland water' (Hemson, 2001: 62). While Durban, like most South African cities, has an abundance of swimming pools, most are either privately owned or located in private schools. Booth (1998) provides photographs that graphically illustrate the differences between the small and dirty public pools in African areas, which were often 'out of commission' (Hemson, 2001: 61), and the pristine Olympic-sized facilities typically found in private schools. Discussing attempts to transform swimming and aquatic sports over the past decade, Desai and Veriava (2010) outline that concerted efforts have been made to promote aquatic skills and competitive swimming for black South Africans. Yet the numbers remain very low because only middle-class black swimmers have access to high-standard swimming facilities and clubs with coaches.[26] Nonetheless, some Africans were finding that surf lifesaving was providing a context for developing swimming competence.

African surf lifesavers in Durban

Professional and voluntary lifesavers are an essential service on Durban's beaches to ensure tourists and visitors stay safe (Hemson, 2001). Like in Australia (see Booth, 2001), surf lifesaving in South Africa has been a popular sporting pursuit, as well as a 'community service and occupation' since the 1920s (Hemson, 2001: 57). Although African lifesavers only emerged in the early 1990s, they have become a feature on most Durban beaches. Crispin Hemson provides a fascinating account of the Thekwini SLC, a club that started in the mid-1970s and remains the only club in Durban that is predominantly African.[27] His research explores the shifting and competing masculine identities among a group of young men who were representative of contemporary African township youth. He illustrates how the surf club provided a space and context through which members could develop a masculine identity, away from the violent and dangerous life of the township (ibid.: 58). My interest here, however, is on the reasons for this rapid increase in African lifesavers, particularly in a context where opportunities to swim were still limited. Traditional cultural values saw the sea as threatening and dangerous, and most of the men lived some distance from the Durban beaches so did not grow up learning the 'physical skills and understanding of surf conditions required for effective lifeguarding' (ibid.: 63).

Lifesaving, in contrast to surfing, provided a relatively well-paid, secure career. Training African lifesavers was seen as a priority: first, as non-black lifesavers had 'difficulty communicating with African beachgoers'; and, second, to compensate for a shortage due to more mobile white lifesavers being lured to higher paying jobs abroad (Hemson, 2001: 63). In 2001, of Durban's 60 lifesavers, 18 were

African, most of which were members of Thekwini; additionally there were a number of seasonally employed members (ibid.). As Hemson explores, despite deep-rooted tensions between traditional and 'new' discursive constructions of masculinity, for the African township youth, lifesaving was seen as a respectable, stable profession, providing opportunities to claim some respect in their communities. The institutionalised, club-based focus also provided a relatively safe and reputable setting, reflected in membership, including youth (from around age eight) and some women.

Despite these social and financial rewards, acceptance of African lifesavers by both beachgoers and township youth remained tenuous. Racism underpinned their experiences, which, as Hemson's interviewees (2001: 71–72) outline below, they learnt to accommodate rather than challenge:

> The way you are treated is not the same [...] people look at you 'Oh a black lifeguard'...

> Although I have a qualification, I can't do [the job], because the situation there is pushing you out.

> There are very few white lifesavers who have a good attitude towards us.

> If you are black you are the first suspect if something is missing.

Thus while lifesaving was providing township youth with an opportunity to experience and break free from some of the constraints of township masculinity, and to gain financial and social rewards, the new-found freedoms were hard-won, contingent on and structured by, wider discourses of masculinity, class, ethnicity and race.

Umthombo's surf club

> On [the street] we share to forget and learn how to ignore the pain. In the water I can laugh, in the water I can dream.
>
> (Street kid surfer, cited in Riaanstoman, 2010)

My initial interest in lifestyle sport in Durban was inspired by reports I had read about Umthombo,[28] an organisation run by ex-street children in Durban. Based near North Beach, it strived to 'empower' street children and to 'change the way that society perceives and treats them' (Trans World Sport, 2010). It had a number of targeted grass-roots actions and outreach projects, and also focused on street children policy and 'strategy development'. One of the projects gaining attention was surfing (2010).[29]

During my visit (in 1996), the Umthombo surfing project was not running; however, I did speak to various people involved and, as documented in numerous news reports,[30] the programme was restarted in 2008, and in 2012 was still running. I was initially rather incredulous that street children, many of whom grew up in inland townships, would have the necessary swimming skills. But as Tom Hewitt, a (white) surfer himself, explained, Durban street kids often grow up in and around the sea, and many have become competent swimmers.[31] In my discussion with the street children at the skate park, several claimed they often swam in the sea, and one boy said that he had been taught to surf by one of the white skaters. Numerous online videos illustrate that some boys have learnt to become very competent surfers.[32] According to one news report, one of the surfing club's participants finished 'eighth' in a regional surfing competition (Keeton, 2008).

The Umthombo 2008 programme involved a group of 10–15 boys who went surfing on a daily basis at some of the most sacred and white-dominated of Durban's surfing spaces under the tutorage of their coach, Sandi Mqadi.[33] Local benefactors and industry provided Umthombo with surfboards and wetsuits. The videos demonstrate that surfing was seen as a group, not a solitary, activity. As Hewitt suggested, 'the coaches and volunteers create a team atmosphere – to make kids feel part of a family again', giving them both 'joy and a sense of belonging' (Trans World Sport, 2010). In contrast to the skate park context, English was not the dominant language used between the boys and adults involved in the Umthombo project. Hewitt saw the all-consuming and 'addictive' nature of surfing participation as being particularly suited to helping these boys break their glue sniffing and other drug habits (ibid.).[34] The surfing coach claimed that among the group who started in 2008, they had all stopped using glue, had rapidly improved their outlook and some had returned home, all of which he attributed to surfing's 'healing properties' (ibid.). Other boys had subsequently found employment in Durban's surfing industry (ibid.).

While the surfing club project has similar aims to the skate project discussed above – namely to use the activity as a way to build relationships, a 'catalyst to re-engage kids, ultimately getting them off the street and back into their communities' (Hewitt, cited in Keeton, 2008) – as it is run by an experienced charitable organisation, with a network of support services, these objectives appeared to be more clearly achievable at Umthombo. It provides, or has links with, services including a mobile health clinic, mentoring and advocacy. 'Safe Space', their 'therapeutic drop-in centre for street children' (Keeton, 2008) based at the Point district, opened in 1998 and serves as a safe space where kids can hang out and get basic needs provided, such as food (Trans World Sport, 2010). There is also a team of professional and social workers offering programmes to deal with the children's complex emotional needs (Keeton, 2008). One of Umthombo's strengths is that former street children, who have a 'unique understanding of the realities of the street child experience and an incredible relationship of trust and respect with the children' (Umthombo website), are included on the staff. In 2008, 15 of the 27 employees formerly lived on the street (Keeton, 2008) and have subsequently been given specialised training for addressing the traumas associated with the children's experiences (Umthombo website). Thus, at

Umthombo, the children's broader welfare is supported and monitored in ways not available to the more piecemeal and individualistic approach at the skate park.

Discussion: lifestyle sport as a tool for social inclusion

This chapter has highlighted how street children in Durban have been targeted through the activities of surfing and skateboarding. While the fascinating stories extend our understanding of the plight of street children, there is a danger in romanticising their experiences, when clearly there is a complex negotiation of power and of identity, particularly in the ways in which race intersects with class, tradition, age and nation in the construction of sporting identity. Indeed, some aspects of North American skateboard and surf cultures, such as male dominance, were replicated in the South African setting, where I observed a complete absence of girls or women.

However, the case studies highlight the ways in which informal lifestyle sports are being targeted by an increasingly wide range of agencies and stakeholders because of their perceived value as a way to address a range of social 'problems' and 'issues', from social inclusion to health (see Bradley, 2010; Gilchrist and Wheaton, 2011; and also the discusion of parkour in Ch. 5). This is a trend worthy of greater reflection and analysis, particularly regarding the ways in which these sports are being adopted outside the Global North and in initiatives for peace and development, which appear to be gaining momentum. Media reports have highlighted a number of such initiatives (e.g. Surfing 4 Peace,[35] and Isiqalo 'Waves for Change' Curriculum [see Drift Surfing, 2011]), including across Africa. The Maloof Skateboarding Global Initiative was (in 2011) undertaking a year-long tour of South Africa, called 'Skateboarding for Hope' (Maloof Money Cup, 2011). Working with the Provincial government, the aims of this initiative included developing skateboarding awareness, providing coaching and equipment to disadvantaged youth and identifying talent. Clearly such seemingly philanthropic operations need careful scrutiny, particularly when driven by commercial companies. As Spaaij outlines, in many sport-for-development programmes there is a danger that sport is 'imposed on disadvantaged communities in a top-down manner, lacking community engagement and shared ownership' (2009: 1109). Yet, their emergence is nonetheless significant, not least because they seem to be proliferating.

Skateistan in Afghanistan, which provides 'formal skate and classroom sessions for more than 300 kids, ages 5 to 17' (Skateistan, 2012), has received considerable press coverage. According to its website (2012), it is:

> Afghanistan's – and the world's – first co-educational skateboarding school. Operating as an independent, neutral, Afghan NGO, the school engages growing numbers of urban and internally-displaced youth in Afghanistan through skateboarding, and provides them with new opportunities in cross-cultural interaction, education, and personal empowerment.

While the project aims to develop skills in skateboarding and skateboarding instruction, the focus is on life skills and education, such as 'healthy habits, civic responsibility, information technology, the arts, and languages'. They claim that Skateistan brings 'Afghan youth of all ethnicities, genders, and socio-economic backgrounds' together. It equips young men and women 'with the skills to lead their communities toward social change and development' (Skateistan, 2012). Awista Ayub (2011) reports on the successful uptake by girls, constituting 120 members of the programme. She highlights that the opening of an indoor facility (October 2009) was foundational, as it allowed girls to participate in an all-female environment, helping to shift the prevalent conservative attitude (held by girls and their parents) that skateboarding was unsuitable for girls.

The organisation portrays itself as well-organised; it has fundraising events and a team of experienced volunteers from across Europe and North America, and has endorsements from industry stars, including Tony Hawk. Ayub claims that 'in a country ravaged by decades of war, Skateistan is truly revolutionary' (2011). Yet, despite such positive commendations, policy makers often know little about the reasons why lifestyle sports are more suited to these communities than other more traditional sporting activities, or for which group of young people the activity is most useful (see Bradley, 2010; Gilchrist and Wheaton, 2011). However, as Spaaij suggests:

> One of the cornerstones of alternative development in the Global South, in which local NGOs play a critical role, is the belief that the *state is often part of the problem*, and that alternative development should occur outside, and perhaps even *against the state.*
>
> (2009: 1109, emphasis added)

As illustrated in the case of skateboarding in Durban, its increased status because it is outside state control and not part of the country's colonial sporting history generated much of the appeal. However, as Gilchrist and Wheaton (2011: 126) concluded: 'There is a need for evaluation of these policy interventions, particularly from the perspectives of participants, to understand the mechanisms leading to the claimed outcomes, and to recognise the specificity of the circumstances leading to changes in people's behaviour' (cf. Coalter 2007). Nonetheless, their analysis of parkour illustrated that a similar range of factors were significant, including: its non-competitive nature; its focus on individual-based and directed skills; its non-club based status; its all-consuming nature; and its individually managed risk-taking opportunity. Across these lifestyle sports, the lack of institutionalisation and adult control, the individualised and non-league based nature, and its play-like character seem to make the activities particularly open to the possibility of re-negotiated and self-generated identities and meanings.

LIVERPOOL JOHN MOORES UNIVERSITY
LEARNING SERVICES

Conclusions

The case studies included in this chapter have provided some partial but reveal-ing insights into the questions posed about the cultural politics of lifestyle sports, particularly about the politics of race and of globalisation. They have also high-lighted the ways in which lifestyle sports have been adopted in communities not generally associated with participation. Despite research in the Global North suggesting that lifestyle sport is a culture produced for and by the white middle-classes, and that participants need high amounts of cultural and economic capital to participate, in some circumstances these barriers can be overcome. Lifestyle sports in some contexts do have the potential to include participants from a range of different backgrounds, including the least privileged. Nonetheless, racialised discourses and ideologies of racial difference continue to be reproduced in both club and informal beach settings.

7 The California beach, whiteness and the exclusion of black bodies

Surfing and whiteness: deconstructing the myth

One issue that has consistently puzzled me is the strength and permanence of the association between surfing and white people. The quintessential image of the surfing body has, since the 1950s, been 'phenotypically White' (Kusz, 2007: 136), specifically, a young, white, male subject, slim, toned, tanned – but not 'too' dark skinned – with a mop of sun-bleached blonde hair. This image has been perpetuated both in the surfing niche media and most significantly through wider mass media surfing discourses. In the USA, the white surfer became so iconic he – and increasingly she (Comer, 2010) – became the face of California, fuelled from the 1950s by the hugely popular Hollywood beach movies and the surf music craze epitomised by the Beach Boys (Booth, 2001; Stenger, 2008). Yet despite this imagery, and in contrast to most lifestyle sports, surfing did not originate as a 'white' sport. Surfing originated as a Polynesian cultural form that was appropriated by white North Americans and Australians in the middle part of the twentieth century, redefining and reorganising the activity in the process. My interest here is to illustrate that surfing's imagery as a white activity and space is a relatively recent and contextually specific social construction.

(Re)reading the global diffusion of surfing: how surfing became white

While California is associated with the birth of modern surfing (Booth, 2001), surfing has a much longer and fascinating history as a pre-colonial black body culture. As Finney and Houston (1996) explore in *Surfing: A history of the ancient Hawaiian sport*, surfing in its 'residual' cultural forms, such as body surfing, existed in many countries, dating as far back as 2000 BC, including among the Maoris in New Zealand, various Pacific Islanders and indigenous people of coastal Africa (ibid.). Dawson documents how surfing was 'invented' by Africans independently of the Polynesian influence, taking place in Senegal, Ivory Coast, Ghana, Gabon and possibly the Congo-Angola region (2006: 1336). Drawings of 'natives' surfing in its broadest sense – for example, body surfing on various implements from coconut fronds to logs – abound in the diaries of

(British, Spanish and Portuguese) missionaries and naval officers travelling in the Pacific and along the west coast of Africa[1] from the early nineteenth century (Finney and Houston, 1996). In an interview, Stevie, a surfer since the 1960s with an interest in surf history, claimed: 'Surfing has always been tied to warm weather, historically around islands, whether it's Fiji or Tonga or Hawaii, wherever, you find people of colour, black people surfing.' Most of the contemporary histories of surfing,[2] however, focus on the role of Polynesians in the Hawaiian archipelago, particularly within the triangle bounded by Hawaii, Easter Island and New Zealand, as it is here that stand-up board-riding as a sport, pastime and culture was most developed (ibid.: 22). Surfing played a pivotal role in Polynesian men's and also women's cultural life. However, colonisation by Europeans and Americans in the eighteenth and nineteenth century changed and eroded the activity. Puritanical American missionaries thought that surfing was immoral and evil, so it was banned, along with most other native sports and pastimes (Booth, 1999: 44). Surfing's decline was therefore part of the 'wider disaster' that European (from 1778) and American (from 1989) colonisation imposed on the Hawaiian people (Finney and Houston, 1996).[3]

It was not until the early twentieth century that surfing was revived, predominantly (but not exclusively) by non-indigenous *haole* (white, European) Hawaiian settlers (Finney and Houston, 1996; Booth, 2001; Canniford, 2009), and reconstructed as a 'hedonistic, erotic form of adventure tourism' (Canniford, 2009: 3) that supported the capital interests of Hawaii's touristic economy. The influence of Hawaiians 'on global surfing culture remains strong, not just in terms of the sport's origins, but also its philosophies, argot and body cultures' (Osmond *et al.*, 2006: 90). Furthermore, as Osmond *et al.* detail, 'resistance to the international diffusion of Californian and other external surfing cultures' was evident from the 1960s onwards (ibid.: 92)[4] and cultural contestation continues. A revival of the Hawaiian surfing heritage in the 1970s was part of a broader Hawaiian cultural (and touristic) renaissance, which included music, Hula, and which saw surfing re-claimed as a 'Hawaiian national institution' through which Hawaii was promoted as a touristic destination (ibid.). Rather than a return to the indigenous cultural system in which surfing had been exercised, 'modern' surfers experienced the beach through a 'hedonistic model', 'a secular celebration of nature, health, physical activity, excitement and outdoor adventure' (Canniford, 2009: 10). Thus, the meaning of surfing – and of Hawaii – continues to be 'located in the struggle between postcolonial and local racial ideologies' (Osmond *et al.*, 2006: 93).

California and the birth of 'modern' surfing

In contrast to this long phase as a black cultural activity, surfing and surf culture in California emerged and then rapidly developed in the 1940s and 1950s in a different ethnic form, fuelled by the broader political and socio-economic circumstances (Booth, 2001). As Stenger (2008: 34) recognises, California 'has a long established if paradoxical history of both exoticizing and Anglicizing surfing and its Hawaiian origins'. Three broad and interconnected factors were central to this process, which are discussed below. First was the discursive construction of the Southern Californian beach as a 'white utopia' (Ibid.), driven by tourism and the media, but especially Hollywood's beach movies. Second was the growth of surf travel; and third, and most significantly, the political context of race segregation that impacted all leisure activities. The beach and beach communities became important sites where racial formations[5] and 'mobilities' could be, and were, policed (ibid.).

I conducted my research in and around Santa Monica, adopting a historic perspective, along with the life histories of contemporary African-American surfers.[6] My discussion also draws on documentary sources and the emerging work of other academics, namely Alison Rose Jefferson. Jefferson's research (2009) involved archival work and interviews with members of the African-American community in Santa Monica to explore how the California beach served as an African-American leisure space during the era of segregation.

Constructing the California beach as white utopia: the role of tourism

Various accounts document that Hawaiian surfers introduced surfing to California at the end of the nineteenth century (e.g. Finney and Houston, 1996: 81). Initially, late in 1885, three Hawaiian princes gave a display of surfing in North California, claimed to be 'the first time black people were found riding waves' in California (Stevie). Then in 1907, George Freeth, a *haole* (European Hawaiian) visited California, sponsored by the Redondo-Los Angeles railroad company, as part of a policy to encourage ocean recreation (Finney and Houston, 1996: 81). However, the arrival of Hawaiian-born surfing legend Duke Kahanamoku (from around 1913), who went on to become the unequivocal 'father of surfing' (Ford and Brown, 2005: 94), is cited as a central feature in the popularisation of surfing in California.[7] The 'Duke', as he became known, was born in Honolulu in 1890 and surfed at Waikiki. However, his international notoriety came initially from his swimming ability, in which he garnered Olympic gold in Stockholm in 1912 (Honolulu.gov, 2010) and subsequently competed for the US team in four Olympic Games (Osmond *et al.*, 2006). In the 1920s, the Duke relocated to Los Angeles, lured by the movie business. Newspaper reports suggested that his surfing exhibitions drew large crowds (*Daily Telegram*, 3 September 1922, cited in Honolulu.gov, 2010) and that he introduced surfing to the 'white folk in Malibu', including Hollywood entertainers such as James Cagney (Stevie).

However, despite his Hawaiian credentials, and the fact that he was generally considered to have been extremely influential in publicising the Hawaiian Islands,[8] Kahanamoku's visits, and eventual relocation, did not bring Pacific culture to California. As Stenger (2008) outlines, at the time of the Duke's visits, the Southern Californian beach was being actively marketed as a *Mediterranean* resort. Touristic imagery was employed to emphasise the region's associations 'with European culture', with its 'connotation of cultural prestige and racial exclusivity', rhetorically repositioning Southern California as a 'white utopia' (ibid.: 34). As a consequence, at that time the Southern California beaches had stronger associations with the 'Mediterranean than the Pacific' (ibid.). Stenger therefore suggests that the Duke's fetishised, exoticised black body – his ethnic and racial otherness – did not present a *threat* to the white landscape, nor to the discursive construction of surfing and whiteness. Rather, he represented the 'civilizing effect of whiteness on the racial Other' (ibid.). Stenger's reading is supported by other commentators (e.g. Osmond *et al.*, 2006) and newspaper reports in the 1920s[9] which assert the Duke 'was a respected and welcomed *guest* of the city' (*Daily Telegram*, 12 July 1913, cited in Honolulu.gov, 2010). The Duke's Olympic sporting prowess positioned him as a respectable, civilised (surrogate white) citizen and the context of his surfing exhibitions as an entertaining tourist attraction. As Willard (2002) argues, the Duke's co-optation 'began with his victories at the 1912 Olympics, when from presumptions of primitivism he and his body became a symbol of a racially unified American nation' (cited in Osmond *et al.*, 2006: 94). He was thus appropriated as an ambassador for the region, which was marketed as both 'exotic paradise and an Anglo arcadia' (Stenger, 2008: 34).

From the 1940s, travel, particularly in the form of tourism, began to play a central part in Californian surfing's diffusion. Booth observes that cheaper airfares from the 1940s fuelled surfers' aspirations to travel, allowing Californians to travel to the surfing Mecca, Hawaii (Booth, 2001: 91).[10] However, the rapid growth of the media industries and emergence of global electronic culture in the 1950s and 1960s led to films, and then magazines, becoming the main forms of cultural exchange for surfers.[11] They depicted the surfer's lifestyle as bohemian and hedonistic; surfing was seen to embrace difference and 'the allure of non-Western cultures' (Rutsky, 1999: 13–14). However, it was the more mainstream genre of beach movies emerging from California's Hollywood studios that were most influential in popularising the surfing lifestyle to non-surfing audiences.

The impact of the Hollywood beach movies

The highly popular and economically successful genre of Hollywood beach movies, such as *Gidget* (1956) produced by Columbia[12] and the AIP (American International Pictures) Beach Party series,[13] reproduced the idyllic fantasy lifestyles of California surfers. The films 'enjoyed vigorous cross-promotion in printed materials, suburban shopping malls and movie theatres', particularly through the surf music 'craze' (Stenger, 2008: 44–45), which in the early 1960s 'defined popular music' in America (Booth, 2001: 93). These films were significant in driving the global diffusion of Californian surf culture, particularly around the Pacific Rim (Booth, 2001).

However, these Hollywood-produced films tended to be shunned by the surfing community, who saw them as a 'criminal misrepresentation of *their* subculture' (Stenger, 2008: 33). As one surfer I interviewed claimed, 'most of the original gang of surfers will tell you, those movies killed surfing as we knew it'.

Nonetheless, they had a widely recognised impact in promoting surfing's values to mainstream audiences (Morris, 1998; Rutsky, 1999; Booth, 2001; Ormrod, 2003) and particular significance for individuals who had never seen, or had the opportunity to experience, the beach. As black surfing advocate Harper claimed, living in the mid-West, it was watching these films that fuelled her desire to surf: 'Ever since I saw *Beach Blanket Bingo*, I have been in love with surfing.' She said these films challenged her views about white society, presenting a more positive image. As Harper suggests:

> It was summer of 1976, I watched *Beach Blanket Bingo*, for the first time I saw a positive view of White America. I grew up in Kansas City, Kansas, where Blacks were still separated from Whites by a railroad track.[14]
>
> (Harper, 2009)

Readings of media texts often differ according to contextual factors, including race and socio-cultural location, and for other African-American surfers growing up in the 1950s and 1960s, these movies were seen to be 'defining surfers' as white (Stevie), creating a myth about beaches being white spaces.

The AIP films have received considerable academic attention, with some divergent views about their motives, impact and cultural politics (e.g. Lawler, 2011; Morris, 1998; Rutsky, 1999; Booth, 2001; Ormrod, 2003; Stenger, 2008). While some academics and critics have dismissed them as apolitical and lacking in social commentary (see discussion in Booth, 2001; Ormrod, 2003; Stenger, 2008), others recognise their relevance as 'aspects of the cultural zeitgeist' (Stenger, 2008: 28) and in their articulation of the values of white middle-class America at that time (Ormrod, 2003).[15] Rutsky discusses how the appeal of surfing and surf culture in the AIP films was linked to an exoticised 'allure of non-Western cultures' (Rutsky, 1999: 13) rooted in both surfing's origins in the Pacific and other cultural elements in the films, such as Beat Culture and its fascination with third world cultures (ibid.: 19). In contrast, Stenger emphasises that: 'The Beach Party films actively *distanced* themselves from its non-Western origins and rejected its non-conformist ethos. Depoliticising the subculture, the films transformed surfing and the beach into palatable commodities for mainstream suburban movie-goers' (2008: 33). Stenger's (2008) insightful analysis using the lens of cultural geography identifies the importance of the dynamics of race and space articulated in these films, illustrating that they presented a 'distinct racialized history of surfing and the beach' in Southern California (ibid.: 34).[16] He locates the films in the historical context of 'the Civil Rights movement, white flight, and anxieties about integration' (ibid.: 28), a period when 'racial formations' were radically realigned (ibid.: 29). He argues that the films constructed the California beach – and indeed surfing – as a 'predictable', white, 'utopian landscape', where racial difference was 'disavowed and contained' (ibid.). This construction not only naturalised whiteness, but regulated 'racial, sexual and geographical mobilities' at a time when, as I discuss below, such mobilities were in crisis for many whites and were a 'precondition for people of colour' (ibid.). By attaching a specific construction of white community onto the 'site of the beach', 'the films not only racialized space, they spacialized race, a key strategy through which racial hierarchies are reified' (Ibid.). In so doing they provided white audiences with an *escape* from the racial and political turmoil of the time (Ibid.).

African-American surfers living through that era concurred with Stenger's analysis. Stevie discussed the conservative, white middle-class image of surfing that the AIP films projected, erasing all reference to the wider racial politics of the era:

> All these white folks, lean, typically middle-class, living in a beach com-munity, 'God bless America'. You never saw no anti-war, you never saw no pro-peace. It was a very right wing conservative image of surfing that was put out there through the films. I figure also stereotypically defined surfing as a white sport.

The surfers I interviewed also pointed to the historical inaccuracies in removing black bodies from these films. It was pointed out that Nick Gabaldon, a promi-nent black surfer and resident of Santa Monica, of 'African-American and Mexican ancestry' (Williams, 2007), was omitted. Gabaldon was the first docu-mented African-American surfing hero (see Williams, 2007). In the late 1940s, Gabaldon was part of the 'in-crowd' at Malibu, the beach that was the basis for, and featured in, the AIP films. He famously died (on 6 June 1951, aged just 24) in a surfing accident in huge waves at Malibu Pier (Ibid.). Whereas the book that *Gidget* was based on (by Frederick Kohner, 1957) mentioned 'the black kid that hit the pier and died' (Jennifer), Gabaldon's death was absent from the film. This erasure of surfing's black history angered those I spoke to: [17]

> I'm angry now, because there was so much information held, especially with Nick [Gabaldon] and talking to his friends [...] I have Deadhead from *Beach Blanket Bin*go [the AIP film] telling me that he knew Nick [Gabal-don]. But if you look at *Beach Blanket* there's not even a token. At least *South Park* has a token [...]. But as a result of that kind of propaganda other people started to buy the lie, and it was kind of like the self-fulfilling prophecy.
>
> (Jennifer)

> You saw people of colour surfing, but they never got in the film! But then again in that period, black folks never got in films unless it was a demeaning role or subservient role, so you know, there's a consistency there with Hollywood [laughs].
>
> (Stevie)

The politics of surfing spaces in California: race and segregation

> Even though segregation was outlawed in the sixties it was de facto. Just because you outlaw something doesn't mean it changes.
>
> (Stevie)

Central to understanding *why* surfing and whiteness became so closely associated is an understanding of the politics and experiences of race segregation in North America, initially as legally instituted in the Jim Crow era[18] (up until the late 1950s) and latterly de facto segregation. This involved a 'complex web of laws regulating housing, land-ownership, labour, and marriage targeted at people of colour' (Jefferson, 2009: 181).

When segregation was legally imposed in the 1920s, the city beaches around Los Angeles, as elsewhere, were typically limited to whites only. In Santa Monica, one small area at the foot of Pico Boulevard marked 'Negroes only' became known as the *Inkwell*. The racial restrictions at public spaces in California were legally invalidated in 1927, yet 'de facto segregation' continued through to the 1960s (Jefferson, 2009: 155). That is, white citizens adopted a range of tactics, from discrimination to harassment, to 'discourage' African Americans from visiting or using public and private facilities, or settling in particular beach locales (ibid.: 180). For example, African Americans were barred from the beach clubs emerging on the Santa Monica coastal strip, such as the Casa Del Mar Hotel, which opened in 1926 and which had a private, fenced-in beach to keep the 'undesirables' out (Williams, 2007). The laws and practices around real estate ownership also became effective ways to exclude people of colour. White land owners added real estate covenants with 'Caucasian restrictions' on their properties, which had a significant – and still enduring – impact on home ownership. When black business owners tried to buy the Crystal Plunge site (at Santa Monica in 1924), an area adjacent to land purchased for a new white hotel and beach club, they were rejected (ibid.). A philosophy was emerging across Southern California beach towns that beaches should be 'reserved for the white public', typified by the 'Save the beaches for the public' campaigns emerging during the 1920s, created initially to stop African Americans creating their own beach clubs (Jefferson, 2009: 180). One notorious example was Bruce's Beach, an African-American-owned resort (in the African-American-designated area of Manhattan Beach), which suffered years of harassment tactics by the Klu Klux Klan (Jefferson, 2009; Project, 2010). When this harassment failed, legal sanctions were used by the City of Manhattan Beach, pressurising the black property owners to sell up at prices well below market value (Project, 2010).[19] In summary then, 'along many stretches of the California coastline, refusal to allow African Americans access to various places of leisure constituted an informal policy that was strictly enforced by many white citizens and policy makers' (Jefferson, 2009: 156). It is important to recognise that, before segregation, the beach was an important leisure space for this African-American community, as well as for other minority groups. Jefferson outlines that, from the turn of the century through to the post-war period, the Southern California beach was a popular place for African Americans to locate for 'relaxation, recreation and vacation' (ibid.). Williams (2007) describes how black churchgoers went to the *Inkwell* Beach to socialise after church, and 'carloads of girls' would arrive at the beach to 'meet suitors and chat', and frequent the bathhouse and dance clubs nearby. Jefferson (2009) outlines how the first wave of African Americans who moved to Santa Monica in the late nineteenth century joined a diverse ethnic community. The town became one of the few seaside communities in the region with a historic African-American community, including thriving black-owned businesses (Williams, 2007). Subsequent migration to the region (between the 1920s and 1940s) was by predominantly the (black and white) middle-classes with financial resources, who were lured by the climate, beauty, employment opportunities and 'more liberated lifestyle' (Jefferson, 2009: 163). For African Americans looking to get away from the 'worst of Jim Crow segregation', California was perceived to be more liberated than many other areas of the USA (ibid.). Thus, at that time (and until legislation was passed to restrict ownership), black businesses and entrepreneurs 'thrived in areas of beach communities around LA' (Stevie), including in Santa Monica (Williams, 2007).

However, as detailed earlier, the beach was increasingly seen by civic leaders and politicians as the 'region's most important recreation and touristic asset' (Jefferson, 2009: 181). This black migration was therefore seen as a *threat*; it was feared that non-white private ownership of beachfront property would make the beaches and beach-area property unattractive to white Americans (ibid.). As Culver (cited in Jefferson, 2009: 181) outlines, by staking a claim to the 'recreational space that stood as the core of the [region's] civic life and identity', African Americans appeared to pose more of a threat to the 'white dominance' than other poorer immigrant communities. So despite the increasingly broad cultural mix in Los Angeles, 'systemised white racism, when manifest in recreation space, was most consistently targeted at African Americans' (Jefferson, 2009: 181). Additionally, racial stereotypes about African Americans, such as being noisy and disorderly, persisted (see also Durrheim and Dixon, 2001) and helped 'perpetuate white belief in a defined racial order predicated on distinct and immutable racial characteristics and an ideology of segregation that depends on identifying the racial other as both dangerous and amusing' (Kahrl, 2008, cited in Jefferson, 2009: 175). The dance halls popular among African-American residents from the 1920s to 1940s, and often located in these beach communities, were a particular focus for white anxieties, and thus were overzealously policed (Jefferson, 2009: 175). Kahrl (2008) notes, therefore, that 'few images were more threatening to the emerging Jim Crow order than that of a black family relaxing on a beach, books in hand, in silence' (cited in Jefferson, 2009: 175).

Economic factors, such as the rising price of beach real estate, also continued to contribute to beach communities becoming increasingly white.[20] As Stenger (2008: 44) argues, 'property ownership' combined with 'class privilege' was effective in restricting beach access. Beachgoing, once important for this

African-American community, became eroded, having, as Jennifer explained, a lasting effect:

> You've got to remember … we're talking generations. So if my Grandmother used to go to the beach and now she's saying 'I ain't going to go down there because the white man used to do this to us', and this and that, and 'this is what happened and all these bad things'. Then that next generation comes along – they're not going. Then that next generation … they're definitely not going.

The significance of the Inkwell

Jefferson discusses the importance of the section of Ocean Park beach in Santa Monica which came to be known as the *Inkwell*, which during the segregation era was a rare leisure site where African Americans were relatively free from discrimination (2009: 158). It became special to the members of the African-American community in Southern California, a place of 'sociability, special significance and warm memories' where they enjoyed the 'sun and surf' (ibid.).

> But the laws changed in about 1925, I think, so that the beach was not allowed to be segregated, and that blacks were allowed to swim in the water. But we didn't and we weren't invited. But we did have that place at the Inkwell, […] So although it was not law, it was as it was.
>
> (Michael)

Ease of access, particularly the Pacific Electric trolley lines from the greater Los Angeles area, made it possible for families from all economic classes and backgrounds to visit. As one of my interviewees recalled: 'Black people that came from the inner city, they took bus lines, and had always taken trolley cars […] and that's where it landed, it landed them at the Inkwell' (Michael). In addition, as noted above, Santa Monica had an ethnically diverse community. Significantly, it was not a popular spot with white beachgoers, and so initially was less densely populated than surrounding areas and African Americans 'felt free to congregate' (Jefferson, 2009: 169). As Michael recounted:

> My grandmother was there [Inkwell] from maybe 1910 through the 1930s, and then my mother was born in 1921, used to go as a child, swimming and playing on the beach, and hanging out at the Inkwell with what you call the black beach boys. And I'd say 'what do you guys do down there?' 'Stuff, all the stuff that all the beach boys did. The other beach boys.' I'd go, 'what was that'? They'd play volleyball, and bodysurf and swim and you know just hang out with the girls, and just do all those activities, and that's what we did in the summer.

The Inkwell also has an important history for the black surfing community because it was here that, in the 1940s, Nick Gabaldon, a Santa Monica High

School student and the first documented black surfer, taught himself how to surf.[21] African-American families and teenagers continued to congregate at the Inkwell as late as the 1960s, the beach spot being popular for 'post-church family outings for picnics, volleyball and fun in the ocean' (Williams, 2007). It was also where many African-American surfers from the broad Los Angeles area said they started to surf, and had been pivotal in their experiences of the beach lifestyle. Michael, who lived in Los Angeles, started going to the Inkwell in 1964, following a family tradition, as his grandmother had been a regular visitor 50 years previously. While the beach was no longer 'known to be a black place', he described it as 'certainly a place where everything could go':

> I never ever experienced any negative comments, any overt racist activities, never any fighting or problems at the Inkwell. Maybe it's because of its tradition, because the heritage from which it came didn't allow it to have that kind of vibe.
>
> (Michael)

The legacy: beach space, access and exclusion

The enduring impact of segregation and the racialisation of space were widely discussed by my interviewees, especially what Stenger calls the 'flight to and fortification of white spaces' by the white middle-classes (2008: 44). They highlighted how political and economic factors – including continued discrimination, limited economic resources and the rise in value of real estate – all contributed to the 'economic segregation' that is now prevalent across the USA (see also Garcia and Baltodano, 2005; Erickson *et al.*, 2009).

> Here the beaches are very, very white, there is no black beaches, at all. There used to be. [...] before integration, under segregation there were areas, there were black beaches. There were actually black communities with only beaches in those areas. But with integration, and the rise of the United States as a capitalist development, the real estate values took off sky high. [...] Because beach real estate is very, very expensive and highly desirable... and because there tends to be very, very conservative elements living along the beach, black folks were discouraged from coming to the beach and using the beach.
>
> (Stevie)

According to recent research (USC Coastal democratic study), people living along the Los Angeles coastline are 'disproportionately non-Hispanic white and wealthy, compared to the state and county: 68 per cent are non-Hispanic white, 16 per cent are Latino, nearly 8 per cent are Asian and less than 5 per cent are black. In all coastal communities, the black population was 'too small to be significant' (Garcia and Baltodano, 2005: 195). That is, the spacialisation of race and racialisation of space continues to the present day. In the affluent beachfront enclaves like Malibu, private ownership of rows of beachfront property has made access to the beach almost impossible other than for residents, for whom the beach becomes a private, secluded garden (field notes). Some residents have sought to cut off beach access to non-residents: 'For years, wealthy Malibu homeowners posted illegal "private property" and "no trespassing" signs, and hired private security guards on all-terrain vehicles that harassed the public and prevented people from reaching the public beach' (Project, 2010). These actions have been fought by a range of bodies, including the California Coastal Commission and State Lands Commission, using legislative actions to preserve and maximise public access to the beach. In the process, some diverse coalitions have been generated, such as between the Surfrider Foundation and the Centre for Law in the Public Interest (Garcia and Baltodano, 2005). For activist groups like The City Project (Project, 2010), the California beach represents 'the latest front in the struggle for equal justice', seeing this racialisation of space as an important way in which racial hierarchies continue to be reproduced (Stenger, 2008). As illustrated further in Chapter 8, similar issues underpinned access to a range of nature-based recreational resources and spaces in California (Wolch and Zhang, 2004; Erickson *et al.*, 2009).

The gentrification of the more ethnically diverse beach suburbs like Venice Beach (just adjacent to Santa Monica) has also contributed to increasingly privileged white communities living by, and controlling access to, the beach. Through the 1970s and 1980s, Venice Beach had the reputation of being a 'hip, non-conformist, third-world beach' (Stevie).[22] Since the 1990s, this once multi-ethnic beach community has become popular with 'creative types', such as (white) musicians and directors, leading to an increasingly segregated and 'much more European' community (Stevie). While Venice has retained its hip and more liberal ethos (Wachs, 2007), it is claimed that the black community has been forced out by rising property prices and 'targeted actions' (Stevie).

Naval communities situated in popular surfing venues were often more ethnically diverse and appeared to provide some exceptions to the white dominance of the California coastal strip. Oceanside, a suburb in San Diego, is 'a military city right on the ocean' (Stevie). According to Steve, its residents – and surfers – had 'less antiquated ideas about race': 'And because it's a military town, there's more minorities there. Asians and blacks and Hispanics and whites and they are all living together, and so the divide is much different. Everybody is much more accepting' (Stevie). Being in naval families or having links with naval communities featured in many interviewees' life stories (see Ch. 8 on family life), and pioneering black surfer Nick Gabaldon honed his water skills in the Navy (Williams, 2007).

The surf media and industry: cultural imperialism and perpetuating the white myth

In this last section, I focus on mediated surfing spaces, exploring some of the ways in which the US surf media and industry continue to perpetuate the association between surfing and whiteness. The sport media clearly play a central role in developing our 'sporting imagination', including the 'embodiment of racialised and gendered sporting bodies' (Azzarito and Harrison, 2008). The surf media is no exception, and for the participants in my research, it was perceived to play a central role in sustaining the myth that surfing was a white activity, and denying or erasing the black surfer subjectivity.

Colonial imaginary and the 'surf safari'

Specialist surf films emerged from the early 1960s and quickly became important subcultural commodities, often consumed in communal settings, 'explaining surfing and surfers to themselves' (Booth, 2001: 94). Soon after, subcultural magazines were launched (ibid.)[23] and quickly became important ways in which surfing's cultural values were diffused and assimilated, particularly across national boundaries. The surfer as nomad in search of the perfect wave[24] became a central discursive feature in all forms of the subcultural media (as well as pro- grammes about surfing travel for 'mainstream' audiences). Comer (2010: 23) highlights that the film *Endless Summer* (1966) produced both 'the initial economy and foundational structures of feeling that underwrite surfing as an international public culture' of six million participants. Embedded in this quest, she suggests, was not just the search for perfect waves but 'alternative ways of living' emerging from a 'disaffection from and critique of mid-century US racial formations' (ibid.: 21).

Yet despite the rhetoric of surfers' bohemian and cosmopolitan disposi- tion, a colonial imaginary underpins the surf safari genre of discovery and travelogues that continued to infuse *all* forms of surfing media (Beattie, 2001; Comer, 2004; Ormrod, 2007; Wheaton, 2003a). The travelogue narrative was based on white, heterosexual, wealthy Western young men searching out perfect waves in 'exotic' distant lands, often around the Global South. Where images of black subjects were used, they tended to be as the 'native' Other, depicted in traditional clothing and/or performing 'primitive' tasks like fishing/hunting for food. Very occasionally (as in *The Endless Summer*), some black surfers are depicted (as my interviewees emphasised). But pre- dominantly the white surfers befriend and tame the primitive native black Other, with whom he shares an affinity for nature and the ocean, the basis of the soul surfing ethos and transcendental experience (Stranger, 1999; Booth, 2001). Racial stereotypes underpin this narrative, emphasising cultural and racial differences, and that post/colonialised countries and subjects are more primitive than the 'civilised' West. Moreover, the 'romantic project' of the surfer seeks to 'parenthesize issues of indigenous poverty, global exploitation and apartheid through good-humoured engagement with locals as curios' (Lewis, 2003: 70). So although the travelling surfer is not oblivious to these issues, they must not detract from the importance of *their* personal journey for spiritual enlightenment, so perpetuating forms of 'Orientalism and exploitation' (ibid.: 71):

The globalism and utopianism paraded by surfing, therefore, are always problematic. Their idealism and political intentions may quite consciously seek to overthrow these hierarchies in some ways. But they can never do so since their own imagining is shaped by uneven distributions of power.

(Ibid.)

The travelogue discourse was widely commented on and criticised. As one interviewee described it:

A crew of white boys go to a break, surf it and never show that anybody else ever surfs here, and then go away [...]. If you watch these other surf movies you will think that's what's going on; nobody else is there and nobody else surfs. And I always thought, I mean that's terrible, because that's sending a message that it's these kids that get to travel around. They are obviously very wealthy because it's very costly, and they get to go to these remote places and ride these beautiful waves. But it's only this pack of kids that get to do that, and that's not true!

(Michael)

While it was recognised that *some* contemporary travelogues had begun to disrupt *aspects* of this discursive construction, such as the all-male environment,[25] they continued to reinforce the naturalness of the surfers' subject position as white and Western. Some surfers I interviewed said this (post)colonial mentality was one of the aspects of surfing culture that most angered them:

Because what you're saying is you're going into these third world countries, *we* are still uncivilised. *You* came, you're going to teach us how to surf! [...] It just, absolutely it amazes me to think that we are so, and I'm going to say United States because I don't see it so much more in other places as we feel like we have to find everything. Our white culture has to discover everything. [...] You don't need to discover us; we've already been here.

(Jennifer)[26]

It is not just the media that exploits the surfer-as-nomad metaphor. Despite various claims to environmental and humanitarian credentials, the operation of the surf travel industry is often exploitative (Wheaton, 2007b; Thorpe and Rinehart, 2010), operating in unethical ways, manipulating various non-Western communities and their resources. Surfing's utopianism as imagined in surf media, and reproduced through the surf industry, ultimately denies 'the hegemonies and injustices that constrain the shoreline' (Lewis, 2003: 70). Jennifer, for example, pointed to the ways the industry appropriated various locations in the developing world, building surf resorts for 'surf adventures' without providing any real support for local communities or understanding how their presence was contributing to various social and political problems in the regions.[27] 'If you ask me it's a takeover of the waves. If you've got a good wave they are going to take it' (Jennifer). It was not just travelogues that perpetuated such images; many aspects of the surf media and industry reproduced dominant stereotypical discourses about black athleticism and, at times, racist imagery.

The surf industry: a 'blonde' tyranny?

> The message is not just that people out there are black and they surf. There's a missing element in the surfing industry, and that's blacks! That's the element, that's the point ... *why* there are no advertising campaigns.
>
> (Rhonda Harper, personal interview)

Rhonda Harper worked as a sport journalist in the action sport industry, so was cognisant of the surf media and lifestyle sports industry more widely. Indeed she saw her role as a watch dog, an insider who would speak out whenever she saw minorities being misrepresented or passed over (see e.g. Harper, 2012). Rhonda discussed the under-representation of black surfers and the stereotypical and at times racist ways in which contemporary surfers were represented in the USA surf-industry advertising (see also Pawle, 2010; Weisberg, 2010).[28] While recognising that black athletes were under-represented across all lifestyle sports, she contended that it was most prevalent in surfing:

> Surfing's the last one; I mean, look at it – you got hockey, they've got their blacks now, skateboarding has got their blacks now, snowboarding has had theirs. There's the Boarder Brothers in Los Angeles, they're a group and they are all professionals. Everybody else has had blacks. This is the one sport that has been consistently white-dominated for decades.

She claimed that there are 'no blacks in any surf advertising', particularly women; she had never seen 'a black female' (see also Comer, 2010). She also criticised the ASP (Association of Surfing Professionals), the most visible and arguably most powerful surfing institution, for its lack of people of colour either as athletes or as representatives of the organisation at contests or in the press. She pointed out that, despite the increasing diversity of surfing in the USA, all of the current USA surf team were 'blonde', arguing that a central reason was the lack of support given to people of colour in the surfing media and industry. Comer (2010) also discusses that the blonde 'California girl' is the dominant female figure in the global surf industry, but the 'fact of this blonde divide' has yet to register as an effect, and hence it must be noticed and explored (ibid.: 153). She describes this visual economy that privileges whiteness as a 'politics of blondness' (ibid.: 154), which, as I outline below, serves to discipline and exclude darker-skinned women.

Several interviewees commented on the costs and difficulties of becoming a professional surfer, particularly for aspiring competitive surfers who do not fit the 'blonde' image. One important factor was the surf media's failure to give aspiring professionals media coverage, the vital link in obtaining sponsorship. Stevie described how this had commenced in the 1960s when corporations became aware they needed a more clean-cut image to sell their products.[29] While the professionalisation of surfing has been well-documented, the impact of race has been ignored from these analyses. That is, implicit in the idea of a respectable and clean-cut athlete was a particularised image of whiteness:

> You've got this clean-cut, short hair, non-tattoo, non-dope smoking kind of European in America to become the image, the visual image of surfing. Typically became blonde haired, blue eyed. Kind of almost the Arian stereotype of a perfect European, and that came from the corporate aspect of surfing. Because I met surfers that should have been world champions, but because they had long hair and tattoos or because, you know, they was kind of rude boys or roughnecks ... I think the corporate role has really driven surfing to become a kind of blonde haired, blue-eyed Malibu kind of image.
>
> (Stevie)

Rhonda discussed several examples of the ways those who did not fit this image of whiteness, including individuals with (various differing) ethnic minority backgrounds, were side-lined by the surf industry, despite, she claimed, having better contest results or performance than the 'white kids' who did gain sponsorship and support. She outlined the career of a prominent Mexican-American surfer, who despite winning many junior competitions did not get a contract. It was 'once he started *winning* the junior pro-tour, and he was winning so much, they had to pay notice to him' and give him sponsorship:

> [They] gave him these big contracts. Next thing you know, they stripped the boy of his entire culture, added in some rock music, thrown him in Mexican coloured shorts and try to get his people to come into the surf community.

Comer (2010) similarly discusses the ways in which the politics of blondness impacted an 'up and coming' elite female Mexican surfer who 'ripped' (meaning she was very skilled). Comer argues that her darker skin was coded as 'ugly'; because 'she did not look a certain way' she didn't receive the media coverage she deserved, and as a result her career 'tanked' (finished prematurely) (ibid.: 154).

Consuming cultural difference

These examples of Mexican surfers aptly illustrate the second broad concern identified in my interviews: the ways in which the surf industry uses cultural difference as a marketing device to sell products and to market itself to new niche audiences, in this case Mexican-Americans. Rhonda claimed that a similar process (of cultural stereotyping) had occurred with the first wave of Brazilian professionals that had emerged a few years earlier. She discussed how she had been approached by a company trying to assess whether the black surfing market was worth investing in.[30] Likewise, Stevie argued:

> Everyone's trying to market their product, and they see this as what they call an emerging market, a budding market, so they want to get on the ground floor, so if it blows up then they will be able to sell more products and make more profit.

In these examples, we see the ways in which, in a neoliberal context, the (post-Fordist) surf industry attempts to tap into new niche markets and audiences, seeing ethnicity as a way of marking the individual as *different* to the blonde, white surfing USA identity (Comer, 2010). Deploying such images of the oriental Other (Said, 1989) to create cultural commodities for consumption and profit, is, as Lewis (2003: 71) argues, a form of 'Orientalism and exploitation'.

It is interesting to reflect on the impact of this process on individual surfers and how participants appear to collude in this process, marketing themselves in ways that reinforce their exoticism, desire and racial otherness.[31] As hooks (2004) asserts, the media sell viewers desire masked as respect, which acts to obscure racism (cited in Smith and Beal, 2007: 123). The media's depiction of professional Bajan windsurfer and 'waterman' Brian Talma is an apposite example of this process. Brian became one of the most well-known international media stars on the professional windsurfing scene in the 1990s, promoted in windsurfing magazines across the world. He became an official ambassador for Barbados, sponsored by various corporations, including Ivory Blue (Virgin Atlantic). Known as the 'irie' man, his identity was constructed as other; his appearance and dark skin were seen as *different* to the dominant white European windsurfing subject.[32] Irie comes from Rasta or Jamaican patois, meaning to 'have respect for yourself', promoting a state of being 'at peace and harmony with yourself and the status quo of your existence'.[33] Talma, as the irie man, was depicted as having a 'natural', laid-back attitude, being a perpetually smiling, happy 'native'. This reading was reinforced by images of the exotic: crystal-blue seas, white beaches and palm trees. Yet the irie man persona was constructed by Brian, not the surf industry (Talma, personal interview, 2010). His business venture, *de Action* Beach Shop, was marketed (in 2010 on its webpage) as 'Home of Brian "Irie Man" Talma, the hub of Barbados' watersports action':

> You can spot Brian 'Irie Man' Talma on a crowded beach from yards away. He's the one with the sun-bleached tousled locks and the broad, welcoming smile. And if he isn't chatting with someone or posing for a camera, he's giving somebody a big thumbs up, accompanied by his trademark beam, 'Yeah, man, action!' ... Born and raised in Barbados, West Indies, Brian represents all that is Caribbean. His distinctive West Indian appearance and warmth garnered him instant popularity among his peers and the fans.
>
> (self-promotion – www.irieman-talma.com/bio.htm, accessed in 2011; see also www.briantalma.com/deactionshop.cfm)

Despite these claims that he 'represents all that is Caribbean' and has a 'distinctive West Indian appearance', Brian discussed how, although he was defined as black in the USA and Europe, in Barbados he was called a Mulatto;[34] 'I'm not white or black, I'm nowhere. I'm not part of the white community, I'm not part of the black community.' While the way he looked 'was not advantageous in Barbados' and he came 'under continual pressure to smarten up', he soon recognised his marketability outside Barbados and consciously manipulated and cultivated this self-image of difference for the European-dominated world tour and tourists:

> I stuck by the way I looked. I realised very early that my subculture was very attractive and my look. So for the media and from the image base I had something that none of them. [...] I'm still in the sport because of it. My image sold beyond [the sport], and so people on the tour [the PBA world tour] were influenced. I made a huge impact on the sport of keeping a mood and selling the sport and image base. I'm one of the best when it comes to promotions. And I'm not the best athlete.
>
> (Talma)

While Talma, and the white Bajan surf and tourism industries, benefitted economically from his irie man image, our conversation revealed the difficulties for him personally in trying to adopt a subjectivity as a Bajan watersport participant. He had experienced widespread resentment, and at times hostility, from the local black community where his beach venture was based. Moreover, despite Brian's personal commitment and effort in helping other aspiring black Bajan participants, his success has had little impact in making the sports of surfing or windsurfing more accessible, culturally, to these communities. These cultural barriers, and the identity of the black surfer, are the focus of Chapter 8.

8 Surfing, identity and race
Belonging and exclusion

Introduction

In this chapter, I explore the formative and contemporary experiences of the African-American surfers I met and interviewed. While some aspects of their experiences and identities were shared with white and other ethnic minority surfers, what was most revealing was the range of difficulties or constraints that many of these African-American surfers had faced and that they saw as barriers to other African Americans becoming surfers. This is the focus of the first section of this chapter ('Examining constraints'), where I explore the cultural and ideological factors that had a negative effect on their experiences. While some had been able to transcend difficulties and had become lifelong surfers, for others, the varying forms of exclusion and white racism they experienced continued to impact on their surfing experiences. In the second section of this chapter ('"Space invaders": African-American surfers' experiences'), I explore how these surfers negotiated space and identity in the surfing subculture, and their experiences of racism and exclusion. I highlight various physical and verbal acts – 'racial microaggressions' (Burdsey, 2011c) – directed at individual black[1] surfers, rather than the institutionally instigated processes discussed in Chapter 7. Nonetheless, these discrete acts need to be understood as an on-going process that was part of the broader discrimination and harassment affecting people's lives (Burdsey, 2013). Given the dearth of research on black surfing experiences, I also offer some insights into the experiences, desires and difficulties of the black surfer subjectivity.[2]

Theoretical approaches

In seeking to understand identity in African-American surfing contexts, and how surfing spaces are subject to diverse and at times competing processes by both those identified as *included* and those identified as *excluded* (Neal and Agyeman, 2006), my analysis is informed by a range of theoretical perspectives. These include: critical whiteness studies, cultural studies (Carrington and McDonald, 2001a; Carrington, 2010), critical race theory (CRT) (Hylton, 2010; Burdsey, 2011a) and Bourdieu's theory of habitus applied to racialised contexts and identities (Puwar, 2004; Erickson *et al.*, 2009). I found work on the sociology and cultural geography of race, place and space exploring 'the racialised experiences of minority groups and how social relations are spatially expressed' (Neal, 2002: 443) particularly useful. Initially this body of research (both in the UK and USA) tended to focus on the experiences of ethnic minorities in urban areas (e.g. Alexander, 2000; Nayak, 2003). These were the spaces where the majority of ethnic minorities lived and therefore were seen as the sites where racism was most likely to occur. However, since the 1990s, a growing body of literature has challenged the idea that race is not relevant in areas dominated by whiteness, recognising the need to explore how race is performed and experienced in different geographical contexts (cf. Nayak, 2010), including rural ones. Coastal areas in the UK and USA often have overwhelmingly majority white populations (Burdsey, 2011b) so have been seen as important 'out of the way places' (Nayak, 2010: 2371) for extending our spatial analyses of race and racism (Burdsey, 2011b). As Chapter 7 illustrated, the California beach suburbs were, and continue to be, constructed through 'imaginary notions of whiteness' (Nayak, 2010: 2375). They are spaces that, fuelled by postcolonial anxiety, have experienced 'white flight' from urban to suburban areas and that still operate as places of 'white retreat and safety' (Neal, 2002: 446) that include practices of white territoriality.

This turn to spatiality has also been influential in recognising how *sporting* spaces are gendered and sexualised[3] (Van Ingen, 2003; Caudwell and Browne, 2011) and increasingly also how the 'power geometries', as Doreen Massey (1994) put it, of 'white space [are] produced and exercised on the bodies of Others' (Carrington, 2009: 201). Puwar's book *Space Invaders* is a seminal text in illustrating that:

> some bodies are deemed as having the right to belong, while others are marked as trespassers, who are, in accordance with how both spaces and bodies are imagined (politically, historically and conceptually), circumscribed as being 'out of place'. Not being the somatic norm, they are space invaders.

(2004: 8)

Puwar's empirical work was developed in the context of the work place. However, her theoretical insights are also applicable to everyday leisure and sporting spaces[4] (see e.g. Hills and Eileen, 2006) and alert us to the value of mapping the articulations of race with gender (sexuality and class) *historically*, *temporally* and as race 'registers and resides in space' (Carrington, 2009: 177). Furthermore, as Ahmed (2006: 111, cited in Carrington, 2009: 177) argues, racism can be considered 'as an on-going and unfinished history, which orientates bodies in specific directions, affecting how they 'take-up space'. In this chapter, therefore, I seek to understand the ways in which black surfing bodies reside and take up space, and if they are made to feel 'out of place', rendered as 'other' to this surfing collectivity.

Examining constraints

Research on black and minority ethnic (BME) usage of various outdoor leisure spaces in the USA has highlighted that nature-based recreational resources are under-utilised (Wolch and Zhang, 2004; Garcia and Baltodano, 2005). This research has identified important socio-cultural, economic and practical barriers, but what is often absent is an 'understanding of the historical and cultural patterns of oppression' which become systematically embedded in 'society's norms and daily practices' (Erickson *et al.*, 2009: 531). Thus, I use constraints as an umbrella term to highlight a range of historical, cultural, ideological and economic factors.[5] I explore how 'racialised structures' and 'ways of seeing the world' (Carrington, 2010: 175) underpin and sustain the difficulties experienced by this group of African-American male and female surfers in California. While some factors are clearly specific to these individuals (even subgroups of individuals) and the context of California, others, such as the myth about swimming competence, are applicable to both other geographic spaces and other groups of minority surfers.[6] Therefore, the research presented here also contributes to extending our currently limited understanding of the cultural and historical factors influencing African Americans', and other ethnic minorities', use of non-urban outdoor recreational spaces more widely (Garcia and Baltodano, 2005; Erickson *et al.*, 2009).

Developing a surfing habitus

Bourdieu's account of how leisure preferences are acquired and reproduced, which he called *habitus* (1984), suggested that a range of cultural factors, including an individual's upbringing (e.g. education, family influence, community, peers) and their values and dispositions, are central in acquiring both the taste for, and experience of, leisure activities. For Bourdieu, taste is not just the result of individualistic choices but is socially patterned and a key means by which the social distribution of symbolic resources is organised. He argued that leisure choices are made in relation to the activities' (or style or spaces') social distribution; for example, whether it is common and easily accessible, or more exclusive. Bourdieu's work, therefore, helps to consider the ways in which participation and accessibility in surfing are related not only to material factors, their cost (termed *economic capital*), but also to the *cultural capital* required. Importantly, the particular and distinctive cultural knowledges they demand and the ways these are embodied, such as in gestures, manners and being in space.[7]

While Bourdieu was primarily concerned with the reproduction of social class, his theories have been used to explore the gendered and racialised aspects of (body) habitus[8] and how they are reproduced historically and spatially (Laberge and Sankoff, 1988; Laberge, 1995; Wacquant, 1995; Kay and Laberge, 2004; Atencio *et al.*, 2009; Thorpe, 2009a, 2010a). Erickson *et al.* propose in their research on African Americans' use of outdoor spaces, employing Bourdieu's concepts of cultural capital and habitus, 'that leisure activity is not simply an action that happens in isolation, but is stringently tied to the history of a population' (2009: 541). Cultural capital in sporting activities like surfing includes a range of cultural, social and historical knowledges and resources a person has and can take various forms, from the embodied to the institutionalised. These knowledges are passed on from generation to generation but can also be learnt through various life experiences. As I explore below, the surfing habitus is also 'corporeally informed by social position and expectations' (Evers, 2008: 413). It is a marker of distinction, and a signifier of identity based on maintaining similarities and differences between selves and 'others'. In her work, Puwar illustrates the ways in which habitus, gender and 'race' operate in 'becoming an insider' in a cultural field: 'people are differentiated in the extent to which they are included, and the extent to which they are insiders in accordance with how well their habitus is adjusted to the demands of the field' (2004: 125). Thus, habitus can help explore the degree to which ethnic minority individuals share or are 'invited to' participate in the 'dominant cultural habitus' (Burdsey, 2004b: 764), and the ways in which they are excluded.

'Water enlightened': childhood experiences and family life

Following Bourdieu's theory (1984), family influences and values are central to acquiring the habitus for visiting the beach and the ocean. Many of those I interviewed were exposed to the beach and the water through their families. Yet they were in the minority, recognising that black families tended not to go to the beach:

> I wouldn't call it a white thing, but we don't do it so regularly. Black families that are quite 'water enlightened' do. But they're still a minority. You know, the majority of people that live in the inner city don't use the facilities of the beach. They don't feel for whatever reason either comfortable because they're brought into it, or because there's not enough black people down there to allow them to feel comfortable.
>
> (Jennifer)

For both Jennifer and Stevie, having fathers in the Navy was a catalyst to providing opportunities to visit the beach, and the water/ocean featuring in family life: 'I was raised around water, because my dad was in the Navy always swimming, surfing, fishing, boating, everything in water. I was very comfortable' (Stevie). Thus, while learning to swim is often constrained by historically based cultural stereotypes (as discussed below), family life also plays an important role.

Despite being water-based families and strong swimmers, none of the black surfers I interviewed had surfers in their families or family-based friendship groups. The attitudes of their parents ranged from support through to ambivalence, to hostility. Josh, who became a competitive surfer, had complete support from his family; his mother saw surfing as something positive, so drove him to the beach and to surf contests: 'My mum was very proud that her son could surf so well and was happy that I found something that I was so passionate about' (Josh). In contrast, Stevie explained how in the 1960s his father banned him from surfing because he saw it as a renegade white activity: 'a bunch of pot heads, [with] long hair' (Stevie). His father's perception of surfing as deviant was not unusual; before the 1950s surfers were seen as non-conformist, unpredictable and less likely to fall in line. They were regarded with suspicion by the middle-classes, who linked surfing with other signs of 'juvenile delinquency', such as biking, hot-rodding and drug-taking (Ormrod, 2003: 2). As Booth explains, for an older generation whose lives were marked by the 'great depression and world war', how could youth who 'shied away from order and structure and who had no formal association, be anything other than indolent, wasteful and selfish?' (2001: 95). Stevie explains how he negotiated his father's attitude:

> So I had to hide my surfboard and [dad said] if he catches me with sand on my feet he'd beat my butt because he told me he don't want me to surf because black people don't surf number one, it serves a bunch of dope-smoking hippies. And you can't get a scholarship to college with surfing.

Evidently, Stevie's father saw surfing as a distraction that would stop his son going to university. Stevie explained that he had 'terrible grades at school' but was a fast runner, so his father believed his best chance for a college scholarship was via sports such as track (sprinting) or (American) football.[9] Stevie continued to surf nonetheless, concealing his involvement from his father (but not his mother), hanging out with a group of school friends whose lifestyles he described as 'non-conformist', surfing and smoking marijuana.

Despite the different historical and cultural context of the Caribbean, for Bajan surfer Talma, growing up in Barbados (in the 1970s and 1980s), surfing was also regarded as 'a full-on outcast sport' related to 'lots of negative things' such as drugs. He recounted that the way he looked – 'long hair, it was blonde and bleached from the sun' – contributed to the 'discrimination' he felt from both the black and white communities in Barbados. Nonetheless, Talma argued that the perception of surfing had shifted, at least for the white community who had recognised the 'cool factor' and surfing's potential role in promoting tourism. As a consequence, he argued that it became acceptable to say to 'parents and peers' you are involved with the beach; that setting up a windsurfing or surfing school was an accepted and legitimate professional path. He continued, however, to experience widespread resentment from the local black community where his beach venture was based.

School and peer group influences

School is foundational in developing sporting preferences. For several interviewees, school-based friendships and associations led to their first surfing experiences. Yet school also presented challenges; Rick and Jennifer both described attending white-dominated schools as difficult experiences: 'I was called a nigger on a daily basis' (Jennifer).

Michael grew up in the 1960s, a time when, in the pursuit of desegregation, children were bussed into different neighbourhoods in an attempt to make the education system more equitable (see e.g. Clotfelter, 2004).[10] Michael was one of these children. He was bussed to a 'high economic standard white school' (Michael) in a middle-class suburb. Racism was prevalent, but being good at 'mainstream' sports, and then lifestyle sports like skateboarding, helped him 'assimilate':

> I mean there was a lot of racism, but because I was good in sports, I could play basketball and football and baseball and things, and so that's how I was able to assimilate. They wanted me on their teams. They might not have wanted me to do a whole lot else, but they needed my friendship because they wanted me on their teams.
>
> (Michael)

For Michael, school was formative in developing an interest in activities popular with his white friends, such as skateboarding, which, he explained, 'allowed me to survive in that kind of environment', and then inspired him to try surfing. This racialised participation pattern of lifestyle sports at school in California that Michael described in the 1960s was reproduced in Gottdiener's (1995) research conducted more than 20 years later. Gottdiener (1995) conducted a study of subcultural identification among a unisex and multiracial high-school student community in California, illustrating that the 'surfies' were almost exclusively male and white. He emphasised that surfers were one of the most gender- *and* race-differentiated of the ten youth subcultures he studied; and that these school-aged surfers in California created their identity in relation to non-white youth.

For Michael, surfing became a cultural space where he felt able to 'escape', to just 'enjoy and be part of' it. However, while his friends accepted him, the attitudes of children's parents and their wider (white) communities were less liberal, and forms of exclusion were instituted. He explained:

> Surfing is an exclusive thing [...] and we could go and just be and enjoy and do that. When it came time to go home and have sleepovers and birthdays parties all that kind of stuff, 'hey, wait a minute maybe you can't come to the party'. Or, 'certainly we would really like you to go on the vacation with us because we know that you're Johnny's best friend, but you're not going, we're taking ...' you know? All those things most certainly happened. [...] So it's when you go home, or you go to school, you go to places where your peers that aren't surfers were, things always got sticky.

He also discussed how attitudes shifted as he got older. As a young child, he was often 'welcome' in these white spaces. But progressing from primary to secondary education (high school), he was increasingly 'shut out', *except* while surfing.

He suggested, however, that once at college (university), where parental and community influence became less influential, difference was less marked:

> Folks do come together in college settings, because they are on their own. They don't carry, you know, their parents' rules and their parents' culture and ideas, quite as much. At least they're not obligated to live up to things that they don't even believe because they are on their own.

Conversely, Michael recounted how his son grew up enjoying beach life and surfing. Then, as a teenager, he rejected surfing in favour of activities popular with his black peers, such as basketball. Josh also highlighted that school was an environment where people had 'an issue' with him surfing and not playing basketball: 'They figured since I surf I was trying to be white, which was totally NOT why I surfed.' As Azzarito and Harrison have discussed in their research, African-American schoolgirls who played 'white sports' were called 'white girls' (2008: 351). Irrespective of experiences, or opportunities, the perception of surfing being a 'white sport' remained an issue for many black families and communities.

'White boy wannabes'

> I think it's a difficult thing when I talk to young black people and I try to encourage them to come out and try the sport. They look at me and just go 'that's a white sport'.
>
> (Jennifer)

My interviewees all discussed how the African-American community in California was suspicious of black people who wanted to surf. Stevie's father – despite spending time in the water swimming, fishing and boating – still held the view that 'black people don't surf' (Stevie). This attitude is still prevalent. Stevie recounted how driving around his neighbourhood with a surfboard on the roof of his car provoked comments like, 'Oh, you're trying to be a white boy.' Michael reflexively narrated the 'personal difficulties' he experienced 'being black, and being a surfer' in the (black) middle-class neighbourhood in which he lived:

> I kind of found myself when I was young in limbo, in no man's lands. You know, I knew I couldn't really fit in with the traditional white surf community down there, so to speak. I didn't really fit in here in the black community because people would call me an Uncle Tom,[11] they'd call me an Oreo, they'd call me a white boy, 'Oh, you're a white boy wannabe.'

As Erickson *et al.*'s research exploring African Americans' use of non-urban leisure spaces in the USA illustrates, because 'recreating in natural areas' is not considered a 'black thing' to do, those who choose to take part risk 'being associated with "white culture" by others in the African-American population, and are perceived as rejecting African-American culture' (2009: 540).

In Barbados, Talma described how, although he faced opposition and discrimination from black and white Bajan communities, it was members of the black community who continued to be the greatest obstacle in his attempts to develop surf-based tourism at South Point (a black community). He attributed this to 'the attitude' of the black community, who, he argued, held entrenched and fixed ideas. As Park and Stonequist (cited in Guss, 2011: 75) suggested, children of first-generation immigrants are often 'marginal men' – integrated into neither the culture of their parents nor their country.

Such cultural values, however, are not fixed, but shift over time. Younger participants also recognised that attitudes have changed, suggesting that parental and community disapproval was less widespread than for previous generations: 'Certainly not as much as previously. Black people are swimming more than before and black kids are relishing all kinds of alternative or 'X' sports: skating, surfing' (Natalia). Nonetheless, these accounts clearly illustrate how ideas about racial difference, 'racialised structures' and 'ways of seeing the world' (Carrington, 2010: 175) were reproduced in school, family life and through sporting participation. Below I explore how stereotypes about race are also reproduced in and through both white and black communities. First, I outline some of the factors that specifically impacted on these female surfers.

Barriers for black female surfers

Surfing remains a male-dominated sport, with female surfing still being considered something to spectate, with limited support.

(Natalia)

Most of the interviewees, male and female, recognised there were particular difficulties for African-American women and girls wanting to surf, even for those exposed to beach culture. Stevie discussed how, as his daughter approached her teenage years, she preferred 'hanging out with friends' than going to the beach (with her family). Given the importance of friendship groups to female teenagers (McRobbie, 1991), factors such as lack of approval from female peers were likely to impact on young black women to a greater extent than young black men.

Commentators have argued that some African-American women and girls avoid getting their hair wet (Dr Downie, cited in Zinser, 2006) as seawater and chlorine can cause 'processed hair popular among black women' to 'break or discolour' (Zinser, 2006). Jennifer observed that, in the surfing 'taster' programmes that she ran, African-American girls were harder to encourage than boys because, she claimed, they 'don't want to get their hair wet', particularly if they had straightened hair, as 'water ruins the look'. Alicia concurred with this analysis; she found getting her hair done was costly: 'so as a black surfer for me, there was a time where I had to say I'm not getting my hair done anymore, I'll just go natural'. However, she recounted that her sister stopped swimming as a teenager because she didn't want her 'hair ruined'.

Cultural stereotypes: 'Blacks can't swim'

> The African is not suited to swimming: in swimming, the water closes their pores so they cannot get rid of carbon dioxide and they tire quickly.
>
> (Frank Braun, president of the South African National Olympics Committee, cited in Booth and Nauright, 2003: 9)

It is a commonly held belief that black people cannot or do not swim. In 1990, at an event in Los Angeles to celebrate Nelson Mandela's release, African-American comedian Nell Carter:

> joked with the seventy thousand spectators, most of whom were black, that swimming was 'un-black' – if blacks knew how to swim, he said, there would be no African Americans because their enslaved ancestors would have all swam back to Africa.
>
> (cited in Dawson, 2006: 1354)

Jennifer suggested that lack of swimming proficiency was 'one of the main reasons why blacks don't surf'.[12] She recounted training to work for the Coast Guard and being amazed that so many of the black recruits could not swim: 'We come from a culture where we don't swim. It's the stereotype that no matter where we live or how we are, we don't surf because we don't swim, and that's crazy.' While such stereotypes about black bodies are rooted in racial ideologies – that is, historically created differences, not biological 'facts' – it is nonetheless a stereotype that, as illustrated above, is widely perpetuated by the media,[13] and by black and white Americans. Statistics also drive these beliefs, illustrating, for example, that more minorities in the USA drown than whites (Dawson, 2006). [14] A study by *USA Swimming* suggested that just under 70 per cent of the African-American children surveyed had no or low swimming ability, in contrast to 42 per cent of white children (Rohrer, 2010).[15] Yet while swimming is clearly a powerful signifier in differentiating the black body from the white body, these pervasive myths about inability to swim have received surprisingly little academic attention (Green, 2010).[16] Given this lack of research, and the on-going relevance of this myth for these individuals' ability to develop a surfing 'habitus', it is worth exploring its historical genesis in some depth.[17]

How swimming became white

In sport, the idea of racial differences in performance tends to be formulated as blacks' innate physical 'edge' and articulated into the 'differing genetic propensities' of black and white bodies (Azzarito and Harrison, 2008: 347). Scientific discourse has played a central role in giving legitimacy to 'common-sense' notions of racial difference, such as white men can't jump (Fleming, 2001; St Louis, 2005; Spracklen, 2008), 'furthering ideas about immutable and scientifically "proven" differences between races, and reinvigorating cultural racism'

(Azzarito and Harrison, 2008: 347). The myth about white swimming superiority is no exception. Pseudoscientific explanations – such as highlighted in the quotation (cited above) from Frank Braun explaining why there were so few black swimmers in the Republic of South Africa – have the 'veneer of rigour and robustness' (Fleming, 2001: 112). They also permeate through 'every layer of society' (ibid.). In North America, the scientific basis of this scientific discourse about biological inferiority appears to be just one 'scientific' study (Allen and Nickel, 1969) published in the *Journal of Negro Education* in 1969 (titled 'The Negro and Learning to Swim: The Buoyancy Problem Related to Reported Biological Difference'). It concluded that blacks could not swim because it was harder for them to keep afloat due to genetic and physical characteristics (such as having heavy bones and longer limbs). Regardless of its (lack of) scientific validity, this *one* study has had an enduring impact in informing common-sense ideas about why blacks do not swim, held by many whites and African Americans as well (Dawson, 2006).[18] For example, in 1987, Los Angeles Dodgers' vice president, Al Campanis, claimed on a popular TV show that blacks are 'not good swimmers' because they *lack buoyancy* (cited in Dawson, 2006: 1355).

What is particularly interesting in understanding how these discourses about white swimming superiority became dominant is that, historically, black Africans were *good* swimmers, while white Westerners were *poor* swimmers. In the colonial period, most Westerners could not swim (Osmond and Philips, 2004), and those that could use a breaststroke–dogpaddle amalgam that was inferior and slower to the strokes used by many black swimmers. Indeed, 'Numerous accounts by European and Euro-American travellers, slave traders, planters and government officials from the sixteenth century through the 1840s reveal fascination with Africans' superiority as swimmers' (Dawson, 2006: 1331). West Africans, Native Americans and Asians used a variety of freestyle,[19] a 'stronger and swifter style', that enabled them to 'incorporate swimming into many daily activities', including diving, fishing and surfing (ibid.: 1330). Thus, as Rommel discusses, it is a myth that Africans did not swim; Africans *and* African slave descendants historically were swimmers, then *became* non-swimmers. However, like black surfing, this appears to be a forgotten history (see Ch. 7). Historian Kevin Dawson's research documents how West Africans often grew up on lakes, rivers and the ocean and were proficient swimmers who 'incorporated their skills' into both work and recreational activities (2006: 1327). Some historians argue these skills then died out during slavery; that slaves born in the USA were not allowed to swim because it was seen as a means of escape, and did not increase their economic values (e.g. Schwartz, cited in Dawson, 2006: 1345). Dawson contests this, suggesting that when 'carried to the Americas, slaves brought this ability with them, where it helped shape generations of bond peoples' occupation and leisure activities' (2006: 1327). He outlines how some slave-holders encouraged swimming as a form of economic capital – for example, using slaves as pearl divers, as salvage divers, in fishing and as lifeguards.

Likewise, the initial European contact with the South Pacific islands saw islanders swimming and surfing. They were seen as 'nimble savages', with 'racially and culturally-determined aquatic ability and advantage', which predisposed them to being such 'natural watermen' (Osmond and Philips, 2004: 312). Likewise, racial stereotypes underpinned white Western beliefs about why Africans were better swimmers. They saw dark-skinned people as genetically predisposed to swimming because, like 'animals, they knew instinctively how to swim' (Dawson, 2006).

Despite the historical fallacy of the belief that swimming has always been a 'white' activity,[20] as Dawson suggests, it is unclear why, after 300 years of retaining their swimming legacy, many twentieth-century African Americans 'abandoned this African' heritage (Dawson, 2006: 1355). Segregation and economic factors help explain lack of access to swimming pools (see Wiltse, 2007, and below), but Dawson asks why the African-American community did not continue to swim in natural waterways. The answer, he suggests, is rooted in swimming *becoming seen* as a white activity, and so being rejected. As I detail below, it seems likely that many of the issues identified in my research about why surfing became associated with whiteness are also applicable to other nature-based, water-focused leisure spaces such as lakes and rivers (see also Erickson *et al.*, 2009).

Numerous economic and culturally based factors contribute to contemporary African-American children being less likely to swim confidently, many of which were alluded to in my interviews.[21] Wiltse's (2007) social history of swimming pools in America details how access to public pools was limited for all blacks during formal segregation, and 'fear of black men interacting with white women in swim wear' kept pools segregated until the mid-1950s (Endo, 2012). Opportunity still remains a factor; many inner-city areas, which have a higher proportion of black residents, are less likely to have public swimming pools (Zinser, 2006).[22] In the US, swimming tuition remains the responsibility of parents not schools (Rohrer, 2010). Jennifer outlined how growing up in the 1970s 'there were no mandatory swim classes' and pools tended to be situated in white suburbs. While she and her siblings could swim – 'my dad was a swimmer so he made sure that we could' – she claimed they were in the minority. Neither her mother nor many of her cousins could swim, despite being from a family that had its own pool.

This reluctance for many black families to encourage swimming was recognised, and some suggestions offered as to why this was the case, including black parents' fear of water (Rohrer, 2010). This fear was then passed on through the generations, with non-swimming parents keeping children away from the water for fear of drowning, effectively creating generations of non-swimmers (Zinser, 2006; Rohrer, 2010). Some attribute this 'fear' to the boats used in slavery:

> I mean it goes back to the boats; we are just not getting into the water the way that we should be, because of fear, the sharks, you know it's the whole [...] there's a whole different dynamic when you talk about blacks getting in the water in the United States. [...] It's more mental than it is actual physical.
>
> (Jennifer)

This fear of water was discussed by both my respondents in California and black water users in Barbados (Green, 2010). Reflecting on his experiences learning to swim in the 1950s, black Baja Rommel Green, discussed his initial apprehension about the ocean, which he saw as a vast untamed expanse that 'had no backdoor' and that was home to dangerous creatures such as sharks and conger eels.[23] For many groups in the African diaspora, nature and the outdoors represented fear. As Erickson *et al.*'s research outlined, African Americans in the US were fearful of travelling outside of their (usually urban) 'comfort zone', based on both perceptions about being in certain spaces and historically rooted 'real' fears about personal safety (2009: 538). They discuss, for example, how the woods continued to have a 'strong negative connotation' because of their association with poverty and lynching (ibid.: 539).

Many of the surfers, however, were cognisant of the fallacy of these discursive constructions of Africans as non-swimmers; 'black surfer and black water men know that there is a heritage, an African heritage, of watermen and water women, and that goes all the way back ... but culture is powerful' (Alicia). Jennifer suggested that 'other minorities', particularly 'the Hispanics', frequented the beach much more than the African-American community, arguing that visiting the beach was a part of their diasporic community's identity and did not seem to have the same connotations as a place of fear. The effect of this, she suggested, was to help break down stereotypes about the beach and surfing as white spaces:

> But things are changing now, because the number of Hispanics in our community, and they do use the beach. And they've got much stronger tradition with the water and using the beach for picnics and for families' events and for parties, because they did it in their homeland. And they felt comfortable doing it and they don't seem to have some of the same stigmas that we have, that belief that if we go down there we're not going to be able to have fun because white people are going to keep us from it. And they go and do it, and it changes the dynamic.

Jennifer's observation is supported by Wolch and Zang (2004) and Garcia and Baltodano (2005: 197), who reported on research exploring the use of beaches and urban parks in the USA, respectively. Both studies suggested that Hispanics used these recreation sites primarily for social gatherings, such as family picnics (ibid.: 250).[24] Their reports highlight the need for further study of beach recreation patterns, recognising that people from different racial and ethnic groups construct 'different meanings for natural space based on their own values, cultures, histories, and traditions' (ibid.: 197).

Constraints: a summary

Surfing is a notoriously difficult and frustrating sport to learn, requiring specific forms of physical capital (Dant and Wheaton, 2007), perseverance and determination. As Stevie contended, beginners rarely 'realise how hard it is. You know, waves knocking you around, trying to stand up on the board, that whole phenomenon.' There are also practical barriers, such as transport, and the financial outlay, particularly buying a surfboard. Garcia and Baltodano's (2005: 201) study confirmed that 'people of color and economically disadvantaged communities disproportionately lack efficient access to the beach' (see also Wolch and Zhang, 2004). They cite bus stops up to 'half a mile from a public path to the beach' that create 'a significant burden', particularly for those with young children or recreational gear (Garcia and Baltodano, 2005: 271). As one interviewee recounted, when 'they made it illegal to take a surfboard on the bus' from South LA to Santa Monica, one of her friends had to stop surfing. It is also the case that the most exclusive beaches, like Malibu (in the most white-dominated communities), were those that were least accessible by public transport (ibid.: 201).

The surfing lifestyle *can* be expensive, with high-performance surfboards and wetsuits costing several hundred dollars; and then the board has to be transported to the beach. Nonetheless, it was argued that, with the increasing availability of cheap products, including boards and wetsuits, the cost of equipment was rarely a constraint. As Jennifer claimed: 'Costco's [a supermarket] got boards now for a hundred bucks; you don't need a *Town and Country* [prominent brand], what you need is a board that you can lie on and have fun.' But the cultural capital required and especially perceptions about surfing's exclusivity as a white sport were widespread. These surfers discussed how they had been affected, at least initially, by stereotypical views about 'what black did and didn't do'. But once they had their first taste of surfing, those 'self-imposed stereotypes' were quickly broken (Alicia). As Alicia contended, as a kid she spent a lot of time with her family at the beach, but 'never asked mum' if she could surf because she assumed 'surfing was for rich people that could afford to buy that stuff'. 'Rich', in this context, equated to white privilege. Thus, as outlined in Wolch and Zhang's analysis of the use of beach space in California, 'race and class matter' (2004: 437).

Yet, as research in other contexts also illustrates, socio-economic factors alone do not account for 'not surfing'. Stories abound – including in the narratives here – illustrating the creative ways (young) people have managed to sustain a surfing lifestyle with minimal financial outlay. In less affluent countries like India (Rahman, 2012), Africa (Leitch, 2009) and particularly Brazil – where surfing is rapidly growing in popularity across socio-economic groups – 'body boarding that is cheaper than surfing, and easier to transport, has become particularly popular' (Jennifer). In cities like Rio, young people from the favelas (shanty towns), who had little money but ample time, could still access the beach fairly easily.[25] Yet, as Jennifer argued, 'even today there are kids in LA who live three miles from the beach' but have 'never walked on the sand'. Racialised social relations continue to be expressed spatially. As these surfers recognised, most outdoor leisure spaces in North America were dominated by the white middle-classes (Wolch and Zhang, 2004; Erickson *et al.*, 2009). Stevie explains:

I think one of the problems is the fact that there has really been a lack of people of colours' access to public spaces in America. Public spaces have been reserved for the more, pretty much for Europeans, whether it's mountains, or deserts, or beaches, or camping, or hiking or all these kinds of things. [...] Europeans have dominated.

As I have outlined (Ch. 7 most extensively), this spacialisation of race is rooted in, and is still influenced by, the historical context of segregation, as well as contemporary political factors that reinforce the socio-economic context of many African Americans in California, and elsewhere.

'Space invaders': African-American surfers' experiences

The title of this section refers to Puwar's (2004) book *Space Invaders*. It highlights that spaces are not blank and open for anyone to occupy, but that some – usually white-bodies are 'tacitly designated as being the natural occupants, 'deemed as having the right to belong' (ibid.: 8). Bodies stand out 'when they are out of place', and such standing reconfirms the 'whiteness of the space' (Ahmed, 2006, cited in Carrington, 2009: 173). Thus, many racialised minorities and women are 'in a tenuous position of being both insider and outsider who are, to varying degrees, rhetorically speaking "space invaders"' (Puwar, 2004: 10). These are insights that resonate through the narratives of the surfers in this study. I draw attention to key themes that resonated among the group, particularly their contradictory feelings of belonging and experiences of exclusion from both white surfing-communities and black, home-based communities.

Exclusion and racism

Sport, both in the USA and in other Western contexts, continues to 'sustain a deeply rooted culture of racism' (Azzarito and Harrison, 2008: 348). Research across an increasingly broad range of sporting contexts has illustrated that sporting 'racism operates in a number of ways and incorporates a plethora of acts and processes' (Hylton, 2010: 350), including individual and institutional practices. These can be either overt or covert in nature and function at levels from the personal to the societal (Hylton, 2010). While sporting racisms operate on many different (but interconnected) levels, from the cultural to the biological (Carrington and McDonald, 2001a), all 'share the belief in the biological separation of the human population into racial discrete groups' (Azzarito and Harrison, 2008: 348). Yet issues related to race and racism are experienced and articulated in diverse ways (Burdsey, 2004a: 297); people have 'differential experiences of racism' (Hylton, 2010: 350). The African-American surfers in my research were not a homogenous group; their surfing identities were shaped by a multitude of experiences that differed in relation to factors including (but not limited to) gender, social class, life stage and where they lived. Therefore, it was not surprising that their experiences ranged from those who claim not to have experienced racism, to those for whom racism has defined their surfing experiences.

Racism was part of everyday life for most of my interviewees, particularly when growing up, and surfing spaces were not immune, as many graphically recounted:

> But you know we experienced racism everywhere, so you know I live in the inner city of Los Angeles, it's a black community in which all my life I've experienced some sorts of racism, and at the beach, I've experienced quite a lot.
>
> (Michael)

> In the sixties and the seventies it was really difficult in [place]. I didn't like to go there because I felt very uncomfortable. People ignored you, they didn't talk to you, they stared at you, they threw things at you, they slit your tyres, they wrote with wax on your car, they keyed your car and scratched names, you know.... Names like 'niggers go home' and things like that, with regularity. So it was really an uncomfortable situation. [...] I got hassled out of [place] from the greasers. They would mess with the surfers, but they really messed with *me like a black person surfing*, oh my gosh! So, sometimes I'd have to stay on the water till after they left because if I come in they will throw rocks and beat me up. So it's pretty, very racist.
>
> (Stevie)

Stevie recounted that one way to cope and 'stay safe' was to try not to surf alone, but to travel with small groups of (predominantly) black friends. He said, 'We either were ignored or we were yelled at, but we could stand firm.'

The conflict between surfers seeking to navigate space in the 'line up' and the aggressive treatment of 'outsiders' – termed localism – is well-documented (e.g. Evers, 2008; Ford and Brown, 2006; Olivier, 2010; Scheibel, 1995; Waitt, 2008; and Ch. 4). It can usefully be thought of as a spatialised form of cultural politics which, while seemingly targeting geographically defined 'outsiders' to that beach break, also extends to anyone who is *different* – including those racialised as non-white (Waitt, 2008).[26] Jennifer admitted she often felt fearful, and at times fear stopped her surfing altogether: 'There were no black people surfing at [surf break]. I would drive up to [place] to sit and watch because I was too afraid to join in.' The 'stare' or 'gaze' operates to make minority ethnic individuals unwelcome or 'out of place' (see Puwar, 2004) and is significant in their 'surveillance' (Burdsey, 2013). Carrington (2002: 277) argues that racialised bodies 'can become subject to a panoptic form of white governmentality' that seeks to oversee, control and regulate the behaviour of black people and is underpinned by the constant threat of racial harassment and violence. As Michael recounted: 'When you're the only black person sitting out there, you know it. And the general vibe in the water sometimes became tense. The staring and the twisted facial expressions sometimes gave way to a slur or negative comment.' While there was a broad recognition that such racist harassment was much less pre-valent and culturally ingrained than it was in the 1960s, racism nonetheless con-tinued to exist, often taking more subtle forms. As Burdsey (2011c: 268) outlines, drawing on Bonilla-Silva's (2006) influential work on the concept of 'colorblind racism', there has been a shift to more subtle form of racism such as *racial micro aggressions*. These are 'brief, everyday exchanges' evident in 'ges-tures, looks, or tones' (Burdsey, 2011c: 268). While surfers who had been the recipients of physical abuse were in the minority, most had experienced or wit-nessed verbal racism in some form, or a particular look or stare. As Alicia claimed, 'I have never been aggressively negatively approached. For the most part you are *looked at* – people *stare* at you.' Alicia believed the stares were benevolent: 'It's just odd, not something that is common, they don't know how to place me and I understand that and accept it' (Alicia). The effectiveness of these micro aggressions is their often 'subtle and unconscious character' and their 'accumulation over a period of time', which can have detrimental con-sequences (Burdsey, 2011a: 268). Contemporary types of racism are often char-acterised by the 'absence of any overt reference to "race" or hierarchy', what Balibar calls 'a racism without races' (1991, cited in Burdsey, 2004a: 287).

The spatialisation of racism

Nonetheless, experiences of racism and exclusion differed widely not only between individuals but also across particular surf spaces and beaches, often depending on the histories of their constituent communities. As discussed in Chapter 7, Santa Monica beach, and the Inkwell specifically, remained popular surfing venues among my interviewees because attitudes were 'more liberated':

> When I got there it wasn't known to be a black place, but it was certainly a place where everything could go. And I never ever experienced any negative comments, any overt racist activities, never any fighting or problem at the Inkwell. Maybe it's because of its tradition, because the heritage from which it came didn't allow it to have that kind of vibe.
>
> (Michael)

Inkwell Beach remains popular with black beachgoers; for example, it has 'black-staffed beach clean-ups', and it is the venue chosen for ' inner-city youth surf camps' (Williams, 2007). As Williams writes, 'The ropes of separation are long gone, but the spirit of our ancestors still exists' (ibid.). The adjacent beach suburb, Venice Beach, has long been viewed as a non-conformist 'hip beach' with a larger ethnic minority community than most LA beaches.[27] Despite recent gentrification, it has retained its openness.

In contrast, beaches in the wealthiest, white, conservative communities were the ones where most prejudice and racism was experienced. Stevie discussed the gentrification of Oakwood and how, for 'a lot of brothers', it was no longer a popular surfing venue. Huntington Beach (located south of LA in wealthy

Orange County) was considered the 'capital of US surfing' (Michael) and was the venue for many of the major surf contests and championships. It was considered to have had a racist culture, particularly in the 1960s. Michael recounted how some of his black friends who favoured 'confrontation', to 'vent their anger', would go to Huntington Beach, knowing that surfing there was bound to provoke 'a fight':[28]

> The real confrontation occurred when we rode as an all black or predominantly black surf crew in our cars. The white Orange County surfers seemed to be more threatened and our black crew felt more rebellious. There was one white surfer who commonly went with us. On quite a few occasions locals would ask him if he was some kind of nigger lover. We became an easy target, but in a larger group we were absolutely unwilling to submit.

These experiences are unlikely to be unique to surfers in California, or throughout the USA. One interviewee described their experiences visiting and living in Hawaii, describing the 'tension between blacks [African Americans] and the locals [Polynesian Hawaiians]' that existed. She outlined that racism towards African Americans was prevalent on the beach and in the water.

The surfing brotherhood, 'race' and belonging: denying racism, externalising race

While angry at those who perpetuated the 'lily-white myth' – namely the surf media and industry (see Ch. 7) – and despite having experienced racist incidents, Michael argued that surfers themselves were more enlightened than most beach users. He saw the values of surf culture as inclusive not excluding: 'Generally the reaction was great. Because surfers I think are enlightened people.' As outlined in Chapter 7, this vision was perpetuated in the popular literature on surfing, emphasising the cosmopolitan inclusive values of their cultures, parenthesising 'race' (Wheaton, 2009b).[29]

Michael was not alone in holding the belief, as well as *desire*, that the surfing brotherhood was inclusive of all ethnic backgrounds. Stevie connected surfing's inclusivity to the culture's 'non-conformist', 'counter-cultural values' (see Lawler, 2011), emphasising links with social movements, including the hippy movement and African movements. He outlined how surfing in the 1960s had 'a sense of communalism' and an openness to difference:

> Surfing in those days, coming out of the sixties, was very non-conformist. So, you could go to beaches and say 'can I use your surfboard?' 'Sure use my surfboard, go and play around in the water.' They don't do that at all now, but that was very common.

Stevie later fell in with a surfing crowd in which, despite being the only non-white surfer, he was soon 'one of the group'. Josh, an elite and life-long surfer in his thirties, claimed not to have experienced *any* racism when surfing, or really even thought about 'race', suggesting that, if anything, black surfers were generally seen as 'cool':

> I've never experienced racism while surfing. Sure, I've had clashes with people in the water but it had nothing to do with my skin colour [...]. Tell you the truth I don't think about skin colour while I'm in the water. I have my focus on getting another wave and thinking about what I'm going to do on it. Maybe if I'm in the water with other black surfers I notice colour but I tell myself that it's nice to see that they discovered surfing.

As Burdsey's research also illustrates, (sporting) racism is not universally present (or absent) but 'operates in complex, covert and frequently ambiguous ways, fluctuating contextually and temporally' (2004a: 288). Yet as his (2004a, 2011c) discussion of racism in professional sports outlines, it is also the case that participants often do not *believe* they have been the recipient of racism, or do not *recognise* racism. In his exploration of British Asian professional footballers, Burdsey discusses that, despite the unequivocal evidence that 'issues relating to "race" evidently contribute to the under-representation of British Asians in English professional football', denying racism was prevalent among players (2004a: 286).[30] More recently, Burdsey (2011c: 275) outlines how 'color-blind ideology' (Bonilla-Silva, 2006) was reproduced by black as well as white groups. He argues 'color-blind ideology is so entrenched in Western sport that minority ethic participants can also enforce its interpretive framework' (Burdsey, 2011c: 275). A range of 'mitigation strategies' exists whereby individuals seek to 'simultaneously downplay or deny incidents of racism while trying to exonerate those accused of engaging in such acts' (ibid.: 268).

Many of the narratives of surfers were also contradictory; their accounts gave numerous examples of ways they were marked as *different* (looks, stares, etc.) and described exclusion or racism instigated by *surfers* (as detailed above). Yet most did not want to see surfers as 'the problem'. Their belief in the inclusivity of the surfing brotherhood and subcultural status made it hard for black participants to hold white surfers accountable. As Puwar (2004: 137) highlights, in many spheres 'the systematic fantasy of imagined inclusiveness makes it difficult to see racism' and to confront the fact that racism exists. Michael blamed those (non-surfers) who lived in middle-class white beach communities:

> See, because a very small percentage of the people that are at the beach are surfers, those are the people that could come from anywhere. The people that dwell there, those people are not necessarily enlightened, and they are not necessarily exposed to a variety of things, one of which is black surfers. And they feel entitled to the ocean already, believing that it's theirs and they could fence it. [...] I mean they don't want white surfers in their water. So they were much more likely to, you know, display racism.

Michael recognised that he did not *want* surfers to be the problem. This is not surprising as, having worked hard to become a surfer and started to see himself as 'surfer', he needed, at least discursively, to disavow surf culture as being excluding or racist. In subsequent conversations, I discussed this contradiction with him and he conceded that the racism he experienced at the beach came from both surfers and non-surfers, although the latter was more prevalent: 'Yes, I do find it difficult to talk badly about anyone or anything that I identify myself with [...] I think you're right about me not wanting to see surfers in that light.' Alicia also acknowledged that a range of views was held by white surfers, from 'respect just for being a surfer, and being good at what I do' to 'exotified, just because you have a different skin colour' (see below). Yet she believed that, once she had developed a level of involvement and commitment to be considered a 'real' surfer, she gained insider status and respect:

> If you get to the level in which you can truly say you *are a surfer*, that level of commitment to the ocean, then you see like-minded people who are doing the same. There are plenty of surfers who surf on the weekend, or only in the summer [...] they get a level of that.[31] But if you get past that threshold, other surfers who are at the same place, some sort of positive energy and connection that's really not about colour or gender or anything, it's just about acknowledging that we are people who love the ocean; and how lucky we are to be able to get to that point. And I just feel very lucky, like being in on a secret, a nirvana with no connection to people, just water.
>
> (Alicia)

As Puwar (2004) discusses, in the process of 'becoming an insider', individuals racialised as non-white develop what Bourdieu (2001: 56) calls a *feel for the game*. This is an 'embodied form of knowledge and skills that operates beneath the level of conscious discourse' and that arises from achieving a level of 'synchrony between their habitus, its social trajectory and the institutional space' (Puwar, 2004: 127) – or here, as Alicia outlines – the field of surfing. As Alicia argued, there is 'unspoken understanding' about being a 'real surfer'. Moreover, implicit in the *feel for the game* is a 'denial of the body', a narrative that 'prides itself on being based on neutral standards that apply across the board to everybody' (ibid.: 132). Thus by describing surfing as a spiritual activity, about connecting to water/nature and not 'bodies', she was able to negate the importance of the visible embodiment of gender and race. As Alicia put it, 'a community was open to me by my commitment to surfing'. This belief that commitment to the surfing *activity* superseded other factors was widespread (see also Comer, 2004). The association between the 'complicity of habitus and field and social capital' that these surfers had achieved through their commitment to surfing has 'immense implications for the opportunities that are made available' (Puwar, 2004: 129). Certainly, in some spaces and contexts, these surfers were able to 'feel at home', become, as Puwar terms it, 'familiar strangers' who have, in Bourdieu's terminology, gained 'ontological complicity' (ibid.). The beach was described as a different and liminal space; as Michael put it, kind of like a 'foreign country' outside of societies and parental control:

> surfing is an exclusive thing, it takes part in the time of day when other people are asleep or doing something else, and we could go and just be, and enjoy and do that ... from six in the morning to you know eleven in the morning ... when we were surfing we were just, you know, we were brothers. [...] And so we all got to just go and be, and hang, and it didn't matter.
>
> (Michael)

When surfing was referred to as a retreat from the problem of wider society, it was not just to white exclusion, but to the ostracisation the surfers had experienced in their (black) community. Some of them had experienced exclusion in the black communities where they lived, ranging from hostility to being called a variety of abusive names, such as 'white boy wannabes', 'Uncle Toms' and 'Oreo cookie'. As Michael reflexively illustrated, he did not fit in with the 'traditional white surf community' or 'here in the black community' but was 'in limbo, in no-man's lands'. A black female surfer who had successfully become one of the elite female surfers in the USA claimed she was 'welcomed with open arms' by the elite surfing fraternity, but experienced 'real issues' with her own (black) community. Thus, as Puwar discusses, the idea of insider and outsider is fluid and complex, also recognising that racialised minorities do 'become, in significant ways, insiders' (2004: 119).

While my analysis has revealed some shared experiences for male and female African-American surfers, it is important to recognise and underline the differences between race and gender, and that an 'analysis that is appropriate for one must not be moved automatically across to the other' (Puwar, 2004: 10). Thus, I briefly highlight some of the specific issues for female black surfers negotiating insider status.

Surfing sisters

Despite claims of a female surfing athletic revolution (Comer, 2010; see also Ch. 4), particularly at the more elite levels surfing remains male-dominated, and black female surfers are a very small minority: 'We could probably count the number of good black female surfers on two hands, and most of us are well over twenty-five years. I think that qualifies us as a rare breed and makes us feel quite *different*' (Natalia). Like many other female surfers, the four female black surfers I spoke to tended to surf predominantly with men, or in mixed sex groups. Black male surfers were positioned by these women as allies, as part of 'their family'. As Alicia recognised, she had benefited from the strides made by earlier black male surfing advocates, making her feel like she was 'part of something larger'. Yet, as Alicia discussed at some length, there were also differences being a black surfing woman. Aspects of their experiences were marked by the same issues experienced by other white female sportswomen, such as objectification and sexualisation.[32] Alicia found that her gender difference, rather than racial difference, provided the greatest challenges 'she had to overcome' when negotiating access to surfing spaces, recognising that 'not everyone wants you out there' (see also Evers, 2009):

> That I was the only female going out there. [...] You want to surf at this spot, you see all males in wetsuits. [...] As a female you had to pump yourself up to get out there not knowing what kind of reaction nor response you are going to have. So initially I was doing that. You have to prove yourself a bit more. At the premier surf spots you need to show what you have.

Gradually over time she became more aware of being one of only a handful of African-American women and the reactions that she provoked, from 'stares' to 'respect', acknowledging that it was often hard to know why she was getting 'a look'. While overt racism was not something she had experienced, the response was generally 'more sexual in nature', which (as she recognised) was nonetheless tied to broader 'stereotypes of black women over history being exotified'. Natalia also said she felt 'different' as a female black surfer and that objectification was an issue: 'In my experience, it seems many white male surfers are caught clumsily between being awed and fascinated by us and seeing us as something to flirt with or conquer' (Natalia). The ways in which these women were made to feel different, as space invaders, were as Alicia explained, often subtle. For example, it was evident in the ways she was spoken to 'slightly differently', or in the ways 'language gets shifted' when she surfed alongside [white] men:

> White males attempt to try to identify with me. [they] 'code switch' and try to speak with an African-American slang. I understand that as their attempt to acknowledge my surfing, but because I am black they seem to be compelled to say 'hey girl' or 'you go girl' [laughs] where normally that wouldn't happen for white female surfers or other surfers, they use this weird language. I understand it is an attempt to acknowledge that I am surfing, my gender, my race, and to say I am doing a good job surfing, but it's just this one little twang [way of speaking] that gets added to it that wouldn't happen if I wasn't black.

As Carrington discusses, being black in a particular white space can provoke intrigue and fascination as well as surveillance. He argues that, while this 'new fact of blackness' appears to be more tolerant, it is nonetheless a 'moment of post/colonial racism, a double bind. Of intrigue and interest and objectification and racialised inscription all at once' (Carrington, 2009: 176). Blackness is still conditional and measured in relation to a narrowly prescribed set of roles and an 'imagined community' from which the black surfer is still, at least partially, excluded. Yet, as the final section explores, black surfers found various ways to negotiate their insider identity and difference in these surfing spaces.

Black surfing brothers ... and sisters

Brothers and sisters this is beautiful! Live your dreams no matter what. After 20 years of denying it, I am a surfer and now know I am a BSB [Black surfing brother] soon to pay my dues of course. I took a lesson in Hawaii last summer and I have not missed a week on the waves. Racism when I was a kid kept me away but nothing stops me now. Anyone surf in Orange County? I surf long board at Seal Beach north of the pier. I am hard to miss (i.e. the only BSB).

(Posting on Black Surfing Association online, 2008)

Being a surfer and being black has always been a dilemma. In the minds of most it is a contradiction, it just can't be possible, and yet here we are.

(Michael)

Insider identity and difference in the surfing space was negotiated in a range of ways. For some, assimilation was a strategy, adopting the subcultural styles of white surfers, such as lifestyle, clothing and dyeing their hair to achieve the sun-bleached look that characterises white surf style. 'A lot of us in the USA die our locks to try and fit in somehow' (Jennifer). Bajan windsurfer Talma described how his look – the sun-bleached hair – helped him to fit into European surf culture (see Ch. 7), and I observed many more black Caribbean and black Hispanic surfers in the Caribbean (Barbados and Dominican Republic) with (natural or chemically produced) 'blonde' streaks. Michael, however, saw black style influencing white surf culture, suggesting that in the 1960s many blacks had joined the 'surfing-craze' and became 'colourful personalities' within the newly developing surf culture, contributing 'greatly in creating the style that surfing would later become' (Jude).

However, not all black surfers want to assimilate; some wanted to be accepted as black surfers, to have the subjectivity of the black surfer and their differences recognised and validated by the dominant white culture. As Michael argued, '*we* are different, different than surfers'. He found, being 'the black surfer' was an uncomfortable subjectivity, personally and culturally: 'We can't fit in the white surf culture. And there is no black surf culture.' The couplet black/surfer embraced two seemingly incompatible subject positions. Discussing the ways in which black bodies are represented in the travelogue, Jennifer's narrative (from Ch. 7) also highlighted the discursive incompatibility of the black surfer in surf media:

Because what you're saying is *you're* going into these third world countries, *we* are still uncivilised. *You* came, you're going to teach us how to surf! You going to tell me that no kid had ever picked up a piece of birch tree or whatever wood they got, or whatever plate they got, and went out and rode waves by themselves. It just, absolutely it amazes me to think that we are so, and I'm going to say United States because I don't see it so much more in other places as *we* feel like we have to find everything. *Our* white culture has to discover everything.... *You* don't need to discover us; *we've* already been here.

Jennifer's shifting use of *us* and *we* in this narrative illustrates her own shifting diasporic black identity.[33] Early in the narrative (lines 1–2), she identifies with the 'uncivilised black natives' being taught to surf by the USA/white surfer ('*you*'); later, however, she appears to identify with the USA surf culture (use of *our* and *we* in the final few lines). For Michael, rather than the surfer subjectivity providing an oppositional space, it was unsettling for his sense of self, making him question if he wasn't really a surfer, or really black:

so all my life people just tell me 'blacks don't surf'. When I say it, I say that's crazy, then one or two things. If blacks don't surf, then what I've been doing for the last forty five years isn't surfing and, you know, and I kind of fancy myself as being able to surf pretty good. Either that what I've been spending all this time my whole life doing isn't surfing or, which is even crazier, I'm not black! So which is it?

(Michael)

However, over time Michael eventually embraced his identity as black surfer, seeing it not as a marker of difference and exclusion, but as a unique cultural identity:

I was offended that people were always identifying me by race. I was always a black surfer, you know, I always wanted to be *a surfer*, I never wanted to be a *black surfer*. And it was uncomfortable because I didn't want to be that, until I, I recognised that, you know, there's no way I'm going to change that. That's really who it is that I am. It was me that was resisting being that, and once I embraced it, once I accepted it, once I realised, you know what, that's something special. It's not a bad thing.

For Jennifer, seeing a photo of a black surfer in *Ebony* magazine was a foundational moment, allowing her to 'embrace it for' herself: 'I said "I can be that".'

Sporting masculinity differs across contexts, and intersects with race, age, sexuality, place and ethnicity (Wheaton, 2004b; Waitt, 2008). The black surfer subjectivity, as understood by many of these African-American surfers, differed in some ways from other (dominant white) surfing identities. It appeared to be more inclusive, and was less competitive, aggressive and territorial than researchers have described among groups of white male surfers in Australia (Waitt, 2008; Evers, 2009), and as has been documented in the global surf media.[34] Whereas dominant white surf culture denigrated body boarding (see Ch. 4), these men saw it as a valid or 'authentic' form of wave riding: 'I take the Hawaiian philosophy – If you ride a wave you're a surfer. Whether you ride a wave with your body, or get a little boogie board' (Stevie). They predominantly described themselves as 'soul surfers', a surfer identity that originated in the 1960s and is still associated with a more relaxed and anti-competitive ethos (Booth, 1994):[35] 'I'm like a sort of soul surfer, you know, I'm into the sport and the communal character of the sport. I don't even look at it as sport, almost like a semi-lifestyle as opposed to a sport' (Stevie). Some of these differences were born out of the difficulties these individuals had to overcome, and their continued minority situation. As Michael suggested, their unique experiences gave them 'something that's special', 'we carry a little greater gratitude'. In rejecting stereotypes and thinking and living differently from most white surfers, 'black surfers bring forth an expanded image of self and black culture' (Michael, email correspondence). These ways of being a black surfer can usefully be examined using Foucault's theory of the *technology of the self* (Foucault, 1988), which emerged from Foucault's conceptualisation of the ways in which individuals are located within power relations. Foucault's concepts have gained popularity, particularly among sports feminists, for understanding how individuals are actively engaged in processes of producing their own subjectivities, particularly those that challenge dominant discourses (Markula, 2003; Markula and Pringle, 2006; see also Ch. 4). *Technologies of the self* is a process, and engagement in it:

> permit[s] individuals to effect by their own means or with the help of others a certain number of operations on their own bodies and souls, thoughts, conduct, and a way of being, so as to transform themselves to attain a certain state of happiness, purity, wisdom, perfection, or immorality.
>
> (Foucault, 1988: 18, cited in Markula and Pringle, 2006: 139)

While gender subjectivity, not race, has been the main focus of empirical study, as a theoretical position, technologies of the self encourages the analyst to explore how individuals occupy shifting positions of power and resistance, some of which offer spaces that potentially disrupt, transform and re-work traditional constructs of race and of white surfing identity. For Alicia, the realisation of being different, a minority (black and female), gradually 'came into play', but was subsumed by her 'own self of happiness', which, she argued, allowed her to transcend her status:

> Over the years you start to make connections between surfing and other things in life, it didn't really occur to me initially about issues of black and white when I began to surf, what occurred to me was I want to be happy and this makes me happy. I loved it. Not connected to anyone or anything, just that feeling. [...] And all that stuff doesn't matter when you are out there trying to catch a wave. That's the stuff you talk about or try to reflect on when you are on land. The purpose of surfing has nothing to do with that.

As Foucault would suggest, however, subjectivity is never final but rather is something continually made and re-made, a process of 'becoming' rather than a finished product. These surfers' selves were clearly crafted at the intersection of multiple, and contradictory, discourses.

Coda

For young people who have, from their childhood, faced discrimination and racism on a daily basis (as manifest in some participants' narratives), to choose such a challenging leisure activity, involving a lifestyle where they would be a minority, a 'space invader' who was excluded by black peers, and vulnerable to white racism, is quite a remarkable path to take. It is, therefore, not surprising that their narratives are riddled with contradictions. However, despite the desire to deny racism, it is undeniable that for these individuals their surfing experience provided a space of relative freedom; as Alicia put it, 'Through surfing I came to realise Bob Marley's lyrics "Heaven is here on Earth"' (Alicia). And for Josh, 'My love of surfing outweighed the negative feelings I had when I was told I was trying to be white.'

Nonetheless, the anger felt by some I spoke to is also a clear thread running through these narratives.[36] Michael was being told continually 'surfing is a white thing'. Jennifer discussed how she saw surfing as having been 'robbed' from 'us', the black community, in the early twentieth century: 'They have taken over what was once, originally, ours' (Jennifer). People articulate their anger in different ways and have a range of strategies for addressing the underlying issues. Some vented their frustration through confrontation. Michael recounted how some of his friends went to beaches where they had experienced racist taunts or were excluded, 'looking for a fight', recognising that 'everyone's got their own take on it, it's just a different way':

> Some of my friends really like to go down there (Orange County) because they like to fight, they want a confrontation. They are looking for somebody to say something, or do something, because they want to stand up. You know, you get so angry about this thing being, you know being put on you, and feeling that, you know, I deserve everything that everybody else has. And when that happens, you get angry and want to stand up. I wasn't one that liked to fight, but those that did, you know, didn't mind going in and standing their own ground. [...] We surfed to experience the freedom and in a group we were sometimes willing to fight for that freedom. It wasn't ideal, but it was all we had, and we were grateful for that.

But for others, the anger was channelled into wanting to *change* the opportunities and experiences of the black surfer, and the culture and representation of surfing. In Chapter 9, I discuss the ways in which, for some black surfers, surfing became an arena through which to confront, contest and attempt to change their individual and collective exclusion and marginality.

9 Challenging exclusion

The Black Surfing Association

Sport has long been seen as a fertile site for political protests against social injustice, including racial exclusion (Carrington and McDonald, 2001b: 416). John Carlos's and Tommie Smith's Black Power salute at the 1968 Mexico Olympic Games remains one of the most prominent examples. In contrast, contemporary black athletes have been criticised for their lack of engagement with race-related activism: '[Since] Harry Edwards's mobilization of efforts towards the end of the Civil Rights Movement in the late 1960s, there have been very few instances of black male athletic activism' (Agyemang *et al.*, 2010: 421). In this chapter, I discuss the ways in which, for some black surfers, surfing has become a politicised arena through which to confront, contest and attempt to change their individual and collective exclusion and marginality. The main collective vehicle for most of my interviewees was the Black Surfing Association (BSA). I outline the formation of the BSA, its aims and objectives, describing what the organisation does and the activities it promotes. Nonetheless, as Carrington advocates, our examinations of such examples of sporting resistance need to be rooted in theoretical questions about their wider impact (Carrington, 2010). Here I explore the reasons why surfing, specifically, was considered an important *political* sphere, also asking what kind of politics was involved, and how individuals' political visions differed. I then assess some of the consequences of their politics for instigating broader social change. I explore the impact of sporting resistance, asking if they were solely 'symbolic gestures or had a wider structural impact on contemporary racial formations and forms of contemporary racism (ibid.: 3).

Introducing the Black Surfing Association

The Black Surfing Association (BSA), in its current configuration, was founded in 1975 (BSA website),[1] although the official history of the organisation's formation is somewhat contested. One interviewee claimed that 'the actual beginning' of the 'Black surfing movement' was in San Diego during the civil rights movement, and by the mid 1960s there were groups of black surfers along the California coast calling themselves BSA.[2] This claim was corroborated by a posting on the BSA website (2009):

The first BSA was created in San Diego, CA in 1966. Just ask Harold Burt, Dana Point, CA; Dr Albert Richardson, Dr Elsworth Pryor, or attorney Diane Ritchey in San Diego. We rode long boards at all the breaks in the area.

The official history of the contemporary Los Angeles-based BSA as documented in the association's web pages, and as recounted by those I spoke to who were involved in its formation,[3] revolved around Tony Corley's 'desire to find, meet, and befriend some of his own surf Brotha's who also sought the oceanic pleasures of the surfing lifestyle'. He therefore sent a letter to *Surfer* Magazine in 1973, subsequently published as a *letter to the editor* in the 1974 January issue:

> The first answer to Tony's plea was delivered to his mail box in Port Hueneme, California, just weeks after the magazine issue reached the newsstands. Following that first letter, the second letter was a racist-hate threat, which he initially thought was a 'joke' from an unmet Black Surfing brother (BSB). The letters continued to trickle in for months, even years after that issue publication. [...] As a result of this initial reaching out, long standing friendships have been established and, of course, the BLACK SURFING ASSOCIATION.
>
> (Corley, n.d.)

Over the past eight years, the association has become more organised and proactive, and despite the focus in California, supporters and some members come from much further afield, including from outside the USA (as evidenced by web pages, guest book, etc.). My focus here is the Southern California Chapter, which appeared to be the hub.

The aims of the association were UMOJA, meaning 'Unity' or 'Together As One'. The objectives, as stated in its lengthy mission statement, were wide-ranging. Some aims, such as promoting athleticism, helping 'to implement aquatic skills' and 'ecological awareness and activism', reflected dominant (white) surfing values (e.g. Wheaton, 2007b). Others were specific to 'wave-riding in the Black communities' so as to promote, educate and implement change:

> To expose and encourage people of African ancestry to witness, experience, participate and enjoy the ancient oceanic activity of surfing throughout the oceans and seas of the world. [...] Ultimately, it is the BSA's goal to expose and advance the sport and activities of wave-riding in the black communities while generating well-being, harmony, and heightened awareness amongst surfing individuals, clubs, organizations, businesses, and related media interest groups. [...] We also encourage and support our members to compete and represent black people and the Black Surfing Association with good sportsmanlike conduct and ethnic ambassatorism.
>
> (BSA website)

Individual members (and presidents) emphasised different aspects of this broad statement; yet for many it was the camaraderie and support they initially sought. For example, Michael wanted:

> to kind of make contact with other people and share experiences [...] Yeah, and then, just to try and develop camaraderie, and to let us know that we weren't alone first, you know, to kind of just touch bases. And then as it grew, and more people started to participate, we decided we wanted to get together more and we wanted to have events, we wanted to come together and share the surfing experience with each other.

And Natalie explains that: 'Challenging stereotypes fits best with how I view the aims of the BSA. Through its existence, surfers (black surfers, in particular) are able to connect, exchange information, create opportunities, and educate each other.' Surfing clubs and associations tend to have fewer regulations and institutional controls than mainstream sports clubs (Ford and Brown, 2005; Wheaton, 2005), so it is not surprising that members of the BSA see it 'not as an organisation' (Michael) but as a relatively 'loose-knit configuration'. Members pay no fees, so there is no budget: 'because we are free. We are people that love freedom and nobody's really buying clubs, regulations and all the laws and that stuff' (Michael). 'This organisation is still growing and taking shape, but I believe it is something truly malleable and not something to become finite' (Natalia). Because of the informal, loose-knit basis of the organisation, and lack of funds, the various activities promoted at any one time appear to be largely dependent on, and reflect the perspectives and political ideologies of, those who are driving activities at that time. As Rick Blocker described in his history of the organisation (www.blacksurfing.com), since the 'seed' planted by Tony Corley, there have been key individuals under whose influence the 'black surfing identity and surfing philosophy' developed in various divergent ways. Rick explained that he set up a website, www.blacksurfing.com, because of his frustration about the inability of the BSA to collectively agree on an activity (such as setting up and paying for a web page):

> At some point in time I just went, 'you know what, I'm going to just do this', [...] everybody started bickering and fighting and arguing on what it was going to be and all that. So what I did was I went like this, 'forget it', OK, this is too important, I'll just do it myself.

Interviewees were cognisant of the differences in their individual visions and thus approaches, and rooted in their own views about 'being political',[4] which at times caused tensions and disagreement. Some black surfers did not support the BSA as an organisation. Harper was a critic,[5] but nonetheless shared many of its objectives, and at times worked alongside the organisation: 'It's more of an individual quest. To me, it hasn't become a unified situation, I wish it would, [...] it's also new, and people are trying to find their place.' In the final section of this chapter, I consider what kind of identity politics the association, or more specifi-cally this loose configuration of individuals, advocated. First, I outline the main activities these surfers were engaged in.

Providing opportunities

> YAY!!! First guestbook message of 2010! I'm really honoured ... I'm not a surfer but I really wanna be. I always thought my race (black) would hold me back ... but the BSA has helped me realize I can surf and be Black!! THANKS.
>
> (Posting on BSA website, 2010)

> I am improving my swimming endurance so that I can begin surfing. I already go kayaking. I had made previous plans for Sept 20, 09 but I will try to make it to your event also. The mere existence of this organization is inspirational.
>
> (Posting on BSA website, 2009)

While the BSA engaged in a range of different activities to address its mission statement, providing various opportunities for members of different black com-munities to get involved in surfing and beach culture was central. However, this was not a liberal drive to increase the numbers of black surfers, but to provide opportunities, to 'open doors':

> It hasn't been my goal to make more black surfers, so to speak. My goal is to give people a positive experience, to let them know that, OK, hey I did that, now if I want to go deep sea diving, or I want to jump out of an aero-plane, or if I want to go climb a mountain, or if I want to run a triathlon, then I can do that. And, when they find the thing that is their individual passion that touches their soul.
>
> (Michael)

Recognising that many members of the black community in California tended not to visit the beach, organised activities, such as kids' surf camps and beach-day outings, often focused on a safe and cheap introduction to the beach, not solely surfing. For example, a poster advertising 'Pan African Beach Days' (Figure 9.1) was subtitled 'Promoting African People using Public Spaces'. While the main image is of an African-American surfer (signified most clearly by his dreadlocks), symbolically, various activities on offer, such as fishing, roll-erskating, skateboarding, cycling, volleyball, a barbecue and fire pit, had for many years all been important aspects of California's white beach culture. Fur-thermore, 'pan-Africanism' was also celebrated with free classes in African dance, drumming and capoeira (a black Brazilian performance/martial art), alongside surfing. Beachgoing, and surfing's place within it, are therefore recon-structed as a hybrid of African diasporic culture and California white beach

Figure 9.1 BSA poster: Pan African Beach Day.

culture, in so doing redefining the surfing space and the identity of the black surfer within it.[6]

Members were also involved with various different projects to enable groups, such as inner-city black youth, who might not otherwise have the opportunity 'to experience the joy of surfing' (e.g. http://legacy.blacksurfing. com/news.htm). Rhonda's company, Inkwell Lifestyle (2005), offered a free 'after school youth programme specializing in action-sport activities', including surfing (Inkwell Lifestyle Brand, 2010). She had 'partnered up with the city's mayoral office' to use school buses to transport children to the beach. They also coordinated 'Giving Back Day', which took individuals from 'a homeless shelter or a battered women's shelter to the beach for a day of relaxation and free surf lessons' (Inkwell Lifestyle Brand, 2010). Laurel was a mentor for *Stoked* mentoring, a youth programme that used 'Action Sport provision' in conjunction with individual mentoring to develop various life skills for 'at-risk and disadvantaged youth'. In Los Angeles, the focus on the *Stoked* programme was the Rampart District of LA, 'home to thousands of immigrants from Central and South America' (Stoked-Mentoring, 2010). While some initiatives were formal projects with funding, many individual supporters showed high levels of personal commitment, offering their time, skills and at times financial resources.

Other activities in which the BSA engaged were reflective of most surfing-based clubs and organisations, such as holding surfing competitions, holding memorial 'paddle outs'[7] after the death of a 'fallen brother', and involvement and support for various environmental organisations, issues and problems, such as beach clean-up days. The online postings on the BSA webpages, mirroring many online surfing forums, focused on the weather conditions and surf sessions; for example, 'Hey Tony, was that some good surf at the rock, yea! Thanks for the leash' (Posting in 2009). Nonetheless, the ways in which these activities were promoted suggested a more inclusive and diverse set of values than those often dominating white surf culture, particularly at the elite end. For example, while a 'BSA Surf Contest'[8] had commercial sponsors and was claimed to be the 'largest Black beach event' ever, it was also characterised as 'more than just a competition', again promoting a broader vision of the surf lifestyle: '500 folks turned out to participate in the fun-filled day which featured a mixture of eclectic cross-cultural elements of urban hip hop, surf, skate and Rasta' (BSA webpages). Highly skilled individuals did aspire to surf in 'mainstream' white competitions. David Lansdowne was cited as one of the few successful competitive black surfers in the 1970s, and was held in high regard. He had continued to develop 'a strong commitment to service' in the black surfing community by 'mentoring the next generation' of black and white surfers[9] (Michael, personal correspondence). One of the surfers I interviewed had competed at regional level and saw his main involvement in BSA as sharing his 'passion' and 'giving advice on how to become a better surfer'.

Black outs: reclaiming space

Reclaiming space, both physical space and virtual or mediated spaces, was a core thread in BSA activities. A *black out* was the name given to an organised day or time when a 'group of black surfers show up together and surf together' (interview), challenging, at least momentarily, the invisibility of black surfers:

> It was an unusual thing because you know especially the surfers in Southern California would see from time to time black surfers in ones and twos, but very rarely would you see a group where there was, you know, twenty black

surfers or thirty black surfers, you know, at a break. So we would do that
and that kind of opened up some eyes.

(Michael)

In some specific cases, legal means were utilised to address exclusion from specific beach spaces, such as the example of Malibu, discussed earlier (Garcia and
Baltodano, 2005). In Asbury Park, a predominantly black community in New
Jersey, surfing had been banned. A legal challenge was made to change the legislation,[10] coordinated by the Surfrider Foundation with support from BSA
members.

For Rhonda, the surfing media were the most visible and influential surfing
spaces in terms of perpetuating what she called the 'lily-white myth'. She saw
herself as a media watch-dog, and was proactive, working to increase the visibility of black surfing and challenging those who perpetuated racist colonial discourses (e.g. Harper, 2010): 'It's kind of like what I do now. It's my expression
of what politically is going on in surfing.' To this end, she wrote blogs and commentaries across a range of media on action sport (such as blackathlete.com),
and used various forms of social media (such as Facebook).[11] She lobbied and
challenged the industry to give black surfing more recognition:

> I'm coming asking questions why. And I'm making a case for ourselves.
> I'm saying we were here. Where were you, for us? Where are you now for
> us, and why fifty years later are we still not represented in the surf industry?

While Rhonda angrily recounted some failures, she claimed nonetheless that the
surf industry was beginning slowly to respond. Her passionate and often con-
frontational style conveyed the importance she attributed to the politics of race
in surfing. For example, in response to an article about a Jamaican surfer titled
'Super Breed Descends' (posted on www.stabmag.com[12]), she wrote:

> I can only think how sad it is that in the year of Obama that people still
> think that it is 'ok' to demean and defame the reputation of a black surfer.
> The article is a ridiculous stab at humour. I personally didn't find it funny or
> entertaining. What I did find is exactly what I had known all along, racism
> in the surf industry is a reality. [...] The color line has been drawn, but we
> can rise above ignorance and become victorious in our progression of the
> sport. [...] This is a new day, a new era and definitely a new attitude in the
> world's view on race relations. *Stab Magazine* and the rest had better play
> catch-up quick. Like it or not, we shall not be moved again.
>
> (Harper, 2010)

While Rhonda saw the white media and industry needing 'education', she was
extremely critical of, and indeed puzzled by, other people of colour in positions
of power who did not share a commitment for change. She singled out a prominent television extreme-sport reporter, who she claimed had not made attempts

to challenge inequality and promote black surfers: 'I mean, he knows everybody and I don't understand where the disconnect came from.'[13]

It was not just Rhonda who recognised the cultural and economic power of the surf industry and media, and how commercial imperatives underpinning the discursive construction of surfing had contributed to the stereotyping and erasure of black surfing bodies. BSA members actively promoted black surfing activities using various media. Rick Blocker used his website, www.blacksurfing.com,[14] to promote the activities of the BSA, and he posted various globally based news stories about black surfing. He set it up 'to spread the word, to get a larger audience, try to carry the message, try to be a hub'. Another member made films which she described as 'a new kind of surf film, shorter, artsy, featuring black surfers ... that paid homage to the humour and beauty of surfing', challenging stereotypes about surfing culture and identity.[15]

Reclaiming surfing histories

It is claimed that contemporary black athletes are not interested in 'the history of the black athlete' and their political struggles: 'Today's black athlete is very different. [...] not many couldn't tell you much. They don't find that history relevant to their world' (Harry Edwards, cited in Agyemang *et al.*, 2010: 421). In contrast, the importance of reclaiming and publicising black surfing history was widely talked about. For example, one person wrote on the BSA website: 'I am appreciative of the African American history in surfing. My membership in the BSA is sure to be both enriching and experiential. Perhaps we can make waves in the Midwest!' (BSA website, 2009). Most black surfers I interviewed made some attempt to discuss the historical roots of surfing in Africa, as well as detailing the histories of African American surfers of the 1950s and 1960s (Williams, 2007).

A commemorative plaque at Santa Monica beach recognising 'the section of beach known as the "Ink Well" and the first African-American surfer, Nicolas Gabaldon' (Jefferson, 2009: 156) was approved by the City of Santa Monica in 2008, due to 'sustained pressure from members of the black surfing community', including BSA members (7 February 2008).[16] The plaque (Figure 9.2) states:

'THE INKWELL'
A Place of Celebration and Pain

The beach near this site between Bay and Bicknell Streets, known by some as 'the Inkwell', was an important gathering place for African Americans long after racial restrictions on public beaches were abandoned in 1927.

African American groups from Santa Monica, Venice, and Los Angeles, as early as the 1920s to the end of the Jim Crow era in the 1950s, preferred

Figure 9.2 The Inkwell plaque.

> to enjoy the sun and surf here because they encountered less racial harass-
> ment than at other Southland beaches.

> In the 1940s, Nick Gabaldon, a Santa Monica High School student and the
> first documented black surfer, taught himself how to surf here.

Jefferson, who wrote the plaque, argues she was 'reclaiming a forgotten history
of beach as leisure space for "African American Angelenos"' (2009: 158). Few
knew of the existence of the Inkwell, nor its history.[17] For Jefferson, the Inkwell
plaque was part of a wider project to document and make public other important
but unmarked and unknown African-American buildings, sites and places (ibid.:
58).[18] Gabaldon, as noted earlier, held particular significance for African-
American surfers, and for Jefferson, his recognition on the plaque 'tells an
American pioneer[19] story about African-Americans who, in spite of challenges,
took agency to participate in the fruits of California' (ibid.: 185). For others,
including Rhonda and Rick, incorporating the histories of black surfing in California was part of the political project, and both were actively publicising these
histories, via websites, books and talks.[20] Rhonda, however, saw Gabaldon's
importance as a black role model, someone who could be identified with:

So I wanted to use him as a catalyst to say here's a hero that's of mixed cultures [...] here's a hero, here's somebody substantial that you can look up to and mould your life, and see how he gave his life for something that he loved.

These histories were also beginning to filter into mainstream surfing spaces, such as an article in *The Surfer's Journal* on Gabaldon (*Surfer's Journal*, 2005) and documentaries (e.g. *Whitewash*[21] and *Soul on a Wave*[22]) that either explored some of the myths about surfing and race or focused on the BSA itself.

I now turn to a more detailed discussion of the ways in which the BSA's activities can be seen to be political. I start with an examination of the politics of the organisation itself and the ways in which claims to recognition of a cultural identity – being black – have shaped their individual and collective political visions.

Identity politics: 'being black'

The identity politics that underpins groups like the BSA, where membership is based on, or linked to, one (essentialised) aspect of identity or standpoint epistemology, has its critics. These debates have been well-rehearsed, particularly in the context of the various identity-based social movements that emerged in the 1960s and 1970s (see Wheaton, 2008a). Their 'intellectual and moral relativism' is problematised and their effectiveness is questioned, seeing them as 'insiderist', defending 'localized, particularistic and overly-narrow subjectivities' (Carrington, 2007: 55). In a provocative polemic, Carrington (ibid.: 50) reviews these debates, challenging the belief that identity politics has gone too far, reading 'politics into every aspect of knowledge production', usually at the expense of 'materialist concerns' (ibid.: 49). Broadly, I share Carrington's position, also arguing that in contrast to this *post*-identity position, identity is often a necessary 'precondition', but not substitute (cf. Gilroy, 2006: 238) 'for any effective oppositional politics' (Carrington, 2007: 49). That is, 'identity needs to be understood as a strategic intervention by marginalized communities for cultural, political and economic *recognition*' (ibid.: 52). Here I make some observations about the nature of 'being black' in the context of the BSA – how questions about African-American diasporic identities framed their political vision, related to questions about inclusion and exclusion.

The active members of the BSA at the organisational level were predominantly, but not exclusively, African-American men and women: 'Anybody can come, but the meetings I go to are pretty much 100% black folks. Because you know there are so many other white surfing associations' (Michael). While the BSA mission statement described the organisation as for 'people of African ancestry', it also discussed being for 'black communities'. These statements were interpreted differently by those I interviewed at the core of the organisation. Stevie felt their focus should be the African diaspora, 'people of African ancestry'. He argued that, despite the wide range of different backgrounds and 'ideological points of view' in the black community, ranging from his 'militant view' to non-political members, 'there's this notion of camaraderie because we're black, black in colour, of African ancestry' (Stevie).

Other members eager to promote the organisation's inclusivity argued for a broader understanding of blackness, a kind of 'strategic essentialism' that embraces all 'people of colour' (Carrington, 2007: 55). For example, Nicholas Gabaldon, a 'Black-Mexican', was often held up as *the* black surfing hero'. Michael argued that the term 'black African descent' is an inclusive idea that 'transcends into everything':

> Not black African, but black African *in origin*, but black African in descent, and that is what it was originally set up as. But black African descent transcends into everything, and that being the case and because you know some of us believe that man having originated in Africa, probably *all of us are really black*. We are all something, we are all the same, but we call it black because we are, and so that includes everybody, and so the organisation *could* embrace *everybody*.
>
> (Michael, emphasis added)

Natalia also claimed it embraced 'all ethnicities': 'Black surfers doesn't segregate itself from anybody, anybody can come to the meetings, white people come, Asians come.' Jennifer, however, was uncomfortable with the label 'black': 'I don't feel like I need to necessarily say black, because it gives off an elitist kind of connotation for me.'[23] Nonetheless, other postings on the BSA forum suggest it was not only African Americans who supported the organisation; for example, one respondent identified himself as 'a Mexican Jew' (14 July 2009). Alicia described the BSA as an 'umbrella' where 'anything can happen or is possible': 'It brought us together, but the *us* is a huge diaspora of black folks, that includes not just African Americans; and not just black people but within that, various views' (Alicia).

Gender politics in the organisation

In contrast, the gendered aspects of the surfing identity politics, or of the organisation itself, were rarely discussed by members. As outlined in Chapter 8, there was some discussion of the particular issues or problems for encouraging black women and girls to surf, recognising the multiple oppressions faced by African-American women. Some BSA activities did focus on women specifically, such as surf clinics targeting women (although not adopting women-only strategies): 'This Spring clinic brought out a strong contingent of black women determined to add surfing to their repertoire. On that day at the Inkwell in Santa Monica, the Sisters charged the waves and dominated the break' (20 May 2006, 'Women dominate Surf Camp Clinic'). Nonetheless, there was also some criticism voiced that the BSA, reflecting white surf culture, was a male-dominated association, with men setting the agenda and holding power. Rhonda's belief that the BSA had side-lined her (Harper, 2007, 2012), which had come to a head in the 'fracas' around Inkwell plague ceremonies,[24] seemed at least in part rooted in gender politics. Natalia, currently on the BSA board, recognised that 'the BSA has been very male dominated', but she adopted a more pragmatic conciliatory position:

> Let's remember it was a male who created the organisation in the first instance. Further I think it is our responsibility as women to find a way to support the males, whilst ensuring the progress of the BSA; if not only because we can.

Given the extremely small numbers of female black surfers, Natalia believed 'there are just not enough of us to make much of a splash', and therefore she needed to, and wanted to, align herself with *black* surfers – male or female – feeling a shared sense of purpose: 'We have another opportunity to learn to work together, building trust and challenging our petty jealousies in order to create something greater than ourselves … still no easy task in today's society.'

Allies to secure change?

Views also differed about whether effective and lasting change was best secured working in partnership with other white organisations or taking a more separatist path. In some contexts, such as fighting various environmental causes, most BSA members worked alongside various other surfing and non-surfing based environmental charities and companies (e.g. Heal the Bay and the Surfrider Foundation for beach clean-ups). For Rhonda, engaging with, even becoming an insider in, the white surf culture was vital to effectively educate, challenge and change the white industry. She recounted how a national not-for-profit surfing organisation had produced what she described as 'racist imagery' based on a spoof of a 'Negro' to promote a comedy event. As a member of the board, she was sent the poster before it was released and was thus able to stop circulation: 'I said, "you guys, you have got to be kidding me! Do you understand the connotations that you will give off? I don't care if it's a comedy night or not, this is not funny"' (Rhonda). She claimed that, once she had pointed out the racist connotation of the image, the executive board quickly retracted the advert.

Jennifer saw her role as an educator, to 'educate white folks', conceding that parts of the white community could be seen as 'allies' in her political project:

> Just by talking to them. They don't have it yet, because they can't see what other surfers are doing. […] I think they're receptive to it because they've been so blind to it, it's just like something that they don't see.

Michael, who was proactive in the Surfrider Foundation, saw it as an opportunity to 'promote the need for unity amongst all surfers'. They had invited him as a guest speaker at a clinic 'to bring urban kids of all ethnicities to the beach and offer them surfing training'.[25] 'Surfrider, therefore, provided a platform for wider exposure of the BSA.' Like Rhonda, he believed in the humanity of surfers, and that change was best achieved working within the industry: 'So things happen. [...] it's not about *who* does it, it's just about that it gets *done*. And, so sometimes we are the same people' (Michael). Michael thus advocated an inclusive politics that worked with different non-political groups, organisations and surfing corporations (for example, for sponsorship and support of their events). He welcomed black entrepreneurialism, describing Patrick Mitchell, who founded the first 'black-owned surfboard company, as 'an icon'. He discussed how Mitchell subsequently used his insider power to support and sponsor black surfers, and eventually the Jamaican national surf team. However, other activists did not want the support of the white surf industry. For Stevie, this was rooted in his class politics: 'Because I'm a socialist, I'm not really chasing corporations for nothing.' He was also sceptical of corporations' motives, recognising the cultural power of the contemporary surfer image, and how it was being mobilised by various voluntary as well as commercial bodies. He discussed how their motives were rarely benevolent, but increasingly represented a form of surveillance and instrumentalism, rooted in wider neoliberal discourses emphasising self-reliance and creativity (Heywood, 2008; Howell, 2008). Jennifer also acknowledged that:

a lot of companies are starting to see how important this whole surfing thing, this whole being able to do it on your own, self-sufficient, self-determination kind of thing that comes from surfing, they are seeing how it's starting to benefit kids so more and more you see these groups starting up.

Given people's different backgrounds, and their varying visions of the association, underlined by their different political positions and affiliations, coordinating strategies was hard. The fragmentation of the organisation I have described was therefore not surprising. While some found this extremely frustrating, and complained about the degree of in-fighting, the 'individualism' and whose voice was heard, others were more accepting of this situation, seeing it as a phase in a longer political project:

So things happen, they kind of happen all over, there are other little small groups, you see them around and individuals that are doing this. And it's really nice and we couldn't all work together because we all work differently, so it really encourages me to see. It's all groups, it's all people. It's white surfers and Asian surfers and Hispanic surfers and black surfers and everybody together and then individually, and women and men and people are trying in their own small ways to offer this to other people because they recognise too that the people that are separated from them are kind of stuck over here and they need an *invitation*. They need to have their hand held while they, while they experience this.

(Michael)

Discussion: surfing and the political

Sport, as Carrington outlines, has often had an 'assumed innocence as a space (in the imagination) and a place (as it physically manifests itself) that is removed from the everyday concerns of power, inequality, struggle and ideology' (2010: 4). It has therefore been seen to offer a 'space for transcendence' and 'utopian dreaming', distinct from seemingly more significant areas of 'civic life' (ibid.). Likewise, the beach has also been constructed as a place of transcendence and freedom, seen as a benign, free and fun-orientated space, rather than recognised to be an important site where racial formations are created and policed (see Evers, 2008; Khamis, 2010). However, for the majority of these individuals, neither the *beach* nor *surfing* was a liminal space beyond 'culture', power and regulation: 'What politically is going on in surfing is that we have been excluded' (Jennifer). Thus, in this final section of the discussion, I further interrogate how surfing for some of these individuals was positioned as a political arena, inherently linked to everyday concerns of inequality, struggle and ideology. I question whether the BSA's activities had an impact that transcended the local and particular context, influencing contemporary racial formations (Carrington, 2010).

Members repeatedly described surfing as political.[26] Jennifer, for example, described this 'whole *black surfing political movement* that I've been on in the last five years'. Their meaning of political, and the types and styles of politics with which they engaged, nonetheless varied. For some it was the freedom to 'just be' in a white space. This is what Carrington terms a 'redemptive' act of resistance – that is 'sport as personal saviour' (Carrington, 2010: 3). Their narratives were replete with examples of the ways surfing enriched their individual lives and provided 'healing-type' experiences, helping them get through difficult times and situations, despite the degree of personal difficulty and struggle involved. For example, as Jennifer claimed: 'In every traumatic situation I have been placed in, surfing has kept me sane and alive.'

However, others advocated more 'transformative' actions, which they believed would lead, eventually, to social change (Carrington, 2010):

> It [change] is going to come slow, and it comes in small pieces. I'm OK with that. I mean, you know, because it's coming, I believe it's coming, I believe it's going to start as a small wave and it's going to grow and it's going to take much longer than it should.
>
> (Jennifer)

These actions involved educating, challenging and changing white surfing. For example, challenging cultural stereotypes (e.g. black outs), intervening in the mass and niche media, and publicising and making visible the black surfer identity.

In summary, political action for the black surfers in this study involved a wide range of activities and interventions, from the macro level, to involvement at local community level, such as engaging with disenfranchised individuals and groups. The black community also needed education and help to transcend long-standing historically rooted perceptions of outdoor space as 'white' and that visiting was not part of black culture (Erickson *et al.*, 2009). As Erickson *et al.* outline, discussing minority patterns of outdoor recreation,[27] and my research confirms, 'because of how individuals have been taught to think about natural areas, invisible lines of segregation continue to exist' (2009: 543). The natural resources of the state, from beaches to mountains, remain the 'purview of the White middle-class visitor' (Wolch and Zhang, 2004: 416):

> So it's kind of been like a, my personal mission to let folks know […] to let black people know, so that we can open the door to new opportunities and new thinking to think differently about ourselves so that we can take advantage of all the things that might be available to us.
>
> (Stevie)

Many of those I spoke to have a sophisticated understanding of the ways in which historical, political and cultural processes impacted on their individual surfing lives, and continued to work against black communities. For some, this understanding translated into political commitment. Michael, for example, discussed how, through trying to understand *his* experiences as a black surfer, he had come to appreciate that the black surfer identity was 'rooted in broader processes about black history, and the beach as it related to civil rights, public access and freedom of opportunity' (personal communication). For others, however, their understanding of surfing as political came from participation in either the civil rights movements or other forms of political activism. Jennifer, for example, described herself as 'an *activist*. I came from a political background, we get on it.' Stevie was a seasoned political campaigner and activist, a former *Black Panther*, who had dedicated his life to various forms of political activism. Despite his continued involvement in a range of global causes, he passionately believed surfing was an important arena of civic life, inherently tied to the continuing 'oppression of black people'. As he eloquently argued, surfing was part of the wider neoliberal capitalist project, intersecting with issues of poverty, poor health and well-being. He championed surfing specifically because he saw it as a relatively cheap, accessible activity, outside of the 'control' either of the state or of commercial leisure providers. Once the financial outlay for the board is made:

> The beach, it's *free*, bring your own food, bring your own blanket, have a fire, play in the water, kids can run as far as they want without worrying about a policeman or a car or a stop sign or perverts, whatever, *they can be free*. Kids freak out at beaches because, especially coming from the city because, 'wow, there's not a building, I can run a mile'. The parents have a good time because they bring their own food, they don't have to worry about having to buy stuff. It's this really phenomenal experience … and *it's free*.
>
> (Stevie)

Paradoxically, by drawing on the dominant discourse of surfing as *freedom*, and suggesting a personal, individualised 'solution' to address a range of deep-rooted socio-economic issues, Stevie appeared to be supporting the neoliberal ideology of individualism. Nonetheless, 'freedom to surf', as this and previous chapters have illustrated, was a hard-won civil rights battle, which for these black surfers took on a different set of meanings to the idea of *freedom* perpetuated in the discourses of white surfing. As Carrington argues, the 'use of sport by the subaltern reproduces and in fact accentuates' paradoxical elements such as that of freedom and constraint; 'a kind of doubling of the effects of freedom and domination' (2010: 91). Or, as Michael put it, 'we surfed to experience the freedom and in a group we were sometimes willing to fight for that freedom'. Nonetheless, as the experiences of the black *female* surfers illustrate, even *among* this small community of black surfers, the *freedom to surf* was contingent and variable, based not just on race but on gender, class and geography. As Natalia argued, male surfers tended to get better support than female surfers, which then 'creates a sense of freedom, fostering the ability and opportunity to express that freedom through surfing'.

Furthermore, although Stevie (above) *appeared* to regard providing opportunity to surf as a *personal* strategy for promoting health, freedom and control, he also recognised that these were fundamentally structural issues rooted in the historical and contemporary 'discrimination against African-American populations in the USA' (Erickson *et al.*, 2009: 537). Providing resources for 'health, well-being and access to public space' (Stevie) were central to tackling discrimination. At the time of my research, the political landscape in the USA was shifting, with reductions in funding to community-based activity programmes and not-for-profit organisations from both corporate and public sectors, being felt in these communities. 'So now we've all these young people with nothing to do' (Stevie). For Stevie, sport generally, and surfing specifically, was 'an important aspect of cultural life of an oppressed people' (Stevie). Taking seriously 'the political nature of the apolitical' (Carrington, 2010: 4) – in this case, the sport of surfing – seemingly directed Stevie, and others, towards a 'richer understanding of politics' (ibid.), one that recognised that what was at stake was how power itself was both manifest and challenged (ibid.). Freedom at the beach was articulated as an important part of this black diasporic group's claim for recognition, equality and identity:

> I don't see the vision of black people surfing as separate from black people's liberation globally.
>
> (BSA member, cited in *A Soul Surfer's Quest*)[28]

> I believe that we are engaged in a civil rights struggle at the beach. That is much different than what white surfers are doing.
>
> (Michael)

> The BSA is simply a chapter in a much larger story about wave-riding as it relates to the African Diaspora (and its black people's relationship to the oceans).
>
> (Alicia, email correspondence)

Conclusions

Because sport is commonly viewed as apolitical, 'it has had an important influence not only on black politics, formally understood, but more widely on how African diasporic peoples have viewed themselves and how these communities have come to be viewed' (Carrington, 2010: 3–4).

While research on activities popular with various black communities (such as basketball in the US) has proliferated, sports with low participation among black communities, like swimming and surfing, have received little academic attention but, as this research has illustrated, also provide important information and understanding about black identities. The politics of surfing and beach access at the 'contested location' of the California beach provides a vivid illustration of the continued racialisation of public space and black communities' continued exclusion from the state's recreational resources, such as mountains and beaches (Wolch and Zhang, 2004; Erickson *et al.*, 2009).

It is also a starting point for understanding cultural identities and the emergence of identity politics in this lifestyle sporting context. While dominant discourses of surfing often emphasise its cosmopolitan idealism and humanity, describing a 'post-racial, meritocratic' brotherhood (Carrington, 2010: 172), this was not the experience for all of the African-American surfers I interviewed. There was a cultural politics in contemporary surfing, centred on who was included and who was excluded; who had the right to be recognised and to belong. Yet racial formations at the beach were not static, and often contradictory. While black surfers continued to experience forms of white racism, they simultaneously felt a bond with white surfers based on the transcendence of subcultural experience, that 'only the surfer knows the feeling'. These African-American surfers continued to create a space for themselves in the white surfing culture, recognising nonetheless the contradictory nature, and at times 'ontological impossibility' (Nayak, 2006), of the black surfer subjectivity. In working through the meaning and context of these lived contradictions, among this small but influential group, surfing has provided a case of sporting political praxis that extends beyond the personal level, allowing (some of) the black surfers to develop a critical consciousness that transcends the context. Carrington suggests that, if sport as a 'racial project can once again be used for progressive purposes', then this will depend largely on the capability of those invested in the sporting cultures to 'hold on to, develop, and articulate a critical consciousness that goes beyond the sport boundary' (2010: 177). If that can be done, he suggests, 'the useless play of sport may turn out to be an important space for the realization of black dreams of freedom in the long struggle accorded the right to occupy the status of the human' (ibid.). The black surfers represented here sincerely hope, and believe, he is right.

10 Coda

As a postgraduate student, grappling with the theoretical challenges of post-modernism, I vividly recall a tutorial with my graduate supervisor, John Hargreaves, a 'devout' (Neo) Marxist, when he gravely declared, 'Belinda, you need to find your framework.' Twenty years later, and this illusive framework still eludes me. Yet the absence of a coherent or all-encompassing metanarrative through which to frame my work is a situation I am more comfortable with; and in this I am not alone. In the preface to his collection of essays titled *The Interpretation of Cultures*, Geertz (2000: v) asks 'did they add up to anything: a theory? A standpoint? An approach?' (cited in McDonald, 2007: 4). Like Geertz (and McDonald), I am also unwilling to *impose* a theoretical framework or claim a theoretical coherence onto what has been an organic process. Research agendas and themes have emerged, been modified and then subsequently led to a range of (mostly) connected themes and theoretical concerns. That is not to say that, in making sense of empirical research, one should not be striving to create a 'critical commentary that not only synthesises, but that "transcends the particular"' (McDonald, 2007: 4). I hope that this ambition has been achieved throughout this book. Yet given the range of ever-changing, boundary-shifting sporting activities that constitute lifestyle sports, and the diverse, selective and partial picture the case studies presented in this book represent, to draw any overarching theoretical conclusion about the cultural politics of lifestyle sports at this conjunctural moment would result in nothing more than an oversimplification. So in this short coda, I briefly reflect back on a question that has framed this journey: whether lifestyle sports have, and can continue to hold, political potential.

The political potential of lifestyle sport revisited

In a climate where political culture is undergoing 'profound transformation' (Anderson, 1997: 206), commentators increasingly hold widely differing visions and explanations about what *being political* is, and how it can, or should, be assessed. This issue has fuelled debate across many disciplinary fields and particularly the sociology of youth cultural practices (e.g. Redhead, 1993; Jordan and Lent, 1999; Martin, 2002; Wilson, 2002; Riley *et al.*, 2010). Traditionally, political engagement was 'thought of as a set of rights and duties that involve formally organized civic and political activities', like voting or joining a political party (Riley *et al.*, 2010: 346). However, new kinds of political arrangements and collectivities are emerging, or intensifying, such as those based around 'alternative' lifestyle interests and their identity politics (Giddens, 1991; Beck, 1992; Maffesoli, 1996).

Examples of these new collectivities include the neo-tribal associations described by Maffesoli (1996), the post-subcultural 'protest formations' outlined by Muggleton and Weinzierl (2003a), as well as the expansion of a range of New Social Movements (NSMs), such as environmentalism.[1] Commentators often differ in their characterisation of these movements, what they are called and how they are theorised. However, they share recognition of their significance; that new political arrangements are being configured which involve *different* and *significant* forms of political participation (Ward and de Vreese, 2011). As Hetherington (1998a: 8) surmises, these new social movements and their lifestyles are seen as 'illustrative of the unbinding of traditional forms of identity and politics in a reflexively modern society'. Muggleton and Weinzierl (2003a) describe how, in what they call 'post-subcultural protest formations', a wave of grass-roots non-violent protests emerged from the mid-1990s, on an unprecedented and transnational scale, ranging from local environmental organisations to those concerned with fair trade, labour rights and so on. In Britain, this 'party and protest' movement of the late 1990s (McKay, 1998) saw a ground-swell of 'interventions' by youth who, like surfers, had previously been characterised as politically dispossessed individualists, their lifestyles based on hedonistic and narcissistic consumption (St John, 2003: 69). Significantly, this upsurge of interventions, which Klein describes as a 'new global political player' (2000: 444), saw adversaries united under the banner of anti-capitalism and anti-globalisation.[2] In these youth and leisure-based cultures, a new identity politics emerged, one that has developed alongside the more ascribed articulations based around class, ethnicity and gender (Hetherington, 1998a: 27). Instead of 'being focused on the removal of structures of inequality and exclusion', these new forms of politics are more concerned with 'facilitating meaningful lifestyles' (Chaney, 2002: 138), converging on questions of identity, self-actualisation and often 'post-materialistic' values (Chaney, 2002; Barker, 2000). As St John outlines:

> fashionably committed to pleasure and politics, such new formations are not disengaged from the political, but are future-directed, pursuing ideals consistent with a historical sensitivity and global sensibilities – as indicated by their reconciliatory gestures, direct action commitments and in their wider cultural outputs.
>
> (2003: 65)

Given the centrality of leisure to identity, it is not surprising that leisure and consumption practices have played a vital part in these formations. Leisure has come to prominence as a central site in which 'social order is either being instituted or resisted' (Chaney, 2002: 127), providing a space to 'redefine, renegotiate and reclaim politics' and citizenship (Riley *et al.*, 2010: 346). Futhermore, as Riley *et al.* (2010: 347) argue, leisure and consumption practices have become important 'tools' in the 'management of the neoliberal self' (Giddens, 1991). In the contemporary neoliberal political context, discourses of collective experiences and struggles are being eroded, accompanied by a general decrease in the sense of the effectiveness of 'representative democracy' (Riley *et al.*, 2010). It therefore makes sense for young people to practice:

> 'aloofness' towards official government organization, turning away from a politics with which they are alienated in favour of engagement in 'everyday politics': participation at the local and informal level where one can gain a sense of sovereignty over one's own existence.
>
> (Ibid.: 347)

These new ways of being political that previously seemed of little significance, including lifestyle sporting practices, hold important insights for understanding this developing field of 'new politics' (Field, 1999; Jordan and Lent, 1999).

As I have advocated through the case studies and commentaries in this book, and in previous work (Wheaton, 2007a, 2007b, 2008a), insights from this interdisciplinary body of work help to understand and assess the contemporary political significance of lifestyle sports. Research in the lifestyle sporting realm has adopted a wide range of different ideas and measures of this new political potential, from the embodied to the spatial (see discussion in Wheaton, 2007a, Thorpe and Wheaton, forthcoming). As discussed in Chapter 5, the emergence of 'new' boundary-shifting activities like parkour, which are (to date) least well understood, have been most enthusiastically pronounced by some academics as transgressive practices. Parkour has been described as having the potential to challenge bodily and spatial norms, contesting the 'institutional control and privatisation of public space' (Guss, 2011: 74), bringing 'forth an aesthetic-spiritual reality of the self' (Atkinson, 2009: 170) through which participants develop an ethic of care (Foucault, 1988) for the self, others and the environment more broadly. Drawing on his thesis of parkour as a microcosm of Hart and Negri's concept of the *multitude*, Guss enthusiastically pronounces that parkour is a 'potentially, emerging democratic political force' (2011: 74) and that it is a 'sign and potentially a harbinger of the emergence of new forms of human relations and *political power*' (ibid.: 83, emphasis added).

Likewise, the culture of surfing, with its iconography of escape, freedom and transcendence – the 'dream for a good life' – has also recurrently been described as holding political potential (e.g. Fiske, 1989; Lewis, 1998; Comer, 2010; Lawler, 2011). Lewis suggests this 'potential' exists in (Australian) surfers' strategic consumption, soul-surfing ethos, bodily pleasure and direct political activism as expressed through environmental lobbying (Lewis, 1998: 65). In Lawler's detailed inspection of the American surfer imagery – both historically and in

contemporary representations – she sees surfing as both signifying *and* producing resistance (2011: 10), principally because of what she sees as its opposition
and challenge to the essential nature of capitalism, work. People are 'collectively
resisting austerity and insisting on constituting time on their own terms' (ibid.:
175), a politics which she believes transcends the context and challenges the
capitalist system itself. Rather than framing commercial expansion in terms of
selling-out an 'authentic image' (as many commentators have), she sees commercial forces as *constituting* and *driving* the very fantasies, memories and
desires that fuel surfers and non-surfers alike, and that ultimately drive this 'subversive politics'.

I have reservations about Lawler's argument, which obscures the complex
ways in which, in late capitalism, the capitalist mode of production operates as
'flexible accumulation' (Harvey, 1990), so over-emphasising the degree to which
the system is challenged. Yet, we converge in proposing that surf culture intersects with various political movements, particularly environmental ones (see also
Ward, 1996; Heywood and Montgomery, 2008; Wheaton, 2008a). From the
1970s, images of the surfer as 'natural environmentalists', along with examples
of surfers using political action in defence of the 'free space of the beach'
(Lawler, 2011: 12), became more explicit in the USA (Garcia and Baltodano,
2005), both in the subcultural media and through organisations such as the Surfrider Foundation. In my own work, I have explored the development and politics
of Surfers Against Sewage (SAS), based in Cornwall, UK (Wheaton, 2007b,
2008a). I illustrated that SAS were part of the wider British 'party and protest'
movement of the late 1990s, described above (McKay, 1998). Like other
environmental protest groups of that era, SAS used a range of creative forms of
political protest, including 'market-based consumer-citizenship measures'
(Parker, 1999: 75) and the adoption of alternative lifestyles. The surfing subculture was the catalyst for politicisation around beach pollution and environmentalism more widely (Wheaton 2007b, 2008a). My case study exemplified how
surfers and participants from other lifestyle sport subcultures (e.g. windsurfing,
body boarding, kayaking) became engaged with environmental politics. The
scale and motivations for participant involvement, and measures of its impact,
still remain unclear. However, the political activism in, and media visibility of,
such new post-subcultural protest formations undermines assumptions that those
who take part in such lifestyle sport subcultures are solely 'politically disen-
gaged' hedonists, or consumers (Muggleton and Weinzierl, 2003b: 14), and
illustrates how the politics of identity operate through such sporting cultures.

Furthermore, while environmental issues have continued to be a focus across
lifestyle environmental groups (e.g. Protect Our Winters, Surfers' Environmental
Alliance), similarly politicised non-profit organisations and movements affiliated
to various lifestyle sport cultures have proliferated. These relate to an array of
social issues, including health (e.g. Boarding for Breast Cancer, Surf Aid International), education (e.g. Skateistan, see Ch. 6), and peace and reconciliation
(Surfers for Peace, aimed at bridging cultural and political barriers between
surfers in the Middle East). Thorpe and Rinehart (2010) drew on Thrift's

non-representation theory, particularly his work on the *politics of affect* and *politics of hope*. They reveal how lifestyle-sports-related social movements were drawing on new technologies to create new forms of 'passionate politics' within communities that spanned the local, global and virtual. Thorpe and Rinehart argue that these communities' use (and abuse) of 'affective practices and political strategies' holds potential for understanding the ways in which they have begun to change the sphere of the political in contemporary lifestyle sporting cultures.

In summary, these subcultural protest movements, including organisations like Surfers against Sewage, the Surfers' Environmental Alliance, the Surfrider Foundation and the Black Surfing Association (BSA; see Ch. 9), provide compelling examples of the politically emancipatory elements (Muggleton and Weinzierl, 2003b) within lifestyle sport cultures. If, as Carrington suggests, the ability for sport to be used for progressive purposes rests, 'in large part, on the ability of those investing in sport cultures to hold on to, develop, and articulate a critical consciousness that goes beyond the sport boundary' (2010: 177), then the BSA provides some optimism. *Despite* the historical and contemporary role played by the white-dominated minority sport of surfing in shaping racial discourse, reproducing dominant discourses about white power and privilege, the BSA has an important place within black diasporic struggles for freedom, equality and identity. The BSA is an example of sporting political praxis that has begun to extend beyond the personal level, allowing *some* participants to develop a critical conscious that transcends the context.

Thus, as critics of these new forms of political engagement maintain, to claim that lifestyle sporting movements have political potential, there is a need to go *beyond* 'interpreting personal lives as political' and develop an agenda for 'social change' where participants engage with institutions of power (Riley *et al.*, 2010: 364). In the context of prominent, environmental, consumer-based protests, it is recognised that politicised consumption alone is unlikely to achieve systematic change (Parker, 1999). The point at which the collective goes macro and the protests transcend 'the subcultural sphere' – which Marchart calls the 'moment of universalization' (2003: 96) – is critical in the politicisation of such formations. In my research on SAS, this universalisation was evident in its concern with *all* water users, not just surfers, and in a campaign that shifted from a local concern to being increasingly 'global' in approach. For example, the organisation campaigns for a range of environmental issues, including renewable energy sources and eco-friendly clothing, and it contributes to global warming/climate change political agendas.[3]

Conclusions

Lifestyle sports continue to provide particularly interesting cases for examining 'binary contradictions' embedded in late capitalist ways of life and potential for 'alternative forms of physical culture' (Atkinson, 2009: 182). As Atkinson has argued, within late modern societies, the destabilisation of modernist boundaries allows the creation of spaces for the 'exploration of non-mainstream athletic forms, identities, lifestyles and physical cultural practices that do not emulate or replicate hyper-competitive, hierarchical and patriarchal modernist sport' (2010: 1250). Whether this potential is, or can ever be, realised in these lifestyle sport cultures has framed large sections of this book and will continue to be the focus of much debate. At their inception, individualised and largely unregulated forms of sport offered participants different and potentially more inclusive spaces for the construction of cultural identities than many traditional institutionalised sports. Yet the research presented in this book suggests that, despite the potential for sporting identities to be different, many lifestyle sports have remained or even *become* the playgrounds of affluent Western white men. Identity and belonging for those outside the male white 'somatic norm' (Puwar, 2004: 8) were more contingent, and many experienced symbolic, material and spatial exclusion from the sporting collectivity. Research needs to continue to illustrate the competing and contradictory messages disseminating through popular forms of (lifestyle) sporting cultures. It needs to map the articulations of gender, sexuality, 'race', class, age, nation and (neoliberal) democracy (Giardina and McCarthy, 2005) disseminating into and through these forms of sporting cultures. The possibility of 'liberating and transformatory scripts for sporting participation' also needs to be understood in the context of the current commercialisation and professionalism (Robinson, 2008: 53) of a range of informal and play-centred lifestyles and sports. In activities like surfing, professionalisation and institutionalisation began several decades ago; for some newly emergent sports, like parkour, their impact is rapidly changing. So we need to consider if it is the particular lifestyle sport itself, its specific characteristics and ethos, or its contextual (historical and temporal) location that allows a sport to retain some autonomy from these processes. Put another way, when new sports are no longer new, is their appropriation – institutional, commercial and educational – inevitable? However, in considering the ways in which lifestyle sports are appropriated and sportised, we need to consider different sites, spaces and expressions of (subcultural) 'resistance' that emerge, and how these articulate with experiences of the gendered, sexualised, racialised and aged (able) body. As explored throughout this book, revealing the gendered and racialised spaces of lifestyle sports (Puwar, 2004), and the ways gender and race articulate with sexuality, age and class, historically and temporally, and as they register and reside in space, remains a key challenge in understanding their cultural politics.

The focus on micro-political struggles in the cultural realm can fail to 'address the actual context of relations, the articulations, between popular culture and systemic politics' (Grossberg, 1997: 236). Yet, as illustrated through the case studies, identity does not need to be a 'barrier to understanding and challenging wider forms of social inequality' (Carrington, 2007: 50); it can be seen as 'a precondition for any effective oppositional politics' (ibid.: 49). Carrington suggests that centring questions of cultural identity helps 'to reveal the play of power and the complex articulations of dominant ideologies while simultaneously recognizing the joy, creativity, and moments of resistance and, occasionally, transformation that popular culture and sport provides us with' (ibid.: 62). Our explorations of different lifestyle sports can, and should, inform our understanding of sport's relationship to wider global and local cultural, economic and political processes. While it is undeniable that lifestyle sports have become willing and perfectly moulded agents to further neoliberal discourses of individualism, self-reliance and health, so too can they be spaces to create and develop the 'critical race and gender consciousness' that commentators like Denzin (2002) suggest research in the twenty-first century demands. Such research means an engagement not only with the potent imagery, symbols and artefacts of these cultures, but also with the experiences and subjectivities of their producers and *all of their* consumers – those who are old and young, able-bodied and not, different genders, ethnicities and sexualities, both in 'the West', and in previously peripheral, but increasingly important spaces like South America, Africa and Asia. Only then can our research contribute to exposing the political possibility of 'sport', leisure and physical culture, and its potential to both establish and challenge social order.

Notes

1 Introduction

1 I am referring here to Raymond Williams' categorisation of residual and emergent (Williams, 1977). Sports like climbing and surfing that have a longer history in the modern period can therefore be thought of as part of the residual (see Rinehart, 2000).

2 Idents are the imagery used between programmes to 'identify' the station.

3 *Roxy* is the female arm of the international clothing (and now lifestyle) brand Quiksilver, which is one of the big three brands across lifestyle sports, including skateboarding, snowboarding and surfing. See Stranger (2011).

4 Theorists have therefore represented the emergence of these sporting activities, and the subcultures and lifestyles that develop around them, as a new phase in the development of sport, characterised by some as postmodern (see Wheaton, 2004a).

5 Some commentators parenthesise the term 'race' to signify its constructed nature; while I subscribe to a constructionist position, given that all identities are constructed, in this book, I will not parenthesise the word.

6 In a sense, this theoretical eclecticism reflects my own academic history, which has straddled sport studies, sociology, media studies and cultural studies.

7 Most recently, the 2008 RAE (Research assessment exercise) and 2014 REF (Research excellence framework). See www.ref.ac.uk.

8 While Brighton has been identified as a hub of this critical work, there are certainly other UK-based scholars of sport, working in similar ways and voicing similar concerns. See, for example, Jarvie (2007).

9 These are debates I revisit below in the context of my multiple and shifting positioning in the surfing culture.

10 For example, reports about Umthombo surfing children on Trans World Sport (Trans World Sport, 2010).

11 This and other names used are pseudo names.

12 Several people helped in the context of developing this research and my interpretations of it. First, Dr Toni Bruce, who was also in Durban for the ISA conference and who, because of limited time (and due to issues around personal security in areas of Durban), accompanied me on my field visits and conducted 'interviews' with the street children. I would also like to thank Mr Mark Walsh, my host and tour guide in Durban. Mark, who has lived in Durban for more than 20 years, helped me gain invaluable insights into the changing context of race in Durban. Subsequently, my thanks to Robert Morell, who agreed to be my academic partner in a follow-up research project that failed to gain funding from the ESRC; and Annelize Gerber, for sharing her expertise on Durban street children with me. Lastly, to Dallas and his team, who answered numerous email requests and who offered to host a researcher.

13 The research was funded by the *Brighton and Sussex Community Knowledge Exchange* programme (BISKE). Our community partners were the *Peacehaven and*

Telescombe Regeneration Partnership (REGEN), who were trying to raise money for the parkour training area.

14 This created some interesting and problematic dynamics in the interview situation, and the need to reflect on this dynamic in the data construction process.

15 As illustrated by this quote, respondents were predominantly well-educated individuals (including teachers, artists and those working in the media), all of whom were self-reflexive about their involvement in surfing.

16 It is also interesting how this same dynamic was played out in the parkour research where I was very much an outsider to the culture and context, and as such was treated with suspicion by some participants.

17 I discussed this with one of my key respondents/gatekeepers and, despite having asked to be named, he agreed with my rationale and decision.

2 Understanding lifestyle sport revisited

1 Tomb stoning is the term given to diving off cliffs or rocks into water (see Laviolette, 2010).

2 Leisure scholars have argued that lifestyle remains an imprecise, nebulous term (Sobel, 1981; Veal, 1993), associated with a 'pluralistic' a-theoretical approach to understanding leisure without consideration of socio-economic, demographic and other structural factors. As Pierre Bourdieu's work in *Distinction* (1984) suggests, cultural capital, leisure and lifestyle, or 'taste', is related to and rooted in economic capital. These criticisms withstanding, notions of lifestyle, and related phrases such as style of life, way of life and leisure lifestyle, have become part of the academic and everyday language of consumer culture (Veal, 1993; Chaney, 1996). In late capitalism, lifestyle is intrinsically linked with patterns of consumption (Featherstone, 1991), and status bestowed by group membership is not linked exclusively to the profession or occupation of the group member, or a specific class background (Chaney, 1996). Bennett suggests that such a use of *lifestyle* does not indicate an abandonment of structural issues, but 'allows for the fact that consumerism offers the individual new ways of negotiating such issues' (Bennett, 1999: 607).

3 Echoing Kellner, who advocates that instead of seeing postmodernity as a 'new cultural totality, I would thus argue that it makes more sense to interpret the many forces of the postmodern as an emergent cultural trend in opposition to residual traditional and modern values and practices' (Kellner, 1992: 171). He outlines that it is precisely this coexistence of traditional, modern and postmodern cultural forms which describes the 'postmodern' (ibid.). Following Kellner, this coexistence of emergent cultural practices with traditional and residual practices and forms found in some lifestyle sport cultures is what constitutes a postmodern sports culture.

4 Bourdieu calls these activities new sports and terms these entrepreneurs the 'new' and 'petite bourgeoisie' (1984: 220).

5 Bale, for example, suggests such activities present a challenge to the 'Western sport model' (Bale, 1994), and Maguire (1999) notes they challenge the 'achievement sport' ideology.

6 Experiences that, as Ford and Brown (2005: 163) contend, participants find extremely hard to express verbally.

7 Although the use of aggressive means in turf wars have been well-documented in skating and surfing. See Chapter 4.

8 For example, as Atkinson and Wilson (2002) have demonstrated, 'notions of subcultural resistance' can benefit from an increased awareness of a 'Foucauldian depiction of surveillance' (Best, 1997, cited in Atkinson and Wilson, 2002: 368–369).

9 Carrington and Wilson (2004) discuss her use of subcultural capital, suggesting that it can be misleading to see it solely as a derivative of Bourdieu's work, given that Bourdieu's concept of taste was underpinned by a particular understanding of class

(and the role of education in the reproduction of social class) based on his empirical work on French society. They conclude that, given the lack of attention to social class in Thornton's analysis and theorisation, her use of the term is at best misleading, at worst 'merely a descriptive category'. Her empirical work is also criticised for not attending to the gendered hierarchies, such as the ways different feminine subjectivities compete for subcultural status (ibid.).

10 For example, in Wheaton's research, the marginalised windsurf widows (see Wheaton and Tomlinson, 1998).

11 In Chapter 4, I explore the ways in which these status hierarchies or authenticity claims in different lifestyle sport subcultures underpin and contribute to gendered and racialised exclusion processes, exploring how gendered and racialised power hierarchies (as well as power differentials based on sexuality, age and class) are reproduced.

12 The gendered use of language and the gender politics underpinning this Othering process is discussed in Chapter 4.

13 This is an interesting example of the ironic postmodern referential style adopted by many lifestyle sport magazines. It is written by the ironically titled Dr Orec in his 'on going phenomenological investigation of kite culture', who interviews some of the 'founding fathers of kite-surfing' to see if kite-surfing has developed its own 'identity' (Orec, 2003).

14 Again, illustrating that insiders in the subcultural media use the term 'lifestyle sport'.

3 Mapping the lifestyle sportscape

1 In activities like surfing, where clubs have been a more long-standing and formal part of the sport's history, they differ in context and meaning from more traditional team-based sport clubs – for example, in facilitating social networks, including inter-club competitive activity. Yet they are not central to the organisation of the activity (Ormrod, 2008).

2 The research and ideas presented in this section are based on a collaborative project with Dr Holly Thorpe and are drawn from the output of that project. See Thorpe and Wheaton (2011a, 2011b).

3 In May 2012, sailing's governing body, the ISAF (International Sailing Federation), had just voted to *include* kite-surfing in the 2012 Games under the sailing discipline, but to *exclude* windsurfing. While kite-surfing had been lobbying for Olympic inclusion for some time (see Thorpe and Wheaton, 2011a), the decision still shocked and outraged parts of the windsurfing community, leading to various protests (e.g. via the Facebook page 'Appeal against kite-surfing in the Olympics put windsurfing back in'). Various petitions were being launched to challenge the decision and reinstate windsurfing. The political and economic imperatives underpinning this decision are certainly worthy of greater reflection.

4 To date, the type of BMX activity is limited to racing, whereas the more popular and aesthetic element of freestyle riding has – for now at least – retained its non-Olympic status.

5 Entertainment and Sports Programming Network, owned by ABC, itself a division of the Walt Disney Group.

6 In a documentary that charts the development of big wave riding, the current generation of big wave riders (e.g. Laird Hamilton), who developed tow-in surfing (being pulled into a big wave by a jet ski instead of paddling), are applauded as the elite of the sport of surfing big waves (Peralta, 2004). Yet, when tow-in surfing emerged, surfing magazines were very critical, seeing it as inferior to 'real' (i.e. not power-assisted) surfing. Interestingly, this documentary makes no mention of this early conflict. It is, however, yet another example of contestation over the meaning of 'authentic' surfing.

7 The feat was later repeated over Brighton pier, gaining even more notoriety. See BBC News (2010).

8 In the discussion of parkour in Chapter 5, I illustrate how this discourse about risk and responsibility is played out in urban familiar spaces, rather than those distant romantic locations, like the mountains and sea.

4 Lifestyle sport, identity and the politics of difference

1 I use the term *race* within a constructionist perspective, recognising that race does not exist as a biological category but that racial identity is a discursive formation, produced by discourses, symbols and practices that construct how people see, understand and live racialised lives.
2 It is evident among participants across a range of adventure sports that women tend to learn in different ways, often needing to feel safe and in control, and are less willing to take unnecessary risk (e.g. Woodward, 1995; Dilley and Scraton, 2010; West and Allin, 2010).
3 The company *Surf Diva* in La Jolla, Southern California is also a focus of Comer's research (2010). She suggests they are the 'industry leader in the girl-business concept' (Comer, 2010: 182), exploring in some depth their devolvement and rationalisation.
4 For a detailed discussion of the third-wave feminism in sport and lifestyle sports, see Comer (2004, 2010), and Heywood and Dworkins (2003). For Heywood and Dworkins, the second- and third-wave approaches are 'not incompatible or opposed' (2003: 10). Yet Caudwell (2011) problematises the notion of a 'third wave' of *sport* feminism. She explores the ways feminist thinking, theory and politics have been framed by some sport feminists in relation to 'waves' of feminism. She discusses how this approach presents developments as 'linear, progressive', which can miss the 'multiple, complex and fragmented nature of feminisms' (ibid.: 111).
5 While an analysis of *Blue Crush* is beyond the scope of this chapter, elsewhere I have analysed the film, and groups of surfer and non-surfer readings of it (Wheaton, 2008b).
6 These are discourses that are also reflective of the complex shifting identities evident in contemporary short-board surf culture (see Waitt, 2008).
7 Heywood and Dworkins discuss the cultivation of what Halberstam (1998) terms athletic 'female masculinity'. The potential for Halberstam's enactment of 'female masculinity' is also evoked in Dilley's research on women's climbing as a serious leisure activity (Dilley and Scraton, 2010).
8 See her website: http://bethanyhamilton.com/about/bio/.
9 The question of surfing's hetero-normativity underpins Ph.D. research by Georgina Roy, exploring female subjectivities in British surfing spaces (Roy, 2011) and how, following Probyn, a sense of belonging to this public space is often complicated, partial or conflicted. Adopting a queer perspective, her empirical research explores surfing femininities in different British surfing spaces.
10 See also Khamis (2010) on the Burquini.
11 See also my discussion of the blonde dictatorship in Chapter 7.
12 Indeed Heywood recognises that girls themselves may not experience the programmes she discusses in these ways. While Comer does interview female surfers, and in her analysis of 'girl localisms' explores the 'counter femininities' (2010: 18) in different surfing spaces, these are often underdeveloped as it is not her central aim.
13 This is discussed in snowboarding; see Thorpe (2008) and below.
14 And in the sports feminism association with the North American Sociology of Sport Association (NASSS), almost an orthodoxy. In particular, Markula was a key proponent (Markula, 2003; Markula and Pringle, 2006).
15 Markula reviews a number of studies that have claimed to detect technologies of the self, arguing that much of the early research conceptualised the concept in rather vague ways and failed to illustrate how self-transformation was occurring (2003).

16 Roy's Ph.D. research into female subjectivities in British surfing spaces also explores the potential of Deleuze and adopts the rhizomatic body model (Roy, 2011).

17 Rooted in the work of Henri Lefebvre (1991), and emerging across many academic fields, the 'spatial turn' (Warf and Arias, 2009) has impacted on both sport sociology (Van Ingen, 2003; Friedman and van Ingen, 2011) and leisure studies (Aitchison, 1999; Caudwell and Browne, 2011).

18 For example, research has illustrated the 'conflicts' between groups of users and cultural 'outsiders' and revealed contestation within (e.g. localism in surfing) and between groups of participants (e.g. skiers and snowboarders; skateboarders and BMXers), exemplifying how different groups of participants make meanings, contesting other uses and representations.

19 The ways in which masculinity performances and 'race' underpin localism is discussed in Chapter 8. See also Evers (2008) and Waitt (2008).

20 He also considers how these are racialised.

21 Approaches to theorising gender have also been increasingly influenced by the performative account of gender offered by Judith Butler. Butler's basic premise is that gender is not something we have or are, but is something that we do; it is a 'discourse we inhabit, employ, a performance with all the connotations of non-essentialism, transience, versatility and masquerade that this implies' (Benwell, 2003: 8). It is appealing because it acknowledges the reflexive, ambiguous, contradictory and fractured processes involved in producing gender in different (sporting) contexts.

22 Numerous excellent assessments of hegemonic masculinity exist; see, for example, Pringle (2005).

23 However, see also discussion of emotions, affect and embodiment in Thorpe (2011), Chivers-Yochim (2010) and Laurendeau (2011).

24 By considering some of the 'emotional specificities of being a traceur that plays with place', Saville draws attention to the limitations of the symbolic or visual 'readings of parkour' (2008: 893) and indeed other lifestyle sports (Evers, 2009; Thorpe and Rinehart, 2010).

25 More detailed research is required to explore if these observations are more widespread than this limited research.

26 *Surfing for Life* is a healthy ageing programme/intervention based around surfing. It includes various literature, including a DVD. See Brown and Earnest (2001) and Gibbons (2008).

27 Saga is a company offering various products and services for the over fifties. See www.saga.co.uk.

28 Paddle-surfing is a form of stand-up surfing that has been gaining in popularity over the past decade. Instead of lying prone and paddling using the arms, participants stand upright and use a paddle to catch the wave. It is well-suited to older participants (and novices) as the boards are bigger and more stable than surfboards, and it does not require the participants to 'pop-up' to their feet, a manoeuvre often cited as the hardest part for older participants (personal interviews, 2010–2011).

29 For a similar set of shifting and contradictory attitudes to and experiences of the older surfer, see Warshaw (2005).

30 Stenger's (2008) insightful analysis of 'race', space and beach culture in the Hollywood beach movies is discussed in Chapter 7, as is the surf-safari genre.

31 Surf films are an increasingly diverse and growing genre, which range from Hollywood blockbusters like *Blue Crush*, to the thousands of DVDs made by the surf industry that Booth categorised as 'pure surf films' – 'that is, films (videos and DVDs) produced by surfers for surfing audiences' (Booth, 1996).

32 The Hawaiian elite surfing setting provided a context in which female surfing bodies were represented in more diverse ways than many previous mainstream and niche surf films.

33 Art house films that have been played at a range of international film festivals, including sport film, surf film and black film festivals.
34 In February 2012, Nike released a film titled *12 Miles North: The Nick Gabaldon Story* (Nike Surfing, 2012), which discussed the forgotten history of African American Nick Gabaldon and how he transcended the race barrier in surfing, which is worthy of analysis, not least in exploring Nike's motivation. The film provoked a range of interesting commentaries. See, for example, Harper (2012) and Yelland (2012).
35 This is also the geographic location of the Inkwell, the black surfing beach discussed in Chapter 7.
36 While, as Kusz discusses, not all these skateboarders are white – several appear to be phenotypically Asian – he argues that their voices have a limited and peripheral position in the film. As Chivers-Yochim (2010: 102) argues, mainstream depictions of skateboarders continue to be 'mainly white' and 'images of diversity' in skateboard media can be 'read as the type of tokenism that maintains the centrality of whiteness'. Furthermore, Kusz argues that the marginalised inclusion of people of colour is crucial to understanding how the film constructs the apparently 'different' white identity of the Z Boys.
37 Brayton (2005), for example, has illustrated that narratives in North American skate magazines can be read not only as bolstering white normativity but as an attempt to escape from white privilege (see also Ch. 7).
38 The work of Colleen McGloin (McGloin, 2005, cited in Waitt, 2008) came to my attention late in this project.
39 The racialised spaces of the Californian surf-beach are discussed in Chapters 7–9.
40 For some participants, this 'outsider status' was tied to a belief that 'minorities' in the US were unfairly 'asserting that their own experiences of oppression are unique' (Chivers-Yochim, 2010: 96). This white backlash is discussed by Kusz (2004). See also Brayton (2005) and Atencio and Beal (2011).
41 In Chapter 6, I explore some of the ways skateboarders in Durban, South Africa challenge and reproduce skateboarding's discursive whiteness.

5 Risk-taking and regulation: examining the sportisation of parkour

1 There are numerous postings on parkour websites and YouTube illustrating moves such as the *cat leap*, where the participant jumps, cat-like, from one ledge/wall/obstacle to another.
2 The civil unrest in France, starting in the autumn of 2005.
3 The Yamakasi founders were Yann Hnautra, Chau Belle, David Belle, Laurent Piemontesi, Sebastien Foucan, Guylain N'Guba Boyeke, Charles Perriere, Malik Diouf and Williams Belle.
4 Atkinson (2009: 170–172) discusses the historical and philosophical foundations of parkour and Hébert's methods in some depth. For a detailed history of parkour, see the work of Julie Angel (2011b).
5 On the nature of the sporting neo-tribe, see Wheaton (2007a).
6 For Guss, the multitude – and parkour – is a 'potentially, emerging democratic political force created in the global information economy' (2011: 74).
7 The current rapid expansion of various Eastern movement forms such as yoga and martial arts as body-self transformative practices in the West is perhaps an important factor contextualising parkour's current popularity. For a fuller discussion of impact and meaning of these Eastern movement forms, see Brown and Leledak (2010).
8 While the links with martial arts are evident, in most respects parkour differs from traditional martial arts.
9 See, for example, www.northernparkour.com/viewtopic.php?f=1&t=4002#p40303 (accessed 20 March 2009).

10 By considering some of the 'emotional specificities of being a traceur that plays with place', Saville draws attention to the limitations of the symbolic or visual 'readings of parkour' (2008: 893) and indeed other lifestyle sports (Evers, 2009; Thorpe and Rinehart, 2010).

11 The *ways* in which these black bodies are represented, however, are worthy of investigation.

12 The Paris suburbs where parkour emerged were categorised as home to low-income and unemployed, 'working-class whites', alongside immigrant and 'racialised' groups (Ortuzar, 2009: 61).

13 See also Nik Walder, interviewed in the documentary *Jump Westminster* (Angel, 2007).

14 See Parkour UK, who include free-running as a discipline of parkour. These definitions are clearly not fixed, and are still shifting and being refined.

15 It is interesting to compare this hybridisation of parkour to the Westernised commoditised version of Eastern movement forms such as yoga and martial arts (see Shilling, 2005; Brown and Leledak, 2010).

16 However, in capoeira these had stemmed from glocalisation of the activity. For a fuller discussion of these authenticity discourses, see Joseph (2009).

17 Bouldering is a type of climbing that takes place on low(er) boulders rather than rock faces.

18 UFF declined an invitation to be involved in the research, so their views are not represented here.

19 It was also apparent that *all* organisations seen to profit financially from parkour were criticised, regardless of their broader philosophy, and *Parkour Generations* also received online critique for engaging in and seemingly profiting from media/stunt work.

20 BBC News, 'World's first free run contest'. Retrieved on 7 October 2008 from http://news.bbc.co.uk/1/hi/england/7597157.stm.

21 In the absence of parkour-approved standards, participant promoters had been quite creative in the ways they provided a duty of care and insurance cover – for example, adopting generic teaching qualifications and forms of protection, such as *Safeguarding Children* certificates, first aid and equity in coaching. One provider claimed he had found it relatively easy to obtain (public liability) insurance cover for teaching in a theatre because he defined parkour as art, as 'physical theatre'.

22 This relationship, however, has subsequently shifted, and at the present time gymnastics organisations and Parkour UK are working together more closely (Minogue, personal correspondence, 2012).

23 The ADAPT qualifications are developed in conjunction with 1st4sport Qualifications, the awarding body for active learning and leisure, and are recognised and accredited by both QCA and Ofqual. See Parkour UK website (www.parkouruk.org) for details of this qualification.

24 Which they had managed to secure because of the backing from Westminster, and they could demonstrate 'a long-standing credibility in the art' (Dan Edwardes).

25 As outlined earlier, *Urban FreeFlow*'s motivation was widely questioned when it tried to introduce competition into parkour, an event that was widely condemned by the majority of the parkour community.

26 It is noteworthy that the first (to our knowledge) parkour training area was funded through the arts, not as a sport.

27 The debate about whether parkour could be, or should be, a sport was also prominent on various chat rooms. For example, see 'Make parkour an official and legal sport' at http://neparkour.ning.com/profiles/blogs/make-parkour-an-official-and (accessed 9 January 2012).

28 This anti-corporate ethos in art and its relationship to lifestyle sport is discussed in Atencio and Beal's analysis of the art exhibit *Beautiful Losers* (2011).

29 Paul advocated accreditation through the arts, a completely different process that he

argued was more student-centred. In addition to the training element, it would involve self-reflection about the discipline and give students flexibility to 'set their own curriculum', reinforcing 'an autodidactic training method'. It should be noted, however, that these comments were made while the ADEPT qualification and governing body was in process and that Parkour UK believes its accreditation *does* allow for creativity (Minogue, 2011).

30 There were mixed views about this development and indeed whether it will fulfil its aims.

31 This shift followed work by Minogue with afPE and the Youth Sport Trust in preparation for the NGB formation.

32 Sport England has a fairly broad definition of 'sport', one that, following the European Council's definition (2001), does not focus solely on *competition* and thus potentially encompasses lifestyle sport activities.

33 In this context, Howell's work intersects with a number of analyses of action/extreme/ lifestyle sports that connect the current expansion of lifestyle sport provision in North America to the growing ethos of neoliberalism within North American (as well as Australasian and many European) societies (e.g. Banks, 2008; Erickson, 2011).

34 Howell (2005) also considers that the impact of Florida's work in promoting the values of this 'creative class' to urban managers is important, influencing the process through which lifestyle sport participants have begun to be seen and utilised as a sign of the economically productive aspects of the global economy (see also Kay and Laberge, 2002b).

35 While the focus has been on participants' engagement with the urban landscape and the transgression of practices of power that regulate bodies and behaviour, unlike skateboarding, research has not to date explored how gendered/racialised bodies are also regulated, reproduced and challenged in these spaces.

36 These can broadly be categorised as sport provision and participation; regeneration projects; social inclusion initiatives and school-based initiatives. In most cases, provision cuts across, and contributes to, several agendas, reflecting New Labour's broad social inclusion agenda, which saw sport centrally placed to contribute to 'community renewal', including 'improving communities' performance in health, crime, employment and education' (Coalter, 2007: 116).

37 Comment on 25 May 2010, 'New England Parkour' http://neparkour.ning.com/profiles/blogs/make-parkour-an-official-and.

38 As well as variations of the parkour training facility, such as a set of movable stages that had been used in schools across Brighton and for a number of public performances.

39 It was suggested this was because of the delay in the park opening not because of the charge.

40 As government reports have repeatedly highlighted, and the media have widely pursued (e.g. Asthana, 2008).

41 As Gilchrist and Wheaton (2011) discuss, while all the policy makers we interviewed across sport, the arts and education had enthusiasm for parkour, detailing the numerous ways it benefited children, there was little evidence or systematic analysis about the effects of these interventions. Despite these widespread endorsements, contradictory discourses of danger and risk infused many of our interviews, and managing the risk, including aspects discussed above, such as providing insurance cover, was one of the central concerns for policy makers across all areas of provision.

42 Regen was an established Area Partnership for Peacehaven and Telscombe.

6 Globalisation, identity and race: lifestyle sport in post-apartheid South Africa

1 Between 2005 and 2009, I conducted a yearly survey of X Games viewing by the sport journalism students at the University of Brighton. Although they tended to be

avid consumers of media sport, initially few had even heard of the X Games. While the percentages who watched the X Games increased, in 2009, half were still unfamiliar and had no idea about its global audience.

2 Exceptions include emerging work on Brazil (Knijnik *et al.*, 2010) and on migration (Thorpe, 2010b).

3 Their paper is a polemic about the interdependence of what they term the sporting *grobal* and the glocal. It is not my intention here to contribute to theoretical debates about sporting globalisation. For the theoretical genesis of these terms, see Wheaton (2005). This is also a focus of Thorpe (2010b).

4 Studies like Joan Ormrod's (2008) research on the ways in which British surfers have expressed regional and national identities help understanding of these processes, particularly what Robertson (1992) termed glocalisation – that is, the global production of the local, and the simultaneous localisation of the global.

5 The apartheid regime classified South Africans into four principle racial groups: *African, Coloured, Asian or Indian*, and *White*. 'Black, the preferred term of the majority non-racial/mass democratic movement, denotes these groups collectively referred to by the government as non-white (broadly non-European)' (Booth, 1998: xi). Racial identities and categories in post-apartheid South Africa continue to be contentious, context-specific and shifting (Pelak, 2005), and in this chapter I use the term black to refer to South Africans of *African, Asian* and *Coloured* identities. However, reflecting their still-widespread use, I also use labels such as *coloured* where appropriate.

6 On the shifting nature of whiteness in South Africa, see Steun (1991).

7 Desai argues that, given sport has been 'trumpeted as a symbol of redress and nation building', the lack of critical analysis of sporting activities is startling; he mentions surfing as one sport needing further analysis (2010: 12).

8 The park has been a focus for several media reports, including a feature by the BBC. See, for example, Pitcher (2006).

9 Singh (2007) discusses how, during the 1996 ISA Conference in Durban that I attended, street children hanging around the conference venues were forcibly removed and transported outside Durban. Similarly, newspaper reports around the time of the football World Cup discussed the ways in which Durban's streets were cleaned of street children (Coyne, 2010).

10 Personal correspondence via email.

11 Gaber nonetheless suggested that, despite the supportive group function, group dynamics fluctuated widely, and ostracism and bullying were also prevalent (2009b).

12 Gaber also observed that the street-kid skaters were younger and smaller than the 'general hangout' (those working at the shop or hanging out there on a regular basis) and some of them were 'babied'.

13 Diverse research on street children in Brazil illustrates their interest in, and knowledge of, brands like Nike and their ability to differentiate fake products.

14 Browsing through South African magazines, it was evident that the ethos of skating was similar and they shared advertisements from global skate brands like Nike, Quiksilver and Elements.

15 Brayton further suggests that white US skaters' fantasies of escaping middle-class *white* suburbia and conformity were realised through an *imagined* and *desired* blackness (2005: 368). However, this desire for blackness was fostered at the level of 'multiracial' commodities, such as style and music, creating a 'symbolic escape' 'contingent on contradictorily romantic and racialised understandings of the ghetto' (ibid.).

16 Gaber suggests that Thalente is using 'gansta' here to refer to stylistic elements, not the violence of South African street culture.

17 Preston-Whyte's more recent exploration of surfing spaces in Durban also revealed that surfers were 85 per cent male, but neither his questionnaire nor his observation across surfing spaces (in 2000) recorded ethnicity.

18 There are similarities here with the ways beach spaces are historically racialised in California. See Chapter 7.

19 This relaxation of the segregation of public amenities, including beaches and swimming pools, during the 1980s was a 'token transformation' in a broader political context of high levels of inter-racial violence and conflict in KwaZulu Natal (Durrheim and Dixon, 2001: 438).

20 There are a number of media-produced accounts of surfing in South Africa, including several films that Thompson discusses.

21 Nonetheless, during my week in Durban, I visited the surfing beaches at North Beach every morning and saw predominantly white surfers.

22 'Stoke' is a word used by surfers to describe the feeling of pleasure when surfing. See Booth (2008).

23 These barriers are also the focus of Chapter 8, which discusses barriers for African American surfers in California, including swimming ability and fear of the water.

24 In terms of developing physical competence, inability to swim is widely cited as a significant factor in other contexts. In Chapter 8, I discuss many of the barriers for African American surfers, outlining how surfing (whether board riding or lifesaving) enjoyment and ability was predicated on confidence in the water.

25 The leash is the line that attaches the surfboard to the surf-rider's ankle.

26 Booth explains that, despite a wealth of development programmes in the 1980s that introduced township children to sports, lack of facilities and infrastructure meant they were unable to continue to pursue these interests (Booth, 1998: 140). Desai and Veriava (2010: 8) suggest that attempts to make swimming more accessible have been hampered not only by the lack of resources, but by a political tension evident across most South African sports – that is, the need to provide grass-roots facilities while also producing black elite performers (e.g. black Olympians).

27 Hemson gained access as one of only three non-African members.

28 See www.umthombo.org/website.

29 Although as Tom Hewitt, their Chair of Board recognised, 'different programmes work for different kids', hence the array of activities and programmes offered in sport and across the arts. Umthombo has become known for organising the Street Child (football) World Cup in Durban, 2010. For details about the activities and aims of Umthombo, see their website at www.umthombo.org/website.

30 Numerous moving-image reports on the surfing project are available (e.g. Trans World Sport and Durban News). These are available on YouTube or the Umthombo website (see www.umthombo.org/website).

31 Personal correspondence with Tom Hewitt.

32 See, for example, a competition training session posted on the Bombsurf.com website, www.thebombsurf.com/thebombsurfvideos/812/ubuntu-surf-challenge (accessed 15 March 2011).

33 Whether this is the same Sandi Mqadi who featured in the *Zulu Wave Rider* documentary is unconfirmed.

34 All the participants in the videos are male, although they also run programmes targeting girls living on the street.

35 See www.surfing4peace.org/s4pindex/Welcome.html. Founded in 2007, 'Surfing 4 Peace is a person 2 person and cross-border cooperation initiative that aims to bridge cultural and political barriers between surfers in the Middle East' (see Olsen, 2012).

7 The California beach, whiteness and the exclusion of black bodies

1 Many of the sources on African surfing (e.g. Dawson, 2006) discuss Sir James Edward Alexander's diaries (1834/1835). One of my interviewees, Stevie, also discussed the significance of these diaries. He also showed me his collection of images illustrating this history of surfing.

2 Numerous excellent academic analyses of surfing's history now exist, which have proliferated over recent years (e.g. Ford and Brown, 2005; Stranger, 2011). In particular, I became aware of Lawler's (2011) book just as it was going to press. She offers a detailed analysis of how the *image* of surfing developed in California from the 1930s to the present day. An explicit analysis of race, however, remains a conspicuous absence in all these academic studies.

3 Indigenous Hawaiians lost their social, economic and political independence, and their population declined sharply due to the introduction of various infectious diseases (Finney and Houston, 1996: 51).

4 See also the surfing documentary *Bustin' Down the Door*, which graphically illustrates this contestation in Hawaii in the 1970s (Gosch, 2009).

5 Racial formations refers to the 'socio-historical process by which racial categories are created, inhabited, transformed, and destroyed' (Omi and Winant, 1994: 55).

6 Research in Chapters 7–9 was conducted during 2009–2010 and focused on California. See Chapter 1 for a more detailed discussion, and the limitations and methodological issues this research raised.

7 The Duke also introduced surfing to Australia, the Eastern Seaboard of the USA and Europe at a similar time (1915; see Booth, 2001; Osmond and Philips, 2004). Osmond *et al.* (2006) explore the symbolism of the Duke via a public statue to commemorate his life in Hawaii, discussing the competing sporting discourses about the Duke's swimming and surfing legacies. See also Chapter 8, the section 'Blacks can't swim'.

8 As Canniford (2009: 10) notes, along with the popularity of surfing, a Hawaiian vogue swept the USA, characterised by Hula dancing and Hawaiian music and song that 'valorised and fetishised a vision of pre-colonial island life'. See also Osmond and Philips (2004) on the exotic appeal of the Pacific islands.

9 For example, *Daily Telegram* and *Long Beach Press*, cited in Honolulu.gov (2010).

10 Air travel, however, was still difficult due to the heavy, long Malibu surfboards used at that time, contributing to the isolation of surfers in more distant locales like Australia (Booth, 2001: 91).

11 New technologies also led to the smaller, more controllable and more transportable surfboards that revolutionised surfing style and culture (Booth, 2001).

12 *Gidget* (1956) was the most famous, followed by sequels *Gidget Goes Hawaiian* (1961) and *Gidget Goes to Rome* (1963), then *Ride the Wild Surf* (1964) (Booth, 2001: 93).

13 The AIP films are *Beach Party* (1963), *Muscle Beach Party* (1964), *Bikini Beach* (1964), *Pyjama Party* (1964), *Beach Blanket Bingo* (1965), *How to Stuff a Wild Bikini* (1965) and *Ghost in the Invisible Bikini* (1966), all directed by William Asher, except *Pyjama Party* and *Ghost in the Invisible Bikini*, directed by Don Weis. Other companies released beach movies, but this is the core group (Morris, 1998).

14 Evident again in this narrative are the ways in which racialised social relations are expressed spatially.

15 There are a range of divergent views on their appeal, the mode of production and how they represent gender and sexuality that is beyond the scope of my discussion here. However, as Booth discusses, academics have warned against over-simple analyses of the era and genre (2001: 94).

16 As discussed in Chapters 4 and 8, Stenger's analysis is rooted in, and supports, a growing body of literature that explores how 'racialised social relations are spatially expressed' (Neal, 2002: 443). Central is the construction of a rural/urban binary, through which rurality is constructed as a place of safety and retreat, collapsed into desirable, idealised forms of whiteness (Neal, 2002).

17 I discuss Gabaldon and this erasure of surfing histories in more depth in Chapter 10.

18 Legal segregation – that is, segregation sanctioned by law – was officially stopped by federal enforcement of a series of Supreme Court decisions after Brown vs. Board of Education in 1954 (www.nationalcenter.org/brown.html). However, the process of

dismantling legal segregation continued through to the 1970s when civil rights demonstrations resulted in public opinion turning against enforced segregation. However,
it is widely recognised that de facto segregation continues to varying degrees without
sanction of law to the present day.

19 Jefferson (2009: 180) also discusses the notorious case of the Pacific Beach Club in
Huntington Beach, an African American-owned resort burnt down by arsonists.

20 Hypersegregation is a term given to racial segregation that consists of the geographical
grouping of racial groups, usually in urban areas, where the residents of the inner city
are African Americans and the suburbs surrounding this inner core are often European
American residents. The idea became known through the work of Massey and Denton
(1993) and their studies of 'American Apartheid', when white flight created the black
ghetto during the first half of the twentieth century in order to isolate growing urban
black populations by segregation among inner-city African Americans (Denton, 2007).

21 I discuss the Inkwell and Nick Gabaldon's significance for contemporary African
American surfers in more depth in Chapter 10. As discussed in Chapter 4, his story
has recently been documented in Nike's film *12 Miles North: The Nick Gabaldon
Story* (Nike Surfing, 2012).

22 See also in Chapter 4 where I discuss skateboarding in this locale, as represented in
Peralta's film *Dogtown and Z-Boys* (Kusz, 2005).

23 See also Chapter 4, which explores how Australian beaches became privileged sites
of whiteness.

24 Exemplifying what Urry calls 'diasporic travellers'; that is, unlike conventional
tourism based upon clear distinctions between 'home' and 'away', s/he has 'no clear
temporal boundaries as one activity tends to flow into the next' (Urry, 2002).

25 Michael discussed *On Safari*, a documentary in the US which, in contrast to the all-
male group, features a (heterosexual, white) couple, both of whom surf and travel
with their baby son; yet there is still an absence of black surfers.

26 Jennifer's shifting use of 'us' and 'we' in this narrative is interesting in illustrating her
own shifting diasporic black identity and the discursive incompatibility of the black
surfer identity, which is discussed in Chapter 9.

27 The exploitative ways in which the surf industry operates are discussed in Wheaton
(2007b) and Thorpe and Rinehart (2010).

28 One unusual, but particularly revealing, example is an article titled 'Super breed
descends' (Smith, 2010) cited in Harper (2010). The article begins with the lines:
'Icah Wilmot is bad for the white devil. Last week this multi-talented Negro became
the first Jamaican winner of the Pan American championships, held in Cuba, signalling, among other things, an uncertain future for the Aryan domination of surfing.'
This article is also discussed in Weisberg (2010), which was originally published, and
then withdrawn, from *Surfer* magazine.

29 Booth (2001) discussed a parallel process in the professionalisation of surfing in
Australia.

30 Interestingly, in her analysis of the scope of the black surfing market, she drew on
stereotypes of race, that black Americans are avid and style-conscious consumers:

> Because if you look at black spending in the United States, blacks will spend more
> money on anything before they buy a home. We have a billion dollar deficit in the
> black community of monies that we spend every single day. I spend more money
> on the surf industry than the surf industry even [laughs].

31 It is also worth noting that a similar process is prevalent among female athletes, black
and white. Elite females (windsurfers, surfers and kite-surfers) I have interviewed and
observed in the surf industry often recognised that to gain maximum photographic
exposure (required for sponsors), they needed to 'play up' the role of 'surf babe'
expected by the male-dominated industry, wearing, wherever possible, skimpy bikinis
that reveal their sexuality. It was a paradox that, when – many years ago – I was an

elite participant, I found myself forced to confront (see my discussion in Wheaton, 1997b). Nonetheless, as Chapter 8 illustrates, the reading and meaning of desire and exoticism are different for black female surfers.
32 IRIE stands for I Respect I Eternally.
33 www.urbandictionary.com/define.php?term=irie (accessed 22 November 2010).
34 Mulatto is a derogatory term that has historically been used to describe people of mixed (usually black and white) heritage.

8 Surfing, identity and race: belonging and exclusion

1 I use the term *black* in this chapter to refer to (self-defined) African-American surfers.
2 Given the small number of surfers I interviewed, and my own (gendered, racialised, Europe) positioning, I would not want to make any claims about the generalisability of their experiences, nor to 'know' or represent their subjectivity as surfers. See Chapter 1 for a fuller discussion of methodology.
3 As sketched out in the discussion of gender and space in Chapter 4.
4 The term *space invader* actually emerged from Doreen Massey's observations about the gendered and racialised spaces of sport (Puwar, 2004).
5 I am mindful that the term *barriers* can invoke a liberal political discourse of equality (Scraton, 2001) that assumes there are particular issues to be overcome that, once achieved, will then lead to equality in opportunity (Carrington and McDonald, 2001a).
6 I, therefore, also draw on interviews and observational work with black water users in Barbados (2010) and past research in locales including Hawaii and the Caribbean (African and Hispanic islands) to contextualise this discussion. See section titled 'A methodological journey' in Chapter 1.
7 Bourdieu calls all forms of power *capital* and discusses different forms such as cultural, symbolic, economic and physical capital, so recognising that wealth is not just economic (or political) but can also be symbolic (Wheaton, 2009a). These different types of wealth, which are inherited or accumulated, tend to be unevenly distributed, and a part of a person's habitus. Through the formation of their habitus people acquire cultural capital, a 'range of cultural competencies', which 'makes particular activities more or less accessible for them' (Haywood *et al.*, 1995: 240). See also discussion of Bourdieu in Chapter 3.
8 Puwar (2004) outlines how Bourdieu's ideas, particularly 'a feel for the game', help understand how ethnic minorities become insiders in institutions dominated by whiteness.
9 It is interesting that Stevie's father viewed his son's best chance to succeed to be his athletic body, despite Stevie's (now proven) intellect. His perception reflects Hoberman's (1997) thesis that, by directing their children into sport, rather than education, black communities unwittingly collude in promoting a broader pro-sport and anti-intellectual culture, which ultimately limits their opportunities. While Hoberman's thesis has been criticised for pathologising black communities and downplaying the more structural barriers, such as education and employment (Carrington and McDonald, 2001a: 11), it is certainly evident that prevalent dominant discourses of race continue to emphasise that black bodies are athletically superior and therefore less rational or intellectual (Abdel-Shehid, 2005).
10 The Brown vs. Board of Education (1954) decision of the Supreme Court, ordering the de jure racial desegregation of public schools in the United States, and subsequently attempts to achieve effective desegregation were made by forced bussing.
11 Derogatory terms like Uncle Tom are discussed in Nayak (2003) and Carrington (2000).
12 She described the documentary *Whitewash*, which 'shows an interview with African-American youth at a basketball court in New York, laughing at the notion of them swimming'.

13 Carrington (2004: 90, 91) discusses the 'racialogical thinking' underpinning media representation of Equatorial Guinea swimmer Moussambaun, dubbed Eric the Eel by the British media in the Sydney Olympic Games, and which drew on wider stereotypes that Africans are non-swimmers (and 'infantalised' via 'animalistic simile').

14 Of course *where* people swim may well be a key factor attributing to this statistic, with whites being more likely to have access to the safer swimming pool environment.

15 In one study, the respondents were asked if they could swim across a 25-yard pool.

16 Particularly in contrast to the wealth of work exploring how sport reinforces dominant racial ideologies about black athleticism.

17 It is also the focus of a recent insightful editorial in *The Inertia* (Endo, 2012).

18 This paper still informs common-sense ideas about why blacks do not swim. For example, it was cited in an article in the *New York Times* in 2006 (Zinser, 2006). Research in South Africa, even 14 years after apartheid, has also demonstrated the enduring impact of this common-sense notion of racial difference (see Ch. 6).

19 It is suggested that freestyle was not adopted in the USA until after 1912. Hawaiian surfer Duke Kahanamoku (discussed in Ch. 7) broke two world records and secured Olympic gold using his 'Kahanamoku kick', despite having never had any formal swimming training (Dawson, 2006: 1334). His subsequent tours of the USA, Australia and Europe demonstrating his swimming and surfing skills popularised both sports (Osmond and Philips 2004; Osmond *et al.*, 2006).

20 The range of racial discourses around aquatic ability is certainly worthy of further reflection. Indeed, mirroring the colonial appropriation of surfing (discussed in Ch. 7), swimming provides a 'classic postcolonial example of the transformation of an indigenous body culture into a more Western sporting activity and its simultaneous appropriation by a colonial nation' (Osmond and Philips, 2004: 313).

21 Of course such experiences are unlikely to be universal but depend on the context. As noted in Chapter 6, African street children in Durban grew up in the proximity of the sea and did learn to swim and surf in the ocean.

22 Zinser (2006) claims that this is, in part, because of prohibitive building and running costs, but clearly there are wider political issues around leisure funding.

23 But as Green's research exemplifies, the reason for this fear was rooted in bodily difference and social inequality, based around swimming's role in the reproduction of class and race in Barbados.

24 The USA Swimming study suggested that Hispanics were better swimmers than African Americans (Rohrer, 2010).

25 See also Chapter 6 on street children using the beach in South Africa.

26 The ways in which masculinity performances and 'race' underpin localism are highlighted by a number of authors detailed in Chapter 4.

27 As outlined in Chapter 4, Venice Beach also played a central role in the development of modern skateboarding culture (Kusz, 2005; Wachs, 2007).

28 This quote again illustrates how localism in surfing is underpinned by a micro politics of gender and 'race'.

29 Media reports about Gabaldon suggested he was 'welcomed' into the

> brotherhood of surfers in the 1940s and 1950s, including at the conservative locale of Malibu. One of Gabaldon's best friends described him as 'a gentleman'. He was accepted and respected by all of us. We didn't look at color, he was just a friend.
>
> (Les Williams, in Gault-Williams, 2010)

Likewise, it was claimed that the white surfers of Malibu 'were in awe at Gabaldon's surfing abilities' and 'counted him as their close friend' (Legendary Surfers, http://files.legendarysurfers.com/blog/labels/Inkwell%20Beach.html). In contrast, when trying to hitch-hike along the Pacific Coast Highway to Malibu (he did not own a car), 'most drivers refused to stop for the tall, muscular African-American man' (Gault-Williams, 2010).

30 In discussing the reasons for this denial, Burdsey highlights that individual players may not have experienced overt racism and that racism in the sport often 'manifests itself in informal, subtle and sometimes unintentional forms', making the detection of racial discrimination hard to detect (Burdsey, 2004a: 287). Burdsey also highlights that players tended not to discuss certain behaviours (such as racist 'industrial language') which are seen to be a legitimate and normal part of the culture of professional sport (see also King, 2004).

31 As discussed in Chapter 3, commitment to the activity was an important way status was marked, and 'authentic' surfers were differentiated.

32 This is not to suggest that these processes are the same for black and white women.

33 The idea of a black diasporic identity is discussed in more depth in Chapter 9.

34 See discussion of surfing masculinity and localism in Chapter 4.

35 In this context, clearly the age of many of these surfers (predominantly over 40), as well as their 'race', is significant in adopting this surfer identity.

36 Anger was experienced in many spheres of their lives, from childhood through to adulthood, not just while surfing.

9 Challenging exclusion: the Black Surfing Association

1 Website refers to the BSA website pages at www.blacksurfingassociation.com.

2 I attempted to corroborate this account, but was unable to make contact with any of these surfers from San Diego.

3 Including Tony Corley, current president Rick Blocker, and previous president Dedon Kamathi.

4 There were also members who did not see surfing as a political issue at all.

5 Her most visible clash with the organisation was during an incident surrounding the ceremony for the plaque at Inkwell (see Harper, 2007). The reasons for these differences are not relevant for the themes in this chapter; however, it should be noted that, while Rhonda was recommended to me via the BSA, and while I am including her interviews in the discussion of the BSA, she is not an active member and lives outside of the LA area.

6 I discuss a similar process of hybridisation or creolisation of lifestyle sport in Africa in Chapter 6.

7 The *paddle out* is a Hawaiian tradition that has been widely (and globally) adopted in surf culture. When a member of the local community has died, surfers take to the water, performing a ceremony sitting on their boards in a circle.

8 'BSA Spring Surf Contest Rocks', 7 May 2006, cited on http://legacy.blacksurfing.com/news.htm.

9 He was regional director/president of the Western Surfing Association between 1980 and 1990.

10 The *Surfer's Path* magazine covered this (23 November 2005). Former BSA president Rick Blocker was involved.

11 See, for example, Inkwell Lifestyle (Inkwell Lifestyle Brand, 2010) and Black Athlete Sports Network (www.blackathlete.net).

12 This article provoked controversy more widely. See Weisberg (2010) and Pawle (2010).

13 I was not able to substantiate these claims.

14 http://legacy.blacksurfing.com/news.htm.

15 For example, when one of her films was screened at a surf film festival, it provoked audience members to visit and write (positive) comments on the BSA forum (e.g. 8 November 2009).

16 As noted above, the plaque caused dispute between various factions of black surfers. See Tojek (2007).

17 Corroborated by my experiences talking to white Angelenos and the news reports about the plaque (Tojek, 2007).
18 A similar campaign, led by the City Project, resulted in a name change at Bruce's Beach in 2007, as part of its campaign to 'completely and accurately celebrate the proud legacy of Bruce's Beach and African-American Los Angeles' (Project, 2010). Bruce's Beach was one of the few beaches in Southern California in the early 1900s that was not off-limits to African Americans. The City Project 'worked with Bernard Bruce, the Bruce's grandson, to change the name of the oceanfront park back to Bruce's Beach' (aka Bruces or Bruce Beach) (ibid.).
19 It is interesting to reflect on how the pioneer has traditionally been marked as a white identity. See, for example, Farley (2005) and Kay and Laberge (2003).
20 Although tellingly, in Lapchick's (2008) book *100 Pioneers: African-Americans who Broke Color Barriers in Sport*, Gabaldon is not mentioned.
21 A discussion of these films would be interesting, but beyond my scope here. White-wash was released but I was unable to watch it.
22 See www.soulonawave.net/Soul_on_a_Wave/Trailer.html. This film was being developed by Portia Scott-Hicks (Los Angeles) and Paul Richardson (Monterey). Most recently, Gabaldon has been the focus of a Nike-sponsored film, *12 Miles North: The Nick Gabaldon Story* (see Nike Surfing, 2012; Yelland, 2012).
23 Evidently some felt the terminology was excluding. One anonymous online posting asked, 'Why are you guys called BSA? Why can't a white guy or Mexican join you? Racist I say ... why does it have to be black only? Why can't you let other races join? Please respond' (Anonymous posting, 23 May 2009). It is not clear if this was a broadly held view and whether this respondent was a black surfer him/herself.
24 In which she was instrumental in getting the Inkwell plaque erected and where she was the surfing ambassador at the civic ceremony.
25 'Surfrider Foundation Invites BSA', 9 June 2005, cited on http://legacy.blacksurfing.com/news.htm.
26 One interviewee, however, did not see surfing as political; given the small selected sample, it is likely that there are others too.
27 And African-American visitation of the Rocky Mountain National Park specifically.
28 www.youtube.com/watch?v=CZH-Up1Kk-g&feature=related.

10 Coda

1 NSMs are increasingly strident political and social collectivities based outside of the workplace, or mainstream political institutions, in which interests are mobilised around a particular goal (Melucci, 1980; Touraine, 1985). They were seen to have emerged in modern Western societies during the 1960s, when they were associated with the student movement, civil rights and anti-Vietnam War protests; however, environmentalism is often taken as archetypal (Anderson, 1997: 77).
2 The 'global carnival against capital' (Klein, 2000: 444) of 18 June 1999 involved protest actions in 70 cities around the world (coinciding with the G-8 meeting in Cologne, Germany) (St John, 2003: 69).
3 In Lawler's analysis, she also argues that surfing's politicisation transcends the context and challenges the capitalism system itself.

References

Abdel-Shehid, G. (2005). *Who Da Man? Black Masculinities and Sporting Cultures*. Toronto: Canadian Scholars' Press Inc.

Aguerre, F. (2009). *Surfing and the Olympics: My Point of View*. Statement from the president of the International Surfing Association. Accessed from www.isasurf.org/olympic-surfing/general-information-olympic-surfing.

Agyemang, K., Singer, J. N. and DeLorme, J. (2010). An exploratory study of black male college athletes' perception on race and athlete activism. *International Review of the Sociology of Sport, 45*(4), 419–435.

Ahmed, S. (2004). Declarations of whiteness: the non-performativity of anti-racism. *Borderlands Journal, 3*(2), 1–6.

Aitch, L. (2008). Event preview: World Freerun Championships. *The Guardian*, 30 August.

Aitchison, C. (1999). New cultural geographies: the spatiality of leisure, gender and sexuality. *Leisure Studies, 18*(1), 19–39.

Alexander, C. (2000). *The Asian Gang: Ethnicity, Identity and Masculinity*. Oxford: Berg.

Allen, R. L. and Nickel, D. L. (1969). The negro and learning to swim: the buoyancy problem related to reported biological differences. *Negro Education, 38*(4, Autumn), 404–411.

Anderson, A. (1997). *Media, Culture and the Environment*. London: UCL Press.

Anderson, K. (1999). Snowboarding: the construction of gender in an emerging sport. *Journal of Sport and Social Issues, 23*(1), 55–79.

Andrews, D. (1993). Desperately seeking Michel: Foucault's genealogy, the body, and critical sport sociology. *Sociology of Sport Journal, 10*, 148–167.

Andrews, D. (2006). Leisure studies: progress, phases and possibilities – an interview with Alan Tomlinson. *Leisure Studies, 25*(3), 257–273.

Andrews, D. (2008). Kinesiology's inconvenient truth and the physical cultural studies imperative. *Quest, 60*(1), 45–62.

Andrews, D. and Cole, C. (2002). On issue: the nation reconsidered. *Journal of Sport and Social Issues, 26*, 123–124.

Andrews, D. and Ritzer, G. (2007). The grobal in the sporting glocal. *Global Networks, 7*(2), 113–153.

Andrews, D. and Silk, M. (2011). Physical cultural studies: engendering a productive dialogue. *Sociology of Sport Journal, 28*(1), 1–3.

Angel, J. (2007). *Jump Westminster* [film]. Julie Angel [dir.]. Accessed from www.julieangel.com/Jump_Westminster.html.

Angel, J. (2011a). *Ciné Parkour* [film]. Julie Angel [dir.]. Accessed from www.juliean-gel.com/Cine_Parkour.html.

Angel, J. (2011b). *Ciné Parkour: A Cinematic and Theoretical Contribution to the Understanding of the Practice of Parkour*. Ph.D., Brunel University, London.

Appadurai, A. (1996). *Modernity at Large: Cultural Dimensions of Globalization*. Minneapolis, MN: University of Minnesota Press.

Archer, N. (2010). Virtual poaching and altered space: reading parkour in French visual culture. *Modern & Contemporary France, 18*(1), 93–107.

Armitage, J., Bishop, R. and Kellner, D. (2005). Introducing cultural politics. *Cultural Politics, 1*(1), 1–4.

Asthana, A. (2003). Girls just want to have fun too. *Observer*, 14 September, 20.

Asthana, A. (2008). Kids need the adventure of 'risky play'. *Sunday Observer*, 3 August.

Ataöv, A. and Haider, J. (2006). From participation to empowerment: critical reflections on a participatory action research project with street children in Turkey. *Children, Youth and Environments, 16*(2), 127–152.

Atencio, M. and Beal, B. (2011). Beautiful losers: the symbolic exhibition and legitimization of outsider masculinity. *Sport in Society, 14*(1), 1–16.

Atencio, M., Beal, B. and Wilson, C. (2009). The distinction of risk: urban skateboarding, street habitus and the construction of hierarchical gender relations. *Qualitative Research in Sport and Exercise, 1*(1), 3–20.

Atkinson, P. (1990). *The Ethnographic Imagination: Textual Constructions of Reality*. London: Routledge.

Atkinson, M. (2009). Parkour, anarcho-environmentalism, and poiesis. *Journal of Sport and Social Issues, 33*(2), 169–194.

Atkinson, M. (2010). Entering scapeland: yoga, fell and post-sport physical cultures. *Sport in Society: Cultures, Commerce, Media, Politics, 13*(7), 1249–1267.

Atkinson, M. (2011). Physical cultural studies [redux]. *Sociology of Sport Journal, 28*(1), 135–144.

Atkinson, M. and Wilson, B. (2002). Bodies, subcultures and sport. In J. Maguire and K. Young (Eds), *Theory, Sport and Society* (pp. 375–395). Oxford: JAI.

Atkinson, M. and Young, K. (2008). Youth tribes in sport. In M. Atkinson and K. Young (Eds), *Deviance and Social Control in Sport* (pp. 51–74). Champaign, IL: Human Kinetics

Ayub, A. (2011). Afghanistan girls take to skateboarding. *ESPNw*, 13 May. Accessed from http://espn.go.com/espnw/features-profiles/6530767/skateistan-challenges-gender-stereotypes-kabul.

Azzarito, L. and Harrison, L. (2008). White men can't jump: race, gender and athleticism. *International Review for the Sociology of Sport, 43*(3), 347–364.

Baker, R. (1999). *Children of the Street: A Reinterpretation Based on Evidence from Durban, South Africa*. Centre for Developing Areas Research, Department of Geography, Royal Holloway University of London.

Bale, J. (1994). *Landscapes of Modern Sport*. Leicester: Leicester University Press.

Banks, M. (2008). The instrumental leisure of the 'creative class'. *CRESC Working Paper Series*, Milton Keynes: CRESC, Open University.

Barclay, R. and West, P. (2006). Racism or patriotism? An eyewitness's account of the Cronulla demonstrations of 11 December 2005. *People and Place, 14*(1), 75–85.

Barker, C. (2000). *Cultural Studies: Theory and Practice*. London: Sage.

Barkham, P. (2006). A bigger splash, a lot more cash. *The Guardian*, 17 July, 6–9.

Bavinton, N. (2007). From obstacle to opportunity: parkour, leisure, and the reinterpretation of constraints. *Annals of Leisure Research, 10*(3/4), 391–412.

BBC News. (2008). Women's surfing campaign. Mike Bushell visits a Devon beach which is playing its part in a worldwide campaign to get more women to surf. *BBC News*, 1 August. Accessed from http://news.bbc.co.uk/1/hi/uk/7538378.stm.

BBC News. (2009). Two kite surfers jump over pier. *BBC News*, 16 November. Accessed from http://news.bbc.co.uk/1/hi/england/sussex/8362671.stm.

BBC News. (2010). Kite surfer 'jumps' over Brighton pier. *BBC News*, 12 November. Accessed from www.bbc.co.uk/news/uk-11748836.

Beal, B. (1995). Disqualifying the official: An exploration of social resistance through the subculture of skateboarding. *Sociology of Sport Journal, 12*(3), 252–267.

Beal, B. (1996). Alternative masculinity and its effect on gender relations in the subculture of skateboarding. *Journal of Sports Behaviour, 19*(3), 204–220.

Beal, B. and Weidman, L. (2003). Authenticity in the skateboarding world. In R. Rinehart and S. Sydnor (Eds), *To the Extreme: Alternative Sports Inside and Out* (pp. 337–352). Albany, NY: SUNY Press.

Beal, B. and Wilson, C. (2004). 'Chicks dig scars': Commercialisation and the transformations of skate boarders' identities. In B. Wheaton (Ed.), *Understanding Lifestyle Sports: Consumption, Identity and Difference* (pp. 31–54). London: Routledge.

Beattie, K. (2001). Sick, filthy, and delirious: surf film and video and the documentary mode. *Continuum: Journal of Media and Cultural Studies, 15*(3), 333–348.

Beaumont, G. (2008). *'Parkour-Related' Activity: afPE's Position Statement and Recommendations*. afPE. Accessed from www.school-portal.co.uk/GroupDownloadFile.asp?GroupId=246156&ResourceID=3578815.

Beck, U. (1992). *The Risk Society: Towards a New Modernity* (M. Ritter, Trans.). London: Sage.

Beedie, P. (2007). Legislators and interpreters: an examination of change in philosophical interpretations of 'being a mountaineer'. In M. McNamee (Ed.), *Philosophy, Risk and Adventure Sports* (pp. 25–42). London: Routledge.

Bell, D., Caplan, P. and Jahan Karim, W. (Eds). (1993). *Gendered Fields: Women, Men and Ethnography*. London: Routledge.

Bennett, A. (1999). Subculture or neo-tribes? Rethinking the relationship between youth, style and musical taste. *Sociology, 33*(3), 599–617.

Bennett, A. (2000). *Popular Music and Youth Culture: Music, Identity and Place*. Basingstoke: Macmillan Press Ltd.

Bennett, A. and Kahn-Harris, K. (Eds). (2004). *After Subculture: Critical Studies in Contemporary Youth Culture*. Basingstoke: Palgrave Macmillan.

Benwell, B. (2003). Introduction: masculinity and men's lifestyle magazines. In B. Benwell (Ed.), *Masculinity and Men's Lifestyle Magazines* (pp. 6–29), Sociological Review Monographs. Oxford: Blackwell.

Birrell, S. and McDonald, M. (2000). *Reading Sport: Critical Essays on Power and Representation*. Boston, MA: Boston Northeastern University Press.

Bonilla-Silva, E. (2006). *Racism Without Racists: Color-Blind Racism and the Persistence of Racial Inequality in the United States*. Lanham, MD: Rowman & Littlefield Publishers Inc.

Bonnett, A. (2000). *White Identities: Historical and International Perspectives*. London: Prentice Hall.

Booth, D. (1994). Surfing 60s: a case study in the history of pleasure and discipline. *Australian Historical Studies, 103*, 262–279.

Booth, D. (1996). Surfing films and videos: adolescent fun, alternative lifestyle, adventure industry. *Journal of Sport History, 23*(3), 313–327.

Booth, D. (1998). *The Race Game: Sport and Politics in South Africa*. London: Frank Cass.

Booth, D. (1999). Surfing: the cultural and technological determinants of a dance. *Culture, Sport, Society, 2*(1), 36–55.

Booth, D. (2001). *Australian Beach Cultures: The History of Sun, Sand and Surf*. London: Frank Cass.

Booth, D. (2003). Expression sessions: surfing, style and prestige. In R. Rinehart and S. Sydor (Eds), *To the Extreme: Alternative Sports, Inside and Out* (pp. 315–336). Albany, NY: State University of New York Press.

Booth, D. (2004). Surfing: from one (cultural) extreme to another. In B. Wheaton (Ed.), *Understanding Lifestyle Sports: Consumption, Identity and Difference* (pp. 94–109). London: Routledge.

Booth, D. (2008). (Re)reading the surfers' bible: the affect of tracks. *Continuum: Journal of Media and Cultural Studies, 22*(1), 17–35.

Booth, D. and Nauright, J. (2003). Embodied identities: sport and race in South Africa. *Contours: A Journal of the African Diaspora, 1*(1), 1–26.

Booth, D. and Thorpe, H. (2007a). *International Encyclopedia of Extreme Sport*. Great Barrington: Berkshire Reference Works.

Booth, D. and Thorpe, H. (2007b). Introduction. In D. Booth and H. Thorpe (Eds), *Berkshire Encyclopedia of Extreme Sports* (pp. ix–xii). Great Barrington: Berkshire Reference Works.

Booth, D. and Thorpe, H. (2007c). The meaning of extreme. In D. Booth and H. Thorpe (Eds), *Berkshire Encyclopedia of Extreme Sports* (pp. 181–197). Great Barrington: Berkshire Reference Works.

Borden, I. (2001). *Skateboarding, Space and the City: Architecture and the Body*. Oxford: Berg.

Bourdieu, P. (1977). *Outline of a Theory of Practice*. Cambridge: Cambridge University Press.

Bourdieu, P. (1978). Sport and social class. *Social Science Information, 17*(6), 819–840.

Bourdieu, P. (1984). *Distinction: A Social Critique of the Judgement of Taste*. London and New York: Routledge & Kegan Paul Ltd.

Bourdieu, P. (2001). *Homo Academicus*. Oxford: Polity Press.

Bowes, G. (2007). Surfing goes indoors. *Observer*, 18 February, 4.

Boyes, M. (2009). Outdoor adventures for the third age. In B. Humberstone (Ed.), *Third Age and Leisure: Research, Principles and Practice* (Vol. LSA No. 108, pp. 81–96). Eastbourne: LSA.

Bradley, G. L. (2010). Skate parks as a context for adolescent development. *Journal of Adolescent Research, 25*(2), 288–323.

Brayton, S. (2005). 'Back-lash': revisiting the 'white negro' through skateboarding. *Sociology of Sport Journal, 22*, 256–372.

Britton, B. (2006). A personal diary account of the surfari. *The Silver Surfari*, 15 October. Accessed from www.irelandsurfari.com/event.html.

Brown, D. and Leledak, A. (2010). Eastern movement forms as body-self transforming cultural practices in the West: towards a sociological perspective. *Cultural Sociology, 4*(1), 123–154.

Brown, D. L. and Earnest, R. (Writers). (2001). Surfing for Life [film]. David L. Brown [dir.] and Roy Earnest [prod.]. www.surfingforlife.com/.

Burdsey, D. (2004a). Obstacle race? 'Race', racism and the recruitment of British Asian professional footballers. *Patterns of Prejudice, 38*(3), 279–299.

Burdsey, D. (2004b). 'One of the lads'? Dual ethnicity and assimilated ethnicities in the careers of British Asian professional footballers. *Ethnic and Racial Studies, 27*(5), 757–779.

Burdsey, D. (2010). British Muslim experiences in English first-class cricket. *International Review for the Sociology of Sport, 45*(3), 315–334.

Burdsey, D. (2011a). 'It still felt like I was going to the end of the earth': the experiences of minority ethnic communities living at the English seaside. Paper given to Centre for Sport Research University of Brighton.

Burdsey, D. (2011b). Strangers on the shore? Racialized representation, identity and in/visibilities of whiteness at the English seaside. *Cultural Sociology, 11*(5), 537–552.

Burdsey, D. (2011c). That joke isn't funny anymore: racial microaggressions, color-blind ideology and the mitigation of racism in English men's first-class cricket. *Sociology of Sport, 28*, 261–283.

Burdsey, D. (2013). 'The foreignness is still quite visible in this town': multiculture, marginality and prejudice at the English seaside. *Patterns of Prejudice, 47*(2), 95–116.

Burnett, C. (2001). Social impact assessment and sport development: social spin-offs of the Australian–South Africa junior sport programme. *International Review for Sociology of Sport, 36*(1), 41–57.

Burton, J. (Writer). (2002). Analysis: popularity of snowboarding and extreme sports [radio]. *Talk of the Nation*, 13 February.

Buscher, M. and Urry, J. (2009). Mobile methods and the empirical. *European Journal of Social Theory, 12*(1), 99–116.

Butler, J. (1990). *Gender Trouble: Feminism and the Subversion of Identity*. London: Routledge.

Butler, J. (1993). *Bodies that Matter: On the Discursive Limits of 'Sex'*. London: Routledge.

Byrne, B. (2006). *White Lives: The Interplay of 'Race', Class and Gender in Everyday Life*. London: Routledge.

Canniford, R. (2009). Culture clash: economic reconstructions of Hawaiian surfing. In J. Ormond and B. Wheaton (Eds), *'On the Edge': Leisure, Consumption and the Representation of Adventure Sport* (Vol. 104, pp. 3–16). Eastbourne: Leisure Studies Association.

Carrington, B. (2000). Double consciousness and the black British athlete. In K. Owusu (Ed.), *Black British Culture and Society: A Text Reader* (pp. 133–156). London: Routledge.

Carrington, B. (2002). Sport, masculinity and black cultural resistance. In J. Sugden and A. Tomlinson (Eds), *Power Games: Theory and Method for a Critical Sociology of Sport* (pp. 275–298). London: Routledge.

Carrington, B. (2004). Cosmopolitan Olympism, humanism and the spectacle of 'race'. In J. Bale (Ed.), *Post-Olympism? Questioning Sport in the Twenty-first Century* (pp. 81–97). Oxford: Berg Publishers.

Carrington, B. (2007). Merely identity: cultural identity and the politics of sport. *Sociology of Sport Journal, 24*(1), 49–66.

Carrington, B. (2008). 'What's the footballer doing here?' Racialized performativity, reflexivity, and identity. *Cultural Studies <=> Critical Methodologies, 8*(4), 423–452.

Carrington, B. (2009). Leeds and the topography of race: in six scenes. In P. Braham and S. Wagg (Eds), *Sport, Leisure and Culture in the Postmodern City* (pp. 99–128). Farnham, Surrey: Ashgate.

Carrington, B. (2010). *Race, Sport and Politics: The Sporting Black Diaspora*. London: Sage.

Carrington, B. and McDonald, I. (2001a). Introduction: 'race' sport and British society. In B. Carrington and I. McDonald (Eds), *'Race' Sport and British Society* (pp. 1–26). London: Routledge.

Carrington, B. and McDonald, I. (Eds). (2001b). *'Race' Sport and British Society*. London: Routledge.

Carrington, B. and Wilson, B. (2004). Dance nations: rethinking youth subcultural theory. In A. Bennett and K. Kahn-Harris (Eds), *After Subculture: Critical Studies in Contemporary Youth Culture* (pp. 65–78). Basingstoke: Palgrave.

Carrol, R. (2009). Brazil's surf sensation inspires girls to take on the big waves. *Observer*, 7 June, 37.

Caudwell, J. (2011). Sport feminism(s): narratives of linearity? *Journal of Sport & Social Issues, 35*(2), 111–125.

Caudwell, J. and Browne, K. (2011). Sexy spaces: geography and leisure intersectionalities. *Leisure Studies, 30*(2), 117–122.

Celsi, R., Rose, R. L. and Leigh, T. W. (1993). An exploration of high-risk leisure consumption through sky-diving. *Journal of Consumer Research, 20*(1), 1–22.

Chaney, D. (1996). *Lifestyles*. London and New York: Routledge.

Chaney, D. (2002). *Cultural Change and Everyday Life*. Basingstoke: Palgrave.

Chetty, V. (1997). *Street Children in Durban: An Exploratory Investigation*. Pretoria: Human Sciences Research Council.

Chiu, C. (2009). Street and park skateboarding in New York city public space. *Space and Culture, 12*(1), 25–42.

Chivers-Yochim, E. (2010). *Skate Life: Re-imagining White Masculinity*. Ann Arbor, MI: University of Michigan Press.

Christie, M. (Writer). (2003). *Jump London* [film]. London: Channel 4.

Christie, M. (Writer). (2005). *Jump Britain* [film]. London: Carbon Media Ltd.

Clarke, S. and Garner, S. (2010). *White Identities: A Critical Sociological Approach*. London: Pluto Press.

Clemmitt, M. (2009). Extreme sports: are they too dangerous? *CQ Researcher, 19*(13), 297–317.

Clifford, J. (1997). *Routes: Travel and Translation in the Late Twentieth Century*. London: Harvard University Press.

Clotfelter, C. T. (2004). *After Brown: The Rise and Retreat of School Desegregation*. Princeton: Princeton University Press.

Coalter, F. (2007). *A Wider Social Role for Sport: Who's Keeping the Score?* London: Routledge.

Coalter, F. (2010). The politics of sport-for-development: limited focus programmes and broad gauge problems. *International Review for the Sociology of Sport, 45*(3), 295–314.

Cole, C. (1991). The politics of cultural representation: visions of fields/fields of vision. *International Review for Sociology of Sport, 26*, 37–49.

Comer, K. (2004). Wanting to be Lisa: generational rifts, girl power and the globalization of surf culture. In N. Campbell (Ed.), *American Youth Cultures* (pp. 237–265). New York: Routledge.

Comer, K. (2010). *Surfer Girls in the New World Order*. Durham, NC, and London: Duke University Press.

Connell, R. (1995). *Masculinities*. Cambridge: Polity Press.

Corley, T. (n.d.). *The Black Surfing Association: History*. Accessed from www.blacksurfingassociation.com/BSA_History.html.

Cornford, C. (2008). Circular 099/2008: guidance on parkour. *CZone* [Online]. Accessed on 12 November 2009 from https://czone.eastsussex.gov.uk/county_information/virtual_schoolbag/document.asp?item=2801.

Couetdic, T. (2011). *Parkour and the Female Practitioner*. Accessed from http://girlparkour.com/articles/2009/15/parkour-and-the-female-practitioner.

Coyne, H. (2010). How art and football gives street children a chance. *BBC Local*. Accessed from http://news.bbc.co.uk/local/cambridgeshire/hi/people_and_places/arts_and_culture/newsid_8733000/8733855.stm.

Cronje, A., Francisco, C. and Nortje, B. (Writers). (2008). *Zulu Surf Riders* [film]. South Africa: Scratch the Surfers.

Crosset, T. (1995). *Outsiders in the Clubhouse: The World of Women's Professional Golf*. Albany, NY: SUNY Press.

Crouch, D. and Tomlinson, A. (1994). Collective self-generated consumption: leisure, space and cultural identity in late modernity. In I. Henry (Ed.), *Leisure, Modernism, Postmodernism and Lifestyles* (pp. 309–321). Eastbourne: LSA Publications.

Dant, T. and Wheaton, B. (2007). Windsurfing: an extreme form of material and embodied interaction? *Anthropology Today, 23*(6, December), 8–12.

Daskalaki, M., Stara, A. and Miguel, I. (2008). The 'Parkour organisation': inhabitation of corporate spaces. *Culture & Organisation, 14*(1), 49–64.

Davidson, L. (2008). Tragedy in the adventure playground: media representations of mountaineering accidents in New Zealand. *Leisure Studies, 27*(1), 3–19.

Dawson, K. (2006). Enslaved swimmers and divers in the Atlantic world. *The Journal of American History, 92*(4, March), 1327–1355.

Denton, N. A. (2007). Hypersegregation. In G. Ritzer (Ed.), *Blackwell Encyclopedia of Sociology* (pp. 2196–2199). Oxford: Blackwell.

Denzin, N. (2002). *Reading Race: Hollywood and the Cinema of Racial Violence*. London: Sage.

Denzin, N. and Lincoln, Y. (1994). *Handbook of Qualitative Research*. Thousand Oaks, CA: Sage.

Derbyshire, D. (2009). Kite surfers leap over seaside pier in death-defying stunt as Met Office warns weather will get worse this week. *Mail Online*, 17 November.

Desai, A. (Ed.). (2010). *The Race to Transform Sport in Post-apartheid South Africa*. Cape Town: HSRC Press.

Desai, A. and Veriava, A. (2010). Creepy crawlies, portapools and the dam(n)s of swimming transformation. In A. Desai (Ed.), *The Race to Transform Sport in Post-apartheid South Africa* (pp. 2–55). Cape Town: HSRC Press.

Dilley, R. and Scraton, S. (2010). Women, climbing and serious leisure. *Leisure Studies, 29*(2), 125–141.

Dionigi, R. (2009). Managing identity in later life through leisure: interpreting the experiences of older athletes. In B. Humberstone (Ed.), *Third Age and Leisure: Research, Principles and Practice* (Vol. LSA No. 108, pp. 59–81). Eastbourne: LSA.

Dionigi, R. and O'Flynn, G. (2007). Performance discourses and old age: what does it mean to be an older athlete? *Sociology of Sport Journal, 24*, 359–377.

Diversi, M. (2006). Street kids in Nikes: in search of humanization through the culture of consumption. *Cultural Studies <=> Critical Methodologies, 6*(3), 370–390.

Dolby, N. (2001). *Constructing Race: Youth, Identity and Popular Culture in South Africa*. Albany, NY: SUNY Press.

Donnelly, M. (2006). Studying extreme sport: beyond the core participants. *Journal of Sport and Social Issues, 30*(2, May), 219–224.

Donnelly, M. (2008). 'Take the slam and get back up': hardcore candy and the politics of representation in girls' and women's skateboarding and snowboarding television. In M. Giardina and M. Donnelly (Eds), *Youth Culture and Sport: Identity, Power, and Politics* (pp. 127–143). New York: Routledge.

Donnelly, P. and Young, K. (1988). The construction and confirmation of identity in sport subcultures. *Sociology of Sport Journal, 5*, 197–211.

Drift Surfing (2011) Isiqalo 'Waves for Change Curriculum', 13 April. Accessed from www.driftsurfing.eu/index.php/archives/7636.

Dumas, A. and Laforest, S. (2009). Skateparks as a health-resource: are they as dangerous as they look? *Leisure Studies, 28*(1), 19–34.

Durrheim, K. and Dixon, J. (2001). The role of place and metaphor in racial exclusion: South Africa's beaches as sites of shifting racialization. *Ethnic and Racial Studies, 24*(3), 433–450.

Dyer, R. (1997). *White*. London: Routledge.

Edwardes, D. (2007). Parkour. In D. Booth and H. Thorpe (Eds), *Berkshire Encyclopedia of Extreme Sports* (pp. 233–236). Great Barrington.: Berkshire Publishing Group.

Edwards, B. and Corte, U. (2010). Commercialization and lifestyle sport: lessons from 20 years of freestyle BMX in 'Pro-Town, USA'. *Sport in Society: Cultures, Commerce, Media, Politics, 13*(7), 1135–1151.

Eichberg, H. (1998). *Body Cultures: Essays on Sport, Space and Identity*. London: Routledge.

Elias, N. and Dunning, E. (Eds). (1986). *Quest for Excitement: Sport and Leisure in the Civilizing Process*. Oxford: Blackwell.

Endo, T. (2012). Debunking the stereotype that blacks don't swim. *The Inertia: Distributor of Ideas*, 20 February. Accessed from www.theinertia.com/surf/12-miles-north-nick-gabaldon-story-exclusive-online-premiere/.

Ennew, J. (2003). Difficult circumstances: some reflections on 'street children' in Africa. *Children, Youth and Environments, 13*(1), Spring.

Erickson, B. (2003). Phantom whiteness: normalizing bodies through race and rock climbing. *Avante, 9*(3), 5–18.

Erickson, B. (2005). Style matters: explorations of bodies. whiteness, and identity in rock climbing. *Sociology of Sport Journal, 22*, 373–396.

Erickson, B. (2011). Recreational activism: politics, nature, and the rise of neoliberalism. *Leisure Studies, 30*(4), 477–494.

Erickson, B., Johnson, C. and Kivel, B. (2009). Rocky Mountain National Park: history and culture as factors in African-American park visitation. *Journal of Leisure Research, 41*(4), 529–545.

Evers, C. (2006). How to surf. *Journal of Sport and Social Issues, 30*(3), 229–243.

Evers, C. (2008). The Cronulla Race Riots: safety maps on an Australian Beach. *South Atlantic Quarterly, 107*(2), 411–429.

Evers, C. (2009). 'The Point': surfing, geography and a sensual life of men and masculinity on the Gold Coast, Australia. *Social & Cultural Geography, 10*(8), 893–908.

Farley, R. (2005). 'By endurance we conquer': Ernst Shackleton and the performances of white male hegemony. *International Journal of Cultural Studies, 8*(2), 231–254.

Farmer, R. (1992). Surfing: motivations, values and culture. *Journal of Sports Behaviour, 15*(3), 241–257.

Featherstone, M. (1991). *Consumer Culture and Postmodernism* (3rd edn.). London, Newbury Park, New Delhi: Sage Publications.

Field, P. (1999). The anti-roads movement: the struggle of memory against forgetting. In

T. Jordan and A. Lent (Eds), *Storming the Millennium: The New Politics of Change* (pp. 68–79). London: Lawrence and Wishart.

Finney, B. and Houston, J. (1996). *Surfing. A History of the Ancient Hawaiian Sport*. San Francisco: Pomegranate Artbooks.

Fisher, K. (2007). Dogtown and Z-Boys. In D. Booth and H. Thorpe (Eds), *Berkshire Encyclopedia of Extreme Sports* (pp. 83–85). Great Barrington: Berkshire Reference Works.

Fiske, J. (1989). Reading the beach. In J. Fiske, *Reading the Popular* (pp. 34–62). London: Unwin Hyman.

Fleming, S. (2001). Racial science and South Asian and black physicality. In B. Carrington and I. McDonald (Eds), *'Race' Sport and British Society* (pp. 105–120). London: Routledge.

Fletcher, R. (2008). Living on the edge: the appeal of risk sports for the professional middle classes. *Sociology of Sport Journal, 25*(3), 310–330.

Ford, N. and Brown, D. (2005). *Surfing and Social Theory: Experience, Embodiment and Narrative of the Dream Glide*. London: Routledge.

Foucan, S. (2008). *Free Running: Find Your Way*. London: Michael O'Mara Books Ltd.

Foucault, M. (1988). Technologies of the self. In L. H. Martin, H. Gutman, P. H. Hutton (Eds), *Technologies of the Self: A Seminar with Michel Foucault* (pp. 16–49). Cambridge, MA: The MIT Press.

Frankenberg, R. (1993). *White Women, Race Matters: The Social Construction of Whiteness*. London: Routledge.

Free, M. and Hughson, J. (2003). Settling accounts with hooligans: gender blindness in football supporter subculture research. *Men and Masculinity, 6*(2), 136–155.

Friedman, T. M. and van Ingen, C. (2011). Bodies in space: spatializing physical cultural studies. *Sociology of Sport Journal, 28*(1), 85–105.

Frohlick, S. (2005). 'That playfulness of white masculinity': mediating masculinities and adventure at mountain film festivals. *Tourist Studies, 5*(2), 175–193.

Furedi, F. (1997). *Culture of Fear*. London: Castells.

Furedi, F. (2006). Making sense of child safety: cultivating suspicion. In S. Waiton and S. Baird (Eds), *Cotton Wool Kids? Making Sense of 'Child Safety'* (pp. 4–6). Glasgow: Generation Youth Issues.

Gaber, A. (2009a). Personal communication [Research with street-based skaters, Durban], 11 January.

Gaber, A. (2009b). Personal communication [Research with street-based skaters, Durban-2], 12 January.

Garcia, R. and Baltodano, E. F. (2005). Free the beach! Public access, equal justice, and the California coast. *Stanford Journal of Civil Rights and Civil Liberties, 143*. Accessed from The City Project.

Gault-Williams, M. (2010). Nick Gabaldon (1927–1951), *Legendary Surfers*. Accessed from http://files.legendarysurfers.com/blog/labels/Inkwell%20Beach.html.

Gemmell, J. (2007). South African cricket: The Rainbow Nation must have a rainbow team. *Sport in Society, 10*(1), 49–70.

Geyh, P. (2006). Urban free flow: a poetics of parkour. *Media Culture Journal, 9*(3), 4.

Giardina, M. D. and Denzin, N. K. (2011). Acts of activism <–> politics of possibility: towards a new performative cultural politics. *Cultural Studies <=> Critical Methodologies, 11*(4), 319–327.

Giardina, M. D. and McCarthy, C. (2005). The popular racial order of urban America: sport, identity, and the politics of culture. *Cultural Studies <=> Critical Methodologies, 5*(2), 145–173.

LIVERPOOL JOHN MOORES UNIVERSITY
LEARNING SERVICES

Gibbons, D. (2008). Surfing for life: it's about much more than catching waves. *Thrive*, *2*(4). Accessed from www.nycplus.com/nyc31/surfingforlife.html.

Giddens, A. (1991). *Modernity and Self-identity: Self and Society in the Late Modern Age*. Oxford: Polity Press.

Gilchrist, P. (2007). Motherhood, ambition and risk: mediating the sporting heroine in Conservative Britain. *Media, Culture & Society, 29*(3), 395–414.

Gilchrist, P. and Ravenscroft, N. (2008). 'Power to the paddlers'? The internet, governance and discipline. *Leisure Studies, 27*(2), 129–148.

Gilchrist, P. and Wheaton, B. (2011). Lifestyle sport, public policy and youth engagement: examining the emergence of parkour. *International Journal of Sport Policy & Politics, 3*(1), 109–131.

Gillis, S., Howie, G. and Munford, R. (Eds). (2007). *Third Wave Feminism: A Critical Exploration* (expanded second ed.). Chippenham: Palgrave Macmillan.

Gilroy, P. (2006). British cultural studies and the pitfalls of identity. In H. Baker, M. Diawara and R. Lindeborg (Eds), *British Black Cultural Studies: A Reader* (pp. 223–239). Chicago: Chicago University Press.

Giroux, H. (2004). *The Terror of Neoliberalism: Authoritarianism and the Eclipse of Democracy*. Boulder, London: Paradigm Publishers.

Giulianotti, R. (2005). *Sport: A Critical Sociology*. Cambridge: Polity.

Giulianotti, R. (2009). Risk and sport: an analysis of sociological theories and research agendas. *Sociology of Sport Journal, 26*, 540–556.

Gorman, B. (2009). ESPN Winter X Games 13 sets records across platforms. *ESPN Press Release*, 2 February.

Gosch, J. (Dir.). (2009). *Bustin' Down the Door* [film]. USA: Fresh & Smoked.

Gottdiener, M. (1995). *Postmodern Semiotics: Material Culture and the Forms of Postmodern Life*. Oxford, UK and Cambridge, MA: Blackwell.

Gratton, C. and Jones, I. (2004). *Research Methods for Sport Studies*. Abingdon: Routledge.

Green, R. (2010). *'The sea en got no back door': black men and swimming cultures in Barbados*. Paper presented at the 'Beyond boundaries: race and ethnicity in modern sport' conference, University of the West Indies, Barbados.

Grossberg, L. (1997). Replacing popular culture. In S. Redhead (Eds), *The Clubcultures Reader: Readings in Popular Cultural Studies* (pp. 199–219). Malden, MA: Blackwell.

Grosz, E. (1994). A thousand tiny sexes. In C. Boundas and D. Olkowsk (Eds), *Gilles Deleuze and the Theatre of Philosophy* (pp. 187–210). New York: Routledge.

Guss, N. (2011). Parkour and the multitude: politics of a dangerous art. *French Cultural Studies, 22*(1), 73–85.

Halberstam, J. (1998). *Female Masculinity*. London: Duke University Press.

Hall, S. (1990). Cultural identity and diaspora. In J. Rutherford (Ed.), *Identity: Community, Culture, Difference* (pp. 222–237). London: Lawrence and Wishart.

Hargreaves, J. (2000). *Heroines of Sport: The Politics of Difference and Identity*. London: Routledge.

Harper, R. (2007). Xtreme Factor: black surfers take a stand for the 'Jena 6'. *Black athlete.com*, 24 September. Accessed from www.blackathlete.com/artman2/publish/X_ Sports_32/Xtreme_Factor_Black_Surfers_Take_A_Stand_For_The_Jena_6.shtml.

Harper, R. (2009). Little black surfer girl. *Blackathlete.net*, 19 October. Accessed from http://blackathlete.net/artman2/publish/X_Sports_32/Little_Black_Surfer_Girl.shtml.

Harper, R. (2010). A 'stab' in the dark: magazine targets Icah Wilmot with racial degradation. *Blackathlete.net*, 22 February. Accessed from http://blackathlete.net/artman2/ publish/X_Sports_32/A_Stab_In_The_Dark.shtml.

Harper, R. (2012). Post in response to 12 Miles North: The Nick Gabaldon Story. *The Inertia: Distributor of Ideas*, 20 February. Accessed from www.theinertia.com/surf/12-miles-north-nick-gabaldon-story-exclusive-online-premiere/.

Harvey, D. (1990). *The Condition of Postmodernity: An Enquiry into the Origins of Cultural Change*. Cambridge: Blackwell.

Harvey, D. (2005). *A Brief History of Neoliberalism*. Oxford: Oxford University Press.

Haywood, L., Kew, F., Bramham, P., Spink, J., Capenerhurst, J. and Henry, I. (Eds). (1995). *Understanding Leisure* (second ed.). Cheltenham: Stanley Thornes (Publishers) Ltd.

Hemson, C. (2001). *Ukubekezela* or *Ukuzithema*: African lifesavers in Durban. In R. Morrell (Ed.), *Changing Men in Southern Africa* (pp. 57–74). Scottsville, South Africa: University of Natal Press.

Hetherington, K. (1998a). *Expressions of Identity: Space, Performance, Politics*. London: Sage.

Hetherington, K. (1998b). Vanloads of uproarious humanity: new age travellers and the utopics of the countryside. In T. Skelton and G. Valentine (Eds), *Cool Places: Geographies of Youth Cultures* (pp. 328–342). London: Routledge.

Heywood, L. (2007). Producing girls and the neoliberal body. In J. Hargreaves and P. Vertinsky (Eds), *Physical Culture, Power, and the Body* (pp. 101–120). Abingdon: Routledge.

Heywood, L. (2008). Third wave feminism, the global economy, and women's surfing: sport as stealth feminism in girls' surf culture. In A. Harris (Ed.), *Next Wave Cultures: Feminism, Subcultures, Activism* (pp. 63–82). London: Routledge.

Heywood, L. and Dworkins, S. (2003). *Built to Win: The Female Athlete as Cultural Icon*. Minneapolis, MN: University of Minneapolis Press.

Heywood, L. and Montgomery, M. (2008). Ambassadors of the last wilderness? Surfers, environmental ethics, and activism in America. In M. Atkinson and K. Young (Eds), *Tribal Play: Subcultural Journeys Through Sport* (Vol. IV 'Research in the Sociology of Sport', pp. 153–172). Bingley: Jai.

Hills, L. and Eileen, K. (2006). Space invaders at Wimbledon: televised sport and deterritorialization. *Sociology of Sport Journal, 23*(4), 419–437.

Hoberman, J. (1997). *Darwin's Athletes: How Sport Has Damaged Black America and Preserved the Myth of Race*. Boston, MA: Houghton Mifflin.

Hodkinson, P. (2002). *Goth: Identity, Style and Subculture*. Oxford: Berg.

Hodkinson, P. (2004). The Goth scene and (sub) cultural substance. In A. Bennett and K. Kahn-Harris (Eds), *After Subculture: Critical Studies in Contemporary Youth Culture* (pp. 353–369). Basingstoke: Palgrave.

Honolulu.gov. (2010). *Duke Kahanamoku*. Accessed from www.honolulu.gov/cameras/waikiki_beach/duke.htm.

hooks, b. (2004). *We Real Cool: Black Men and Masculinity*. New York: Routledge.

HOPE HIV. (2006). 10 September. Accessed from www.hopehiv.org.

Howe, J. (2003). Drawing lines: a report from the extreme world. In R. Rinehart and S. Sydor (Eds), *To the Extreme: Alternative Sports, Inside and Out* (pp. 353–369). Albany, NY: State University of New York Press.

Howell, O. (2005). The creative class and the gentrifying city: skateboarding in Philadelphia's Love Park. *Journal of Architectural Education, 4*, 32–45.

Howell, O. (2008). Skateparks as neoliberal playground. *Space and Culture, 11*(4), 475–496.

Humberstone, B. (2009). Third age and leisure research: principles and practice –

introduction. In B. Humberstone (Ed.), *Third Age and Leisure: Research, Principles and Practice* (Vol. LSA No. 108, p. v). Eastbourne: LSA.

Humberstone, B. (2011). Embodiment and social and environmental action in nature-based sport: spiritual spaces. *Leisure Studies, 30*(4), 495–512.

Humphreys, D. (1997). 'Skinheads go mainstream?' Snowboarding and alternative youth. *International Review for Sociology of Sport, 32*(2), 147–160.

Humphreys, D. (2003). Selling out snowboarding: the alternative response to commercial co-optation. In R. Rinehart and S. Sydor (Eds), *To the Extreme: Alternative Sports, Inside and Out* (pp. 407–428). Albany, NY: State University of New York Press.

Hylton, K. (2010). How the turn to critical race theory can contribute to our understanding of 'race', racism and anti-racism in sport. *International Review for the Sociology of Sport, 45*(3), 335–354.

Inkwell Lifestyle Brand. (2010). Meet the company. *Inkwell Lifestyle Brand*. Accessed from www.facebook.com/pages/Inkwell-Lifestyle-Brand/102706206455675.

Jackson, S. (2005). I'm afraid of Americans? New Zealand's cultural resistance to violence in 'globally' produced sports violence. In S. Jackson and D. Andrews (Eds), *Sport Culture and Advertising* (pp. 192–212). London: Routledge

Jackson, S. J. (2004). Exorcizing the ghost: Donovan Bailey, Ben Johnson and the politics of Canadian identity. *Media, Culture & Society, 26*(1), 121–141.

Jarvie, G. (2006). Sport, lifestyles and alternative culture. In G. Jarvie, *Sport, Culture and Society: An Introduction* (pp. 267–282). London: Routledge.

Jarvie, G. (2007). Sport, social change and the public intellectual. *International Review for the Sociology of Sport, 42*(4), 411–424.

Jefferson, A. R. (2009). African American leisure space in Santa Monica: the beach sometimes known as the 'Inkwell', 1900–1960s. *Southern California Quarterly, 91*(2), 155–189.

Johnson, A. and Wroe, S. (2009). Free running could be taught in secondary schools. *Independent*, 25 January.

Jones, S. and Graves, A. (2000). Power plays in public space: skateboard parks as battlegrounds, gifts, and expression of self. *Landscape Journal, 19*(1–2), 136–148.

Jordan, T. and Lent, A. (Eds). (1999). *Storming the Millennium: The New Politics of Change*. London: Lawrence and Wishart.

Joseph, J. (2009). The logical paradox of the cultural commodity: selling an 'authentic' Afro-Brazilian martial art in Canada. *Sociology of Sport Journal, 25*(4), 498–515.

Kay, J. (2005). Extreme sports and national sport policy in Canada. In A. Flintoff, J. Long and K. Hylton (Eds), *Youth, Sport and Active Leisure: Theory, Policy and Participation* (pp. 47–56). Eastbourne: Leisure Studies Association.

Kay, J. and Laberge, S. (2002a). Mapping the field of 'AR': adventure racing and Bourdieu's concept of field. *Sociology of Sport Journal, 19*(1), 25–46.

Kay, J. and Laberge, S. (2002b). The 'new' corporate habitus in adventure racing. *International Review for the Sociology of Sport, 37*(1), 17–36.

Kay, J. and Laberge, S. (2003). Oh say can you ski? Imperialistic constructions of freedom in Warren Miller's *Freeriders*. In R. Rinehart and S. Sydor (Eds), *To the Extreme: Alternative Sports, Inside and Out* (pp. 373–380). Albany, NY: State University of New York Press.

Kay, J. and Laberge, S. (2004). 'Mandatory equipment': women in adventure racing. In B. Wheaton (Ed.), *Understanding Lifestyle Sports: Consumption, Identity and Difference* (pp. 154–174). London: Routledge.

Kay, T. (2009). Developing through sport: evidencing sport impacts on young people. *Sport in Society, 12*(9), 1177–1191.

Keeton, C. (2008). Surfing provides greater high than sniffing glue for street kids. *The Times*, 15 December.

Kellner, D. (1992). Popular culture and the construction of postmodern identities. In S. Lash and J. Friedman (Eds), *Modernity and Identity* (pp. 141–177). Oxford, UK and Cambridge, MA: Blackwell.

Kelly, D., Pomerantz, S. and Currie, D. (2005). Skater girlhood and emphasized femininity: 'You can't land an Ollie properly in heels'. *Gender and Education, 17*(3), 129–148.

Kelly, D., Pomerantz, S. and Currie, D. H. (2006). 'No boundaries'? Girls' interactive, online learning about femininities. *Youth Society, 38*(1), 3–28.

Kelly, D., Pomerantz, S. and Currie, D. H. (2007). 'You can break so many more rules': The identity, work and play of becoming skater girls. In M. D. Giardina and M. Donnelly (Eds), *Youth Culture and Sport: Identity, Power, and Politics* (pp. 113–126). London: Routledge.

Khamis, S. (2010). Braving the burquini: re-branding the Australian beach. *Cultural Geographies, 17*(3), 379–390.

Kiewa, J. (2002). Traditional climbing: metaphor of resistance or metanarrative of oppression? *Leisure Studies, 21*, 145–161.

Kincheloe, J. and McLaren, P. (2005). Rethinking critical theory and qualitative research. In N. Denzin and Y. Lincoln (Eds), *The Sage Handbook of Qualitative Research* (pp. 303–342). Thousand Oaks, CA: Sage.

King, C. (2004). Race and cultural identity: playing the race game inside football. *Leisure Studies, 23*(1), 19–30.

Klein, N. (2000). Beyond the brands: the limits of brand-based politics. In N. Klein, *No Logo* (pp. 421–438). London: Harper Collins Ltd.

Knijnik, J. D., Horton, P. and Cruz, L. O. (2010). Rhizomatic bodies, gendered waves: transitional femininities in Brazilian surf. *Sport in Society: Cultures, Commerce, Media, Politics, 13*(7), 1170–1185.

Kusz, K. (2003). BMX, extreme sports, and the white male backlash. In R. Rinehart and S. Sydor (Eds), *To the Extreme: Alternative Sports, Inside and Out* (pp. 145–152). Albany, NY: State University of New York Press.

Kusz, K. (2004). 'Extreme America': the cultural politics of extreme sports in 1990s America. In B. Wheaton (Ed.), *Understanding Lifestyle Sports: Consumption, Identity and Difference* (pp. 197–213). London: Routledge.

Kusz, K. (2005). Dogtown and Z-Boys, white particularity, and the new, *new* cultural racism. In R. King and D. Leonard (Eds), *Visual Economies* (pp. 135–164). New York: Peter Lang Publishing.

Kusz, K. (2007). *Revolt of the White Athlete: Race, Media and the Emergence of Extreme Athletes in America*. New York: Peter Lang Publishing.

Laberge, S. (1995). Towards an integration of gender into Bourdieu's concept of cultural capital. *Sociology of Sport Journal, 12*, 132–146.

Laberge, S. and Sankoff, D. (1988). Physical activities, body habitus and lifestyles towards an integration of gender into Bourdieu's concept of cultural capital. In J. Harvey and H. Cantelon (Eds), *Not Just a Game: Essays in Canadian Sport Sociology* (pp. 267–288). Ottawa: University of Ottowa Press.

Laing, J. (Producer). (2008). 'Silver surfers'. The growing number of older women riding the waves. *Woman's Hour*, BBC Radio, 6 May.

L'Aoustet, O. and Griffet, J. (2001). The experience of teenagers at Marseilles' skate park: emergence and evaluation of an urban sports site. *Cities, 18*(6), 413–418.

Lapchick, R. E. (2008). *100 Pioneers: African-Americans who Broke Color Barriers in Sport*. Morgantown, WV: Fitness Information Technology.

Laurendeau, J. (2004). The 'crack choir' and the 'cock chorus': the intersection of gender and sexuality in skydiving texts. *Sociology of Sport Journal, 21*, 397–417.

Laurendeau, J. (2008). 'Gendered risk regimes': a theoretical consideration of Edgework and gender. *Sociology of Sport Journal, 25*, 293–309.

Laurendeau, J. (2011). 'If you're reading this, it's because I've died': masculinity and relational risk in BASE jumping. *Sociology of Sport Journal, 28*(4), 404–420.

Laurendeau, J. and Sharara, N. (2008). 'Women could be every bit as good as guys': reproductive and resistant agency in two 'action' sports. *Journal of Sport and Social Issues, 32*(24), 24–47.

Laviolette, P. (2007). Editor's introduction: special issue on hazardous sport. *Anthropology Today, 23*(6), 8–12.

Laviolette, P. (2010). *Extreme Landscapes of Leisure: Not a Hap-Hazardous Sport*. Farnham, Surrey: Ashgate.

Law, A. (2001). Surfing the safety net: 'dole bludging', 'surfies' and governmentality in Australia. *International Review for the Sociology of Sport, 36*(1), 25–40.

Lawler, K. (2011). *The American Surfer: Radical Culture and Capitalism*. New York: Routledge.

Le Breton, D. (2000). Playing symbolically with death in extreme sports. *Body and Society, 6*(1), 1–12.

Lefebvre, H. (1991). *The Production of Space* (D. Nicholson-Smith, Trans.). Oxford: Blackwell.

Leitch, L. (2009). Alfred Lomax: the man who could be Liberia's first professional surfer. *The Times online, 27* May.

Lewis, J. (1998). Between the lines: surf texts, prosthetics, and everyday theory. *Social Semiotics, 8*(1), 55–70.

Lewis, J. (2003). In search of the postmodern surfer: territory, terror and masculinity. In A. Edwards, K. Gilbert and J. Skinner (Eds), *Some Like it Hot: The Beach as a Cultural Dimension* (pp. 58–76). Oxford: Meyer and Meyer Sport.

Lewis, N. (2004). 'Sustainable adventure': embodied experiences and ecological practices within British climbing. In B. Wheaton (Ed.), *Understanding Lifestyle Sports: Consumption, Identity and Difference* (pp. 70–93). London: Routledge.

Lincoln, Y. and Denzin, N. (1994). Part V. The art of interpretation, evaluation, and presentation. In N. Denzin and Y. Lincoln (Eds), *Handbook of Qualitative Research* (pp. 479–484). Thousand Oaks, CA: Sage.

Loret, A. (1995). *Génération Glisse: Dans L'Eau, L'Air, La Neige.... La Révolution Du Sport des 'Années Fun' [The Glide Generation: On Water, Air, and Snow. The Sport Revolution of the 'Fun Years']*. Paris: Edition Autrement.

Lucia Stasia, C. (2007). 'My guns are my Fendi': the postfeminist female action hero. In S. Gillis, G. Howie and R. Munford (Eds), *Third Wave Feminism: A Critical Exploration* (expanded second edition edn, pp. 237–249). Chippenham: Palgrave Macmillan.

Lyng, S. (1990). A social psychological analysis of voluntary risk-taking. *American Journal of Sociology, 95*, 851–886.

Lyng, S. (2005). Edgework and the risk-taking experience. In S. Lyng (Ed.), *Edgework: The Sociology of Risk-Taking* (pp. 3–14). New York: Routledge.

Lyng, S. (2008). Risk-taking in sport: Edgework and reflexive community. In M. Atkinson and K. Young (Eds), *Tribal Play: Subcultural Journeys through Sport* (Vol. IV 'Research in the Sociology of Sport', pp. 83–109). Bingley: Jai.

MacKay, S. and Dallaire, C. (2013). Skirtboarder net-a-narratives: young women creating their own skateboarding (re)presentations. *International Review for the Sociology of Sport,* 48(2), 171–195.

Madden, D. (2010). Revisiting the end of public space: assembling the public in an urban park. *City and Community,* 9(2), 197–206.

Maffesoli, M. (1996). *The Time of the Tribes: The Decline of Individualism in Mass Society* (first published in 1991 in French). London: Sage.

Maguire, J. (1999). *Global Sport: Identities, Societies, Civilizations.* Cambridge: Polity Press.

Maloof Money Cup (2011). Maloof skateboarding global initiative. *Maloof Money Cup.* Accessed from www.maloofmoneycup.com/skateboarding/index.php?option=com_con tent&view=article&id=275:maloof-skateboarding-global-initiative&catid=86:2011-sa-blogs&Itemid=182.

Mansfield, R. (2009). *The Surfing Tribe: A History of Surfing in Britain.* Newquay: Orca Publications.

Marchart, O. (2003). Bridging the micro-macro gap. In D. Muggleton and R. Weinzierl (Eds), *The Post-Subcultures Reader* (pp. 83–97). Oxford: Berg.

Marcus, G. (1994). What comes (just) after 'Post'? In N. Denzin and Y. Lincoln (Eds), *Handbook of Qualitative Research* (pp. 563–574). Thousand Oaks, CA: Sage.

Markula, P. (2003). The technologies of the self: sport, feminism, and Foucault. *Sociology of Sport Journal,* 20(2), 87–107.

Markula, P. (2006). Deleuze and the body without organs: disreading the fit feminine identity. *Journal of Sport and Social Issues,* 30(29), 29–44.

Markula, P. and Pringle, R. (2006). *Foucault, Sport and Exercise.* London: Routledge.

Martin, G. (2002). Conceptualizing cultural politics in subcultural and social movement studies. *Social Movement Studies,* 1(1), 73–88.

Massey, D. (1994). *Space, Place and Gender.* Cambridge: Polity Press.

Massey, D. S. and Denton, N. A. (1993). *American Apartheid.* Cambridge, MA: Harvard University Press.

McDermott, L. (2007). A governmental analysis of children 'at risk' in a world of physical inactivity and obesity epidemics. *Sociology of Sport Journal,* 24, 302–324.

McDonald, I. (2002). Critical social research and political intervention: moralistic versus radical approaches. In J. Sugden and A. Tomlinson (Eds), *Power Games: Theory and Method for a Critical Sociology of Sport* (pp. 100–116). London: Routledge.

McDonald, I. (2007). *Critiquing Sport: Policies and Practices.* Ph.D., University of Brighton.

McGloin, C. (2005). *Surfing Nation(s), Surfing Country(s).* Ph.D., University of Wollongong.

McKay, G. (Ed.). (1998). *DIY Culture: Party and Protest in Nineties Britain.* London: Verso.

McKay, J., Messner, M. and Sabo, D. (Eds). (2000). *Masculinities, Gender Relations, and Sport.* Thousand Oaks, CA: Sage.

McLean, C. R., Houshian, S. and Pike, J. (2006). Paediatric fractures sustained in parkour (free running). *Injury,* 37(8), 795–797.

McNamee, M. (Ed.). (2006). *Philosophy, Risk and Adventure Sports.* London: Routledge.

McRobbie, A. (1980). Settling accounts with subcultures: a feminist critique. *Screen Education,* 34, 37–49.

McRobbie, A. (1991). *Feminism and Youth Culture.* Basingstoke: Macmillan.

McWaters, P. (2008). The rise of the silver surfer. *Coast online,* 10 June. Accessed from www.allaboutyou.com.

Mellgren, D. (1998). AP reports Terje boycotting Nagano? *Transworld Snowboarding*, 7 January. Accessed from http://snowboarding.transworld.net/1000025710/news/ap-reports-terje-boycotting-nagano/.

Melucci, A. (1980). The new social movements: a theoretical approach. *Social Science Information, 19*(2), 199–226.

Midol, N. (1993). Cultural dissents and technical innovations in the 'whiz' sports. *International Review for Sociology of Sport, 28*(1), 23–32.

Midol, N. and Broyer, G. (1995). Towards an anthropological analysis of new sport cultures: the case of whiz sports in France. *Sociology of Sport Journal, 12*, 204–212.

Miles, S. (2000). *Youth Lifestyles in a Changing World*. Buckingham: Open University Press.

Miller, J. and Demoiny, S. (2008). Parkour: a new extreme sport and a case study. *The Journal of Foot and Ankle Surgery, 47*(1), 63–65.

Minogue, E. (2011). Parkours? Parce que! *The Leisure Review*, February. Accessed from www.theleisurereview.co.uk/articles11/articles11pdf/parkours2.pdf.

Moore, L. (2011). *Understanding the Rise of Mindful Fitness: Women's Experiences of Yoga and Body Balance*. MA thesis, University of Brighton, Eastbourne.

Morrell, R. (Ed.). (2001). *Changing Men in Southern Africa*. Scottsville, South Africa: University of Natal Press.

Morris, G. (1998). Beyond the beach: AIP's beach party movies. *Bright Lights Film Journal, 21*, May. Accessed from http://brightlightsfilm.com/21/21_beach.php.

Mould, O. (2009). Parkour, the city, the event. *Environment and Planning: Society and Space, 27*, 738–750.

Muggleton, D. (2000). *Inside Subculture: The Postmodern Meaning of Style*. Oxford: Berg.

Muggleton, D. and Weinzierl, R. (Eds). (2003a). *The Post-Subcultures Reader*. Oxford: Berg.

Muggleton, D. and Weinzierl, R. (2003b). What is 'post-subcultural studies' anyway? In D. Muggleton and R. Weinzierl (Eds), *The Post-Subcultures Reader* (pp. 3–23). Oxford: Berg.

Nauright, J. (1997). *Sport, Cultures and Identities in South Africa*. Leicester: Leicester University Press.

Nayak, A. (2003). *Race, Place and Globalization: Youth Cultures in a Changing World*. Oxford: Berg.

Nayak, A. (2006). After race: ethnography, race and post-race theory. *Ethnic and Racial Studies, 29*(3), 411–430.

Nayak, A. (2010). Race, affect, and emotion: young people, racism, and graffiti in the postcolonial English suburbs. *Environment and Planning A, 42*(10), 2370–2392.

Neal, S. (2002). Rural landscapes, representations and racism: examining multicultural citizenship and policy-making in the English countryside. *Ethnic and Racial Studies, 25*(3), 442–461.

Neal, S. and Agyeman, J. (2006). Introduction. In S. Neal and J. Agyeman (Eds), *The New Countryside? Ethnicity, Nation and Exclusion in Contemporary Rural Britain* (pp. 1–18). Bristol: Policy Press.

Nike Surfing (2012) 12 Miles North: The Nick Gabaldon Story. *The Inertia: Distributor of Ideas*. Accessed from www.theinertia.com/surf/12-miles-north-nick-gabaldon-story-exclusive-online-premiere/.

Nortje, B. (2008). Zulu Surfrider – the beginning of a special story. *Umzumbe Surfrider's Club*, 17 June. Accessed from http://zulusurfrider.blogspot.com/.

Olivier, S. (2010). 'Your wave, bro!': virtue ethics and surfing. *Sport in Society: Cultures, Commerce, Media, Politics, 13*(7), 1223–1233.

Olsen, M. (2012). Surfing 4 Peace. *World Policy Journal,* Summer. Accessed from www.worldpolicy.org/journal/summer2012/surfing-4-peace.

Omi, M. and Winant, H. (1994). *Racial Formation in the United States: From the 1960s to the 1990s.* New York: Routledge.

Orec, D. (2003). Kite culture: the insiders. *Kiteworld,* April–June, 96–97.

Ormrod, J. (2003). Issues of gender in Muscle Beach Party (1964). *Scope Online Journal of Film Studies,* 15 July. Accessed from www.scope.nottingham.ac.uk/.

Ormrod, J. (2006). 'Just the lemon next to the pie': apocalypse, history and the limits of myth in Big Wednesday (1978). *Scope Online Journal of Film Studies,* February. Accessed from www.scope.nottingham.ac.uk/.

Ormrod, J. (2007). Endless Summer: consuming waves and surfing the frontier. In R. Briley, M. K. Schoenecke and D. A. Carmichael (Eds), *All Stars and Movie Stars: Sports in Film and History (2008)* (Vol. 35, pp. 17–39). Lexington: University Press of Kentucky.

Ormrod, J. (2008). *Expressions of Nation and Place in British Surfing Identities.* Ph.D., Manchester Metropolitan University.

Ormrod, J. (2009). 'On the edge': leisure, consumption and the representation of adventure sports. Introduction. In J. Ormrod and B. Wheaton (Eds), *'On the Edge': Leisure, Consumption and the Representation of Adventure Sport* (Vol. 104, pp. v–xvii). Eastbourne: Leisure Studies Association.

Ormrod, J. and Wheaton, B. (Eds) (2009). *'On the Edge': Leisure, Consumption and the Representation of Adventure Sport.* Eastbourne: Leisure Studies Association.

Ortuzar, J. (2009). Parkour or l'art du deplacement. *The Drama Review, 53*(3), 54–66.

Osmond, G. and Philips, M. (2004). 'The bloke with a stroke': Alan Wickham, the crawl and social memory. *The Journal of Pacific History, 39*(3), 309–324.

Osmond, G., Phillips, M. and O' Neill, M. (2006). 'Putting up your Dukes': statues, social memory and Duke Paoa Kahanamoku. *International Journal of the History of Sport, 23*(1), 82–103.

Parker, G. (1999). The role of the consumer-citizen in environmental protest in the 1990s. *Space and Polity, 3*(1), 67–83.

Parkour UK (2011). *What is Parkour/Art du Deplacement?* Accessed from www.parkouruk.org/#Definition.

Pawle, F. (2010). Racism and drug abuse stories covered up in the endless summer of sycophancy. *The Australian,* 5 April. Accessed from www.news.com.au/breaking-news/racism-and-drug-abuse-stories-covered-up-in-the-endless/story-e6frfkp9-1225849637570.

Pearson, K. (1979). *Surfing Subcultures of Australia and New Zealand.* St Lucia, Queensland: University of Queensland Press.

Pearson, K. (1981). Sub-cultures and sport. In J. Loy, G. Kenyon and B. McPherson (Eds), *Sport, Culture and Society: A Reader on the Sociology of Sport* (pp. 131–145). Philadelphia: Lea & Febiger.

Peck, S. and agencies. (2008). 2012 Games could see skateboarding debut. *The Telegraph,* 16 July. Accessed from www.telegraph.co.uk/news/uknews/1553957/2012-Games-could-see-skateboarding-debut.html.

Pedersen, P. and Kelly, M. (2000). ESPN X Games: commercialised extreme sports for the masses. *Cyber-Journal of Sport Views and Issues, 1*(1).

Pelak, C. F. (2005). Negotiating gender/race/class constrains in the new South Africa. *International Review for Sociology of Sport, 40*(1), 53–70.

220   *References*

Pender, P. (2007). 'Kicking ass is comfort food': Buffy as third wave feminist icon. In S. Gillis, G. Howie and R. Munford (Eds), *Third Wave Feminism: A Critical Exploration* (expanded second edition ed., pp. 224–236). Chippenham: Palgrave Macmillan.

Peralta, S. (Writer) (2001). *Dogtown and Z-Boys* [film]. USA: Sony Pictures.

Peralta, S. (Writer) (2004). *Riding Giants* [film]. USA: Sony Pictures.

Pfeil, F. (1995). *White Guys: Studies in Postmodern Domination and Difference*. London and New York: Verso.

Phoenix, C. and Sparkes, A. (2009). Being Fred: big stories, small stories and the accomplishment of a positive ageing identity. *Qualitative Research,* (9), 219–236.

Pike, E. (2010). Growing old (dis)gracefully? The gender/ageing/exercise nexus. In E. Kennedy and P. Markula (Eds), *Women and Exercise: The Body, Health and Consumerism* (pp. 180–196). London: Routledge.

Pike, E. C. (2011a). Aquatic antiques: swimming off this mortal coil? *International Review for the Sociology of Sport,* 11 March (online).

Pike, E. (2011b). The active ageing agenda, old folk devils and a new moral panic. *Sociology of Sport Journal, 28*(2), 209–225.

Pitcher, G. (2006). In pictures: South Africa skateboarders, *BBC News,* 5 August. Accessed from http://news.bbc.co.uk/1/shared/spl/hi/picture_gallery/05/africa_sa_skateboarders/html/1.stm.

Pomerantz, S., Currie, D. H. and Kelley, D. M. (2004). Sk8er girls: skateboarders, girlhood and feminism in motion. *Women's Studies International Forum, 27,* 547–557.

Porter, N. (2003). Female skateboarders and their negotiation of space and identity. *Journal for the Arts, Sciences and Technology, 1*(2), 75–80.

Preston-Whyte, R. (2002). Construction of surfing space at Durban, South Africa. *Tourism Geographies, 4*(3), 307–328.

Pringle, R. (2005). Masculinity, sport and power: a critical comparison of Gramscian and Foucauldian inspired theoretical tools. *Journal of Sport and Social Issues, 29*(3), 256–278.

Probyn, E. (1993). True voices and real people: the problem of the autobiographical in cultural studies. In V. Blundell, J. Shepherd and I. Taylor (Eds) *Relocating Cultural Studies* (Chapter 4). London: Routledge.

Probyn, E. (2003). The spatial imperative of subjectivity. In K. Anderson, M. Domosh, S. Pile and N. Thrift (Eds), *Handbook of Cultural Geography* (pp. 290–299). London: Sage.

Project, T. C. (2010). Bruce's Beach: The City Project celebrates Black History Month. *The City Project Blog* (Vol. 10, December), Los Angeles.

Pronger. (1998). Post-sport: transgressing boundaries in physical culture. In G. Rail (Ed.), *Sport and Postmodern Times* (pp. 277–298). Albany, NY: SUNY.

Puwar, N. (2004). *Space Invaders: Race, Gender and Bodies Out Of Place*. Oxford: Berg.

Rahman, M. (2012). India discovers the joys of surfing. *Guardian,* 21 February. Accessed from www.guardian.co.uk/world/shortcuts/2012/feb/21/india-discovers-joys-of-surfing.

Rawlinson, C. and Guaralda, M. (2011). Play in the city: parkour and architecture. *The First International Postgraduate Conference on Engineering, Designing and Developing the Built Environment for Sustainable Wellbeing,* 27–29 April, Queensland University of Technology, Brisbane.

Redhead, S. (1993). *Rave Off: Politics and Deviance in Contemporary Youth Culture*. Aldershot: Avebury.

Reed, R. (2005). *The Way of the Snowboarder*. New York: Harry N. Abrams, Inc.

Riaan Stoman. (2010). *Umthombo – Street Spirit*, 7 October. Accessed from www.youtube.com/watch?feature=player_embedded&v=LM9O_ApRbzY#at=38 or www.umthombo.org/website/.

Riley, S., Griffin, C. and Morey, Y. (2010). The case for 'everyday politics': evaluating neo-tribal theory as a way to understand alternative forms of political participation, using electronic dance music culture as an example. *Sociology, 44*(2), 345–363.

Rinehart, R. (1998). *Players All: Performances in Contemporary Sport*. Bloomington and Indianapolis: Indiana University Press.

Rinehart, R. (2000). Emerging arriving sport: Alternatives to formal sport. In J. Coakley and E. Dunning (Eds), *Handbook of Sport Studies* (pp. 504–519). London: Sage.

Rinehart, R. (2008). ESPN's X Games, contests of opposition, resistance, co-option, and negotiation. In M. Atkinson and K. Young (Eds), *Tribal Play: Subcultural Journeys Through Sport* (Vol. IV 'Research in the Sociology of Sport', pp. 175–196). Bingley: Jai.

Rinehart, R. and Sydor, S. (Eds). (2003). *To the Extreme: Alternative Sports, Inside and Out*. Albany, NY: State University of New York Press.

Robertson, R. (1992). *Globalization: Social Theory and Global Culture*. London: Sage.

Robinson, V. (2004). Taking risks: identity, masculinities and rock climbing. In B. Wheaton (Ed.), *Understanding Lifestyle Sports: Consumption, Identity and Difference* (pp. 113–130). London: Routledge.

Robinson, V. (2008). *Everyday Masculinities and Extreme Sport: Male Identity and Rock Climbing*. Oxford: Berg.

Rohrer, F. (2010). Why don't black Americans swim? *BBC News US and Canada*, 3 September. Accessed from www.bbc.co.uk/news/world-us-canada-11172054.

Roy, G. (2011). Exploring the feminist potential of the female surfer: surfing, spaces and subjectivities. In B. Watson and J. Harpin (Eds), *Identities, Cultures and Voices in Sport and Leisure* (Vol. LSA Publication, no. 116, pp. 141–158). Eastbourne: LSA.

Rutsky, R. L (1999). Surfing the other: ideology on the beach. *Film Quarterly, 52*(4), 12–23.

Sacramento News. (2008). Parkour investigated in teen's death. *KCRA.com*. Accessed from www.kcra.com/news/21503335/detail.html.

Said, E. (1989). Representing the colonized: anthropology's interlocutors. *Critical Inquiry, 15*(2), 205–225.

Sail-World. (2010). IKA launches bid for inclusion at the Olympic Sailing Regatta 2016. *Sail-World.com*. Accessed from www.sail-world.com/index.cfm?nid=64477.

Saukko, P. (2003). *Doing Research in Cultural Studies: An Introduction to Classical and New Methodological Approaches*. London: Sage.

Saville, S. J. (2008). Playing with fear: parkour and the mobility of emotion. *Social & Cultural Geography, 9*(8), 891–914.

Scheibel, D. (1995). 'Making waves' with Burke: surf Nazi culture and the rhetoric of localism. *Western Journal of Communication, 59*, 253–269.

Scraton, S. (1994). The changing world of women and leisure: feminism, 'postfeminism' and leisure. *Leisure Studies, 13*(4), 249–261.

Scraton, S. (2001). Reconceptualizing race, gender and sport: the contribution of black feminism. In B. Carrington and I. McDonald (Eds), *'Race' Sport and British Society* (pp. 170–187). London: Routledge.

Scraton, S., Caudwell, J. and Holland, S. (2005). 'Bend it like Patel': centring 'race', ethnicity and gender in feminist analysis of women's football in England. *International Review for the Sociology of Sport, 40*, 390–402.

Shilling, C. (2005). *The Body in Culture, Technology and Society*. London: Sage.

Silk, M. and Andrews, D. (2006). The fittest city in America. *Journal of Sport and Social Issues, 30*, 315–327.

Silk, M. and Andrews, D. (2008). Managing Memphis: governance and regulation in sterile spaces of play. *Social Identities, 14*(3), 395–414.

Silk, M. and Andrews, D. (2011). Toward a physical cultural studies. *Sociology of Sport Journal, 28* (1), 4–35.

Singh, S. (2007). Challenging stereotypes of street children. In R. Pattman and S. Khan (Eds), *Undressing Durban* (pp. 90–194). Durban: Madiba Press.

Sisjord, M. K. (2009). Fast-girls, babes and the invisible girls. Gender relations in snowboarding. *Sport in Society, 12*(10), 1299–1316.

Skateistan. (2012). Afghanistan: what we do. Accessed from http://skateistan.org.

Skelton, T. and Valentine, G. (Eds). (1998). *Cool Places: Geographies of Youth Cultures*. London: Routledge.

Smith, M. and Beal, B. (2007). 'So you can see how the other half lives': MTV cribs' use of 'the Other' in framing successful athletic masculinities. *Journal of Sport and Social Issues, 31*(2), 103–127.

Smith Maguire, J. (2002). Michel Foucault: sport, power, technologies and governmentality. In J. Maguire and K. Young (Eds), *Theory, Sport and Society* (pp. 293–314). Oxford: JAI.

Sobel, M. (1981). *Lifestyle and Social Structure: Concepts, Definitions and Analyses*. New York: Academic Press.

Song, M. and Parker, D. (1995). Commonality, difference and the dynamics of disclosure in in-depth interviewing. *Sociology, 29*(2), 241–256.

Spaaij, R. (2009). The social impact of sport: diversities, complexities and contexts. *Sport in Society, 12*(9), 1109–117.

Sparkes, A. (2009). Ethnography and the senses: challenges and possibilities. *Qualitative Research in Sport and Exercise, 1*(1), 21–35.

Spowart, L., Burrows, L. and Shaw, S. (2010). 'I just eat, sleep and dream of surfing': when surfing meets motherhood. *Sport in Society: Cultures, Commerce, Media, Politics, 13*(7), 1186–1203.

Spracklen, K. (2008). The Holy Blood and the Holy Grail: myths of scientific racism and the pursuit of excellence in sport. *Leisure Studies, 27*(2), 221–227.

St John, G. (2003). Post-rave technotribalism and the carnival of protest. In D. Muggleton and R. Weinzierl (Eds), *The Post-Subcultures Reader* (pp. 65–82). Oxford: Berg.

St Louis, B. (2005). Brilliant bodies, fragile minds: race, sport and the mind/body split. In C. Alexander and C. Knowles (Eds), *Making Race Matter: Bodies, Spaces and Identity* (pp. 113–131). Basingstoke: Palgrave Macmillan.

Stebbins, R. (1992). *Amateurs, Professionals and Serious Leisure*. Montreal: McGill Queen's University Press.

Stebbins, R. (2007). *Serious Leisure: A Perspective for our Time*. London: Transaction Publishers.

Stenger, J. (2008). Mapping the beach: beach movies, exploitation film and geographies of whiteness. In D. Burnardi (Ed.), *The Persistence of Whiteness: Race and Contemporary Hollywood Cinema* (pp. 28–50). Abingdon: Routledge.

Steun, M. (1991). *Whiteness Just Isn't What It Used To Be: White Identity in a Changing South Africa*. Albany, NY: SUNY.

Stockwell, J. (Writer). (2002). *Blue Crush* [film]. B. Grazer (Producer). USA: Universal Pictures.

Stoked-Mentoring (2010). Our programs. *Stoked.org*. Accessed from www.stoked.org/our-programs/.

Stranger, M. (1999). The aesthetics of risk: a study of surfing. *International Review for the Sociology of Sport, 34*(3), 265–276.

Stranger, M. (2010). Surface and substructure: beneath surfing's commodified surface. *Sport in Society: Cultures, Commerce, Media, Politics, 13*(7), 1117–1134.

Stranger, M. (2011). *Surfing Life: Surface, Substructure and the Commodification of the Sublime*. Farnham, Surrey: Ashgate.

Stratford, E. (2002). On the edge: a tale of skaters and urban governance. *Social & Cultural Geography, 3*(2), 193–206.

Strauss, A. and Corbin, J. (1990). *Basics of Qualitative Research*. London: Sage.

Strauss, A. and Corbin, J. (1994). Grounded theory methodology: an overview. In M. Miles and A. M. Huberman (Eds), *Qualitative Data Analysis* (pp. 273–285). Thousand Oaks, CA: Sage.

Sugden, J. (2004). Is investigative sociology just investigative journalism? In M. McNamee (Ed.), *Philosophy and the Sciences of Exercise, Health and Sport*. London: Routledge.

Sugden, J. and Tomlinson, A. (1999). Digging the dirt and staying clean: retrieving the investigative tradition for a critical sociology of sport. *International Review for the Sociology of Sport, 34*, 385–397.

Sugden, J. and Tomlinson, A. (2002). Theory and method for a critical sociology of sport. In J. Sugden and A. Tomlinson (Eds), *Power Games: Theory and Method for a Critical Sociology of Sport* (pp. 240–266). London: Routledge.

Surfer's Journal (2005). Nick Gabaldon. *The Surfers Journal, 14*(1), 123.

Swartz, S. (2003). Is Kwaito South African hip hop? Why the answer matters and who it matters to. *The World of Music, 50*, 15–33.

Swink, S. (2003). *Kwaito: Much More Than Music* [Online]. Accessed on 22 November 2006 from www.southafrica.info/what_happening/news/features/kwaitomental.htm.

The Petition (2010). No skateboarding in the Olympics! *The Petition Site*. Accessed from www.thepetitionsite.com/takeaction/656763888?ltl=1146760863.

Thompson, D. (2008). Jump city: parkour and the traces. *South Atlantic Quarterly, 107*(2), 251–263.

Thompson, G. (2001). Making waves, making men: the emergence of a professional surfing masculinity in South Africa during the late 1970s. In R. Morrell (Ed.), *Changing Men in Southern Africa* (pp. 91–104). Scottsville, South Africa: University of Natal Press.

Thornton, A. (2004). 'Anyone can play this game': Ultimate frisbee, identity and difference. In B. Wheaton (Ed.), *Understanding Lifestyle Sports: Consumption, Identity and Difference*. London: Routledge.

Thornton, S. (1995). *Club Cultures: Music, Media and Subcultural Capital*. Cambridge: Polity Press.

Thorpe, H. (2008). Foucault, technologies of self, and the media: discourses of femininity in snowboarding culture. *Journal of Sport and Social Issues, 32*(2), 199–229.

Thorpe, H. (2009a). Bourdieu, feminism and female physical culture: gender reflexivity and the habitus-field complex. *Sociology of Sport Journal, 26*, 491–516.

Thorpe, H. (2009b). The psychology of extreme sport. In T. Ryba, R. Schinke and G. Tenenbaum (Eds), *The Cultural Turn in Sport and Exercise Psychology* (pp. 361–384). Morgantown: Fitness Information Technology.

Thorpe, H. (2010a). Bourdieu, gender reflexivity and physical culture: a case of masculinities in the snowboarding field. *Journal of Sport and Social Issues, 34*(2), 176–214.

Thorpe, H. (2010b). 'Have board will travel': global physical youth cultures and trans-national mobility. In J. Maguire and M. Falcous (Eds), *Sport and Migration* (pp. 73–87). London: Routledge.

Thorpe, H. (2011). *Snowboarding Bodies in Theory and Practice*. Basingstoke: Palgrave Macmillan.

Thorpe, H. and Rinehart, R. (2010). Alternative sport and affect: non-representational theory examined. *Sport and Society, 14*(7/8), 1268–1291.

Thorpe, H. and Wheaton, B. (2011a). 'Generation X Games', action sports and the Olympic movement: understanding the cultural politics of incorporation. *Sociology, 45*(5), 830–847.

Thorpe, H. and Wheaton, B. (2011b). The Olympic movement, action sports, and the search for Generation Y. In J. Sugden and A. Tomlinson (Eds), *Watching the Olympics: Politics, Power and Representation* (pp. 182–200). London: Routledge.

Thorpe, H. and Wheaton, B. (forthcoming). Dissecting action sports studies: past, present and beyond. In D. Andrews and B. Carrington (Eds), *Blackwell Companion to Sport*. Oxford: Blackwell.

Tojek, J. (2007). Surfing controversy, *KCAL9 News*, 12 September. Accessed from www.youtube.com/watch?v=ZKMd7uoYFiI.

Tomlinson, A. (2001). Sport, leisure and style. In D. Morley and K. Robins (Eds), *British Cultural Studies: Geography, Nationality, and Identity* (pp. 399–415). Oxford: Oxford University Press.

Tomlinson, A. (2005). *Sport and Leisure Cultures*. Minneapolis: University of Minnesota Press.

Tomlinson, A., Ravenscroft, N., Wheaton, B. and Gilchrist, P. (2005). *Lifestyle Sport and National Sport Policy: An Agenda for Research*. Report to Sport England. Accessed from   www.sportengland.org/research/idoc.ashx?docid=a6554a47-29b1-4b02-b3ac-600f3144bf8b&version=1.

Touraine, A. (1985). An introduction to the study of new social movements. *Social Research, 52*(4), 749–787.

Trans World Sport (2010) Umthombo surfing children South Africa. Accessed from www.youtube.com/watch?v=F_JMdueDV4w&feature=player_embedded   or   www.umthombo.org/website/.

Travlou, P. (2003). *Teenagers and Public Space: Literature Review: Openspace: The Research Centre for Inclusive Access to Outdoor Environments*. Edinburgh College of Art and Heriot-Watt University. Accessed from www.openspace.eca.ac.uk/pdf/teenagerslitrev.pdf.

Tulle, E. (2008a). *Ageing, the Body and Social Change: Running in Later Life* (Vol. 14). Basingstoke: Palgrave Macmillan.

Tulle, E. (2008b). The ageing body and the ontology of ageing: athletic competence in later life. *Body & Society, 14*(1), 1–19.

Urry, J. (2002). *Globalising the Tourist Gaze*. Department of Sociology, Lancaster University. Accessed from www.lancs.ac.uk/fass/sociology/research/publications/papers/urry-globalising-the-tourist-gaze.pdf.

Van Bottenburg, M. and Salome, L. (2010). The indoorisation of outdoor sports: an exploration of the rise of lifestyle sports in artificial settings. *Leisure Studies, 29*(2), 143–160.

Van Ingen, C. (2003). Geographies of gender, sexuality and race: reframing the focus on space in sport sociology. *International Review for the Sociology of Sport, 38*(2), 201–216.

Veal, A. (1993). The concept of lifestyle: a review. *Leisure Studies, 12*(4), 233–252.

Vivoni, F. (2009). Spots of spatial desire: skateparks, skateplazas, and urban politics. *Journal of Sport and Social Issues, 33*(2), 130–149.

Wachs, F. (2007). Venice Beach. In D. Booth and H. Thorpe (Eds), *Berkshire Encyclopedia of Extreme Sports* (pp. 336–337). Great Barrington: Berkshire Reference Works.

Wacquant, L. J. D. (1995). Pugs at work: bodily capital and the bodily labour among professional boxers. *Body and Society, 1*(1), 65–94.

Waitt, G. (2008). Killing waves: surfing, space and gender. *Social and Cultural Geography, 9*(1), 75–94.

Waitt, G. and Warren, A. (2008). Talking shit over a brew after a good session with your mates: surfing, space and masculinity. *Australian Geographer, 39*, 353–365.

Ward, J. and de Vreese, C. (2011). Political consumerism, young citizens and the Internet. *Media, Culture & Society, 33*(3), 399–413.

Ward, N. (1996). Surfers, sewage and the new politics of pollution. *Area, 28*(3), 331–338.

Warf, B. and Arias, M. (Eds). (2009). *The Spatial Turn: Interdisciplinary Perspectives*. Abingdon: Routledge.

Warshaw, M. (2005). Winterland. Fred Van Dyke and the dynamics of the aging surfer. *The Surfers Journal, 14*, 46–59.

Weigel, D. (2007). Sebastien Foucan. In D. Booth and H. Thorpe (Eds), *Berkshire Encyclopedia of Extreme Sports* (pp. 96–97). Great Barrington: Berkshire Reference Works.

Weisberg, Z. (2010). Diversity in surfing: we need more of it. *The Inertia: Distributor of Ideas*, 13 September. Accessed from www.theinertia.com/business-media/diversity-in-surfing-we-need-more-of-it/.

West, A. and Allin, L. (2010). Chancing your arm: the meaning of risk in rock climbing. *Sport in Society, 13*(7–8), 1234–1248.

Wheaton, B. (1997a). *Consumption, Lifestyle and Gendered Identities in Post-Modern Sports: The Case of Windsurfing*. Ph.D. thesis, University of Brighton.

Wheaton, B. (1997b). Covert ethnography and the ethics of research: studying sport subcultures. In A. Tomlinson and S. Fleming (Eds), *Ethics, Sport and Leisure: Crises and Critiques* (pp. 163–172). Aachen: Meyer & Meyer Verlag.

Wheaton, B. (2000). Just do it: consumption, commitment and identity in the windsurfing subculture. *Sociology of Sport Journal, 17*(3), 254–274.

Wheaton, B. (2002). Babes on the beach, women in the surf: researching gender, power and difference in the windsurfing culture. In J. Sugden and A. Tomlinson (Eds), *Power Games: Theory and Method for a Critical Sociology of Sport* (pp. 240–266). London: Routledge.

Wheaton, B. (2003a). Lifestyle sports magazines and the discourses of sporting masculinity. In B. Benwell (Ed.), *Masculinity and Men's Lifestyle Magazines* (pp. 193–221.). Oxford and Malden, MA: Sociological Review, Blackwell.

Wheaton, B. (2003b). Windsurfing: a subculture of commitment. In R. Rinehart and S. Sydor (Eds), *To the Extreme: Alternative Sports, Inside and Out* (pp. 75–101). Albany, NY: State University of New York Press.

Wheaton, B. (2004a). Introduction: mapping the lifestyle sport-scape. In B. Wheaton (Ed.), *Understanding Lifestyle Sports: Consumption, Identity and Difference*. London: Routledge.

Wheaton, B. (2004b). New lads? Competing masculinities in the windsurfing culture. In B. Wheaton (Ed.), *Understanding Lifestyle Sports: Consumption, Identity and Difference* (pp. 131–153). London: Routledge.

Wheaton, B. (Ed.). (2004c). *Understanding Lifestyle Sports: Consumption, Identity and Difference* (pp. 1–28). London: Routledge.

Wheaton, B. (2005). Selling out? The globalization and commercialisation of lifestyle sports. In L. Allison (Ed.), *The Global Politics of Sport* (pp. 140–161). London: Routledge.

Wheaton, B. (2007a). After sport culture: rethinking sport and post-subcultural theory. *Journal of Sport and Social Issues, 31*(3), 283–307.

Wheaton, B. (2007b). Identity, politics, and the beach: environmental activism in Surfers Against Sewage. *Leisure Studies, 26*(3), 279–302.

Wheaton, B. (2008a). From the pavement to the beach: politics and identity in Surfers Against Sewage. In M. Atkinson and K. Young (Eds), *Tribal Play: Subcultural Journeys Through Sport* (Vol. IV 'Research in the Sociology of Sport', pp. 113–134). Bingley: Emerald/Jai.

Wheaton, B. (2008b). *Surf Film and Female Spectatorship*. Paper presented at the North American Sociology of Sport Conference, Denver.

Wheaton, B. (2009a). Habitus. In S. Wagg, B. Wheaton, C. Brick and J. Caudwell (Eds), *Key Concepts in Sport Studies* (pp. 102–108). Thousand Oaks, CA: Sage.

Wheaton, B. (2009b). The cultural politics of lifestyle sport (re)visited: beyond white male lifestyles. In J. Ormond and B. Wheaton (Eds), *'On the Edge': Leisure, Consumption and the Representation of Adventure Sport* (Vol. 104, pp. 131–160). Eastbourne: Leisure Studies Association.

Wheaton, B. (2010). Introducing the consumption and representation of lifestyle sports. *Sport in Society: Cultures, Commerce, Media, Politics, 13*(7), 1057–1081.

Wheaton, B. and Beal, B. (2003a). 'Keeping it real': subcultural media and the discourses of authenticity in alternative sport. *International Review for the Sociology of Sport, 38*(2), 155–176.

Wheaton, B. and Beal, B. (2003b). Surf divas and skate betties: consuming images of the 'other' in lifestyle sports. In S. Fleming and I. Jones (Eds), *New Leisure Environments: Media, Technology and Sport* (Vol. LSA Publication No. 79, pp. 69–90). Eastbourne: Leisure Studies Association.

Wheaton, B. and Tomlinson, A. (1998). The changing gender order in sport? The case of windsurfing. *Journal of Sport and Social Issues, 22*, 252–274.

Williams, M. (2007). Legendary surfers: Nick Gabaldon (1927–1951). *Surfing Heritage and Culture Center*, 2 May. Accessed from http://files.legendarysurfers.com/blog/labels/Inkwell%20Beach.html.

Williams, R. (1977). *Marxism and Literature*. Oxford: Oxford University Press.

Wilson, B. (1997). 'Good blacks' and 'bad blacks': media construction of African-American athletes in Canadian basketball. *International Review for Sociology of Sport, 32*, 177–189.

Wilson, B. (2002). The Canadian rave scene and five theses on youth resistance. *Canadian Journal of Sociology, 27*(3), 373–412.

Wilson, B. (2008). Believe the hype? The impact of the internet on sport-related subcultures. In M. Atkinson and K. Young (Eds), *Tribal Play: Subcultural Journeys Through Sport* (Vol. IV 'Research in the Sociology of Sport', pp. 135–152). Bingley: Emerald/Jai.

Wiltse, J. (2007). *Contested Waters: A Social History of Swimming Pools in America*. Chapel Hill, NC: The University of North Carolina Press.

Wisse, E. (2009). *The Development of Capoeria as a Western Lifestyle Sport*. Hertogenbosch: Mulier Institute, Centre for Research on Sport in Society.

Wolch, J. and Zhang, J. (2004). Beach recreation, cultural diversity and attitudes to nature. *Journal of Leisure Research, 36*(3), 414–443.

Woodward, V. (1995). *Windsurfing Women and Change*, Masters thesis, University of Strathclyde.

Wooley, H. and Johns, R. (2001). Skateboarding: the city as a playground. *Journal of Urban Design, 6*(2), 211–230.

Yelland, R. (2012). Director's Cut: Inside 12 Miles North. *The Inertia: Distributor of Ideas*, 8 February. Accessed from www.theinertia.com/business-media/12-miles-north-black-surf-documentary/.

Young, A. and Dallaire, C. (2008). Beware *#! Sk8 at your own risk: the discourses of young female skateboarders. In M. Atkinson and K. Young (Eds), *Tribal Play: Subcultural Journeys Through Sport* (Vol. IV 'Research in the Sociology of Sport', pp. 235–254). Bingley: Jai.

Young, K. and Atkinson, M. (2008). Introduction: a subcultural history. In M. Atkinson and K. Young (Eds), *Tribal Play: Subcultural Journeys Through Sport* (Vol. IV 'Research in the Sociology of Sport', pp. 1–46). Bingley: Jai.

Zinser, L. (2006). Dive in: everyone into the water. *New York Times*, 19 June. Accessed from www.nytimes.com/2006/06/19/health/healthspecial/19swim.html.

Index

Taylor & Francis

eBooks

FOR LIBRARIES

ORDER YOUR FREE 30 DAY INSTITUTIONAL TRIAL TODAY!

Over 23,000 eBook titles in the Humanities, Social Sciences, STM and Law from some of the world's leading imprints.

Choose from a range of subject packages or create your own!

Benefits for you
- ▶ Free MARC records
- ▶ COUNTER-compliant usage statistics
- ▶ Flexible purchase and pricing options

Benefits for your user
- ▶ Off-site, anytime access via Athens or referring URL
- ▶ Print or copy pages or chapters
- ▶ Full content search
- ▶ Bookmark, highlight and annotate text
- ▶ Access to thousands of pages of quality research at the click of a button

For more information, pricing enquiries or to order a free trial, contact your local online sales team.

UK and Rest of World: **online.sales@tandf.co.uk**

US, Canada and Latin America: **e-reference@taylorandfrancis.com**

www.ebooksubscriptions.com

ALPSP Award for BEST eBOOK PUBLISHER 2009 Finalist

Taylor & Francis eBooks
Taylor & Francis Group

A flexible and dynamic resource for teaching, learning and research.